Essay Index

6-14-76 h3

STYLE AND STRUCTURE
IN LITERATURE

STYLE AND STRUCTURE IN LITERATURE

Essays in the New Stylistics

Edited by Roger Fowler

CORNELL UNIVERSITY PRESS

ITHACA, NEW YORK

First published 1975 by Cornell University Press

*This edition is not for sale in the United Kingdom and
British Commonwealth*

International Standard Book Number 0–8014–0949–7

Library of Congress Catalog Card Number
74–24277

Printed in Great Britain

CONTENTS

PREFACE

The present collection of essays grew out of a one-day conference held at the University of East Anglia, Norwich, England, on June 6, 1972. This conference had two objectives. First, in acknowledgement of the great diversification of research into linguistic aspects of literature in the past few years, several experts of rather diverse backgrounds and persuasions were assembled for the purpose of exchange of information among specialists in different corners of the field. Second, we wished this to be an occasion on which there would be not only exchange of views among experts, but also dissemination of information to a more general audience. Papers were to be presented in such a way that a relatively uninformed audience (but with good background in literature) could glean information about new, and somewhat technical, approaches in stylistics.

We hoped to say something about both poetry and narrative, and the morning session was devoted to the former, the afternoon to the latter. Papers delivered by Donald C. Freeman, Edmund L. Epstein, L. M. O'Toole and Jonathan Culler were rewarded by the attention and enthusiasm of around one hundred members of faculty and graduate students from several different universities, not only UEA but also Cambridge, Essex, London, Lancaster, York. (The London contingent included Professor Frank Kermode and the members of his graduate seminar from University College, London.) The good reception which the papers received encouraged the Editor (and conference organizer) to plan a volume of essays using the revised conference papers as a nucleus, and the speakers readily concurred. We have not attempted to produce a volume literally reporting the proceedings of the conference, but rather a book of essays having the same aims as the conference, and built around the original papers. The conference papers were augmented by essays by John Rutherford (who attended the conference but did not address it), Seymour Chatman (who was unable to attend) and by the Editor. Within the compass of a short book, we have tried to give an impression of the variety of technique and theory to be found within contemporary stylistics and generative poetics, and to exemplify these approaches in analyses of texts with a range of different origins and genre affiliations. The papers have been selected and composed with a view to balancing theory and practical criticism, and their arguments related to live issues in present-day stylistics.

Producing this book has depended on the co-operation of many people and circumstances. I am much in the debt of the contributors, who not only delivered their essays with great despatch, but also willingly and rapidly revised them where changes were necessary to fit in with the overall design of the book. The University of East Anglia supported the initial conference by providing rooms, equipment and hospitality; and Brown University supplied an appropriate intellectual and social atmosphere while I was engaged on the most crucial and interesting stages of writing and editing.

Providence, Rhode Island, April, 1973   Roger Fowler

Note: the papers by E. L. Epstein and by myself make some use of phonetic transcriptions of passages of verse. Our dialects (American and British English) are very different, and it would be inappropriate to normalize the conventions for notation. The values of the phonetic passages are, we believe, clear from their contexts.

THE NEW STYLISTICS

Roger Fowler

The one-day conference held at the University of East Anglia on June 6, 1972 was designed partly to offer a progress report on work in the linguistic and structural analysis of literature. It was prefaced by a brief introduction, by the present Editor, called 'Language and Style: Stocktaking' (not printed here). In offering that short paper, I wanted to sketch a historical perspective from which the audience could receive and make use of the more substantial presentations which were to follow. However, the speakers were not briefed to address themselves explicitly to the history of stylistics or to the state of the art. In this Introduction I shall attempt to characterize the nature of these speakers' contributions to the progress of stylistics, and by the way allude to some general ideas which have to bear on the present state and future prospects of linguistics and structuralism in literary studies.

The more violent reverberations of early battle-cries have, it appears, faded. There was Harold Whitehall's 'as no science can go beyond mathematics, no criticism can go beyond its linguistics'; Roman Jakobson's 'Poetics deals with problems of verbal structure. . . . Since linguistics is the global science of verbal structure, poetics may be regarded as an integral part of linguistics'.[1] Taking into account the historical and polemic contexts in which these statements were made, and the senses intended for the terms of their phrasing, they do not appear

[1] Respectively, *Kenyon Review*, 13 (1951), 713; *Style in Language*, ed. T. A. Sebeok (Cambridge, Mass.: MIT Press, 1960), p. 350.

now to be particularly outrageous. As an over-stated, program-
matic assertion about technical apparatus in criticism, Whitehall's claim makes some sense; as for Jakobson, close inspection
of his essay, and of his subsequent work, shows that he is using
'poetics' and 'linguistics' as idealized terms in a special logical
relationship: he does not threaten us by proposing the sub-
servience of all literary studies to linguistics.

If we strip these two assertions of their pugnacious connotations, and consider their content soberly, we come to realize
that they point in two different directions. Whitehall considers
that linguistics is naturally an available technique within criticism. A specific science may be dependent on mathematics,
but it nevertheless preserves its identity as a specific science;
so criticism is accepted as an independently defined field of
endeavour or knowledge, and linguistics an indispensable aid
to that discipline. Whitehall's formulation allows us to accept
criticism as a discipline with its own canons. But Jakobson
proposes a new discipline 'poetics' (the word does not have the
traditional meaning 'science of literature' or 'theory of literature' common to Aristotle's *Poetics* and other enterprises within
that area of speculation, down to Todorov's *poétique*) whose
definition, and necessarily its techniques and metalanguage,
are dependent on a prior conception of linguistics.[2] Linguistics
includes poetics, whereas for Whitehall critical technique
includes linguistics. Consequently, Jakobson's strategy narrows
to an analytic procedure which derives all its terms from
linguistics (rejecting all which are not so defined) and which
claims absolute reliability and pertinence for those terms.
Jakobson has demonstrated the application of this procedure in
several papers which have become famous or even notorious.[3]
Jakobsonian analysis is highly distinctive. When Jakobson
squares up to a poem, his stance suggests that he faces a completely unknown adversary. Everything that can be known,

    [2] This is the aim, but the practice differs: in effect, Jakobson offers a re-
definition of linguistics, widening it to include his poetics and perhaps re-
designing it according to his conception of poetics.
    [3] For references to Jakobson's writings, and to some critiques of his method,

and/or is relevant to know, can, it seems, be revealed by a technique of minute linguistic annotation at the levels of sound and syntax. The approach seems to be about as positivistic as one could get. The analyst accumulates a bank of minute observations of phonetic and syntactic patterning, sorts them, and invokes their frequency and distribution in support of the existence of larger, abstract but spatially conceivable, structural patterns in poems. On pp. 82–8 below I describe the method and some of its effects more fully. To summarize the more important premisses of the approach, they appear to be: (a) poetics (in the relevant sense) yields a specific and sufficient technique of literary analysis; (b) it is validated, both for theory and results, by the science of linguistics; (c) exhaustive analysis is possible; (d) all linguistic facts are poetically relevant; (e) there is no hierarchy of value among these facts. It seems also to be assumed that description can be conducted independently of evaluation and interpretation. If interpretation is indulged, it is unconnected to the description—a trivial semantic paraphrase—and if evaluation is attempted it is clear that this does not guide the description except crudely, by selecting the poem for analysis.[4]

Now Jakobson has been bolder than most in announcing and exemplifying these principles, but they are not restricted to his work alone. Explicit or implicit reliance on some or all of these assumptions characterizes a whole tradition of early work in stylistics. The critical limitations of this approach are obvious. Fortunately, the greater part of recent work in stylistics is much more generous in its aims and procedures.[5] I use the

---

see ch. iv below. An extensive bibliography of Jakobson's writings in poetics up to 1967 is given on pp. 602–3 of his 'Poetry of Grammar and Grammar of Poetry', *Lingua*, 21 (October, 1968), 597–609.

[4] Cf. Tzvetan Todorov on 'description', *Poétique de la prose* (Paris: Seuil, 1970), pp. 246–7; Fowler, 'Linguistics, Stylistics; Criticism?', *Lingua*, 16 (1966), 153–66, rpt. in *The Languages of Literature* (London: Routledge and Kegan Paul, 1971), pp. 32–42.

[5] Stanley Fish, in a paper delivered at the English Institute, Harvard, September, 1972 ('What is Stylistics and Why are they Saying such Terrible

4 ROGER FOWLER

phrase 'The New Stylistics' in my sub-title with some confidence. Even though 'stylistics' is a tricky term if we attempt to tie it down to a hard and fast theory of style, it is operationally straightforward if we use it pragmatically, to refer to the collected work of the writers who have contributed to the various anthologies from Sebeok's *Style in Language* down to the recent collection of Kachru and Stahlke, *Current Trends in Stylistics*. The two most recent anthologies, that of Kachru and Stahlke just cited, and Chatman's *Literary Style: A Symposium*—display a remarkably wide range of topics and approaches.[6] We are not offered simple applications of single linguistic models to favourable literary texts, but complex essays employing the analogy, or the theory, or some of the techniques, of general linguistics in the context of a rich variety of literary-critical, literary-theoretical, and literary-historical, problems. Another characteristic of the New Stylistics is its theoretical catholicity and flexibility. One of the principal achievements of generative-transformational linguistics has been its influence in broadening the scope and affiliations of language-studies, in making it amenable (as American structural linguistics of the previous generation was not) to fruitful contacts with many other humane disciplines: various branches of philosophy, psychology, anthropology, sociology, mathematics, not to mention general structuralist theory in the tradition of Saussure, Lévi-Strauss and Barthes. In the past ten years or so, stylistics has grown alongside generative linguistics, and has remained sensitive and receptive to developments in linguistics: I believe this is the main reason why stylistics is so much more varied,

---

'Things about it?', published in Seymour Chatman, ed., *Approaches to Poetics* (New York and London: Columbia Univ. Press, 1973), 109–52) suggests that such positivistic assumptions are inevitable to, and fundamentally damaging to, any attempt to link linguistics and literature. I do not believe that this failing is essential to stylistics, nor that it is wholly characteristic of the work of some of the stylisticians whom Mr. Fish discusses.

[6] Braj B. Kachru and Herbert F. W. Stahlke, eds., *Current Trends in Stylistics* (Edmonton, Alberta: Linguistic Research, Inc., 1972); Seymour Chatman, ed., *Literary Style: A Symposium* (New York and London: Oxford University Press, 1971).

both in its ambitions and its apparatus, than it was just a few years ago.

One aspect of the New Stylistics which deserves special comment is its vital relationship with the contemporary structuralism/formalism of the French *nouvelle poétique*. I will have more to say about this connexion as this Introduction proceeds.

Every paper in this volume reflects interests recognizable as traditional and important to established literary studies. In no case does an author simply 'apply' linguistic technique to literary texts, nor does anyone strain to present any special technique claimed as 'linguistic stylistics'. Of course, the book's coherence, its justification, comes from the fact that all contributors make use of concepts and procedures drawn from linguistics and from other linguistics-like sciences treating the structure of communicative systems. All the papers are set in motion by intuitions, hypotheses, problems, which are external to linguistics itself, but even if the motive force for each of these papers derives from problems in literary criticism, these problems are assailed with the equipment of an established battery of language sciences. Linguists have addressed their interests to literature for some twenty years, and, while respecting the innocence of the non-specialist, this book builds on the foundations laid by those endeavours. But we hope that, being conscious of the occasional *critical* blindness of our predecessors, we succeed in communicating a direct engagement with questions of an essentially literary origin. If this optimism is justified, our book should be readily accessible to readers of a predominantly literary background.

The first paper in this collection, by Donald C. Freeman, is typical of recent stylistics in adopting a powerful and complex critical hypothesis as the point of departure. Freeman's chosen text—three poems by Dylan Thomas—is not offered as virgin territory to be probed by a perfectly neutral analytic machine. Nor does Freeman select Thomas for the utilitarian motive which drew earlier linguists to his poetry—fragments of his work have often been served up out of critical context because they conveniently illustrate striking forms of syntactic and semantic deviation.[7] Freeman approaches Thomas with a specific line of enquiry or field of interest: the poet's habitual synthesizing, identifying, generalizing preoccupations: 'he sought to fuse natural process and human physiology, the forces of nature and human mortality, and . . . man's individual life and death with collective human and cosmic history' (p. 21 below). This preoccupation is assumedly encoded in the artistic design of Thomas's poems; and the artistic design both resides in the language and is discovered by the reader in his language-induced experience of the poems. Freeman claims that those parts of the poems which are particularly significant, aesthetically, are 'foregrounded' by exceptional manipulations of syntax, bendings but not breaches of the rules. At these points of syntactic strain, the reader's attention and interpretative skills are commanded, and the mental gymnastics he must perform in order to penetrate the syntax force him to perceive the values and perspectives which Thomas's metaphors insist on.

Demonstration of this argument calls for a specifically adapted form of linguistic analysis, a careful preselection of relevant linguistic technique and of verbal patterns to be observed. Any attempt to write a complete grammar of the poem would be gratuitous and would obscure the object of the analysis, for 'one doesn't want to know every syntactic fact about a poem; one wants to know the significant ones . . .' (p. 21 below). Freeman, unlike many of his predecessors in stylistics, is conscious that different grammatical models are selective in different ways; and he has the advantage over his predecessors that a range of models are available to him. He chooses to present his syntactic observations in the terms of transformational-generative grammar, a choice which is peculiarly appropriate to the specific enterprise in hand. TG provides a delicate analytic apparatus for just the kinds of

[7] Stanley B. Greenfield, in a lecture at London University, once proposed a moratorium on discussions of 'a grief ago'. The lecture was subsequently published and provides a valuable guide to early work in 'linguistic stylistics'. See 'Grammar and Meaning in Poetry', *PMLA*, 82 (1967), 377–87.

structures Freeman needs to describe. Moreover, its advocates conceive of it as having *psychological* validity. Though transformational rules do not represent actual procedures which a speaker or hearer runs through as he constructs or decodes an utterance, the structures these rules describe have psychological implications for users of language, and differences among these implications account for variable stylistic effects experienced by readers.[8] Thomas's foregrounded syntax happens to answer to a class of constructions on which Noam Chomsky has specifically commented, those which are 'unacceptable' but not 'ungrammatical'.[9] These do not transgress any rules of the grammar, but are nevertheless extremely difficult to 'process'—for instance, they impose an inordinate burden on short-term memory. Freeman shows how such structures, in Dylan Thomas, arrest the reader and, as he unravels their contorted syntax, guide him to the heart of the author's artistic design. In the relation he sets up between grammatical model and critical problem, Freeman illustrates not a mechanical transposition of a text into linguistic jargon, but a dialectical process in which the linguistics and the literature are mutually responsive.

Edmund L. Epstein's paper, which sustains one of the most ambitious arguments of any advanced in this volume, at the same time demonstrates copiously a practical quality fundamental to any application of linguistic technique to literary style. I refer to the extensive and penetrating explication of stylistic texture: a demand that the reader (the reader studying the illustrative citations in order to follow Epstein's argument) attend closely to the minutiae of phonetic, syntactic and rhetorical arrangement; an assumption (as in Freeman) that the experiences of someone reading poetry are under the control of

---

[8] In addition to the writings of Richard Ohmann cited by Freeman in support of this view, see J. P. Thorne, 'Generative Grammar and Stylistic Analysis', in *New Horizons in Linguistics*, ed. John Lyons (Harmondsworth: Penguin, 1970), pp. 185–97.

[9] See *Aspects of the Theory of Syntax* (Cambridge, Mass.: MIT Press, 1965), pp. 10–15.

these verbal particulars; and a sharply focused description of the significant features, rendered in the reliable vocabulary of linguistic science. Of course, 'reliability' in the sense of dispassionate reproduction of the linguistic facts is not the aim of this study, nor is that, unqualified, a valuable aim in stylistics in any case. Epstein selects his verbal structures according to clearly articulated criteria of rhetorical significance. And it is noteworthy that, although his paper almost continuously refers to precise aspects of language structure, and in doing so persistently confronts us with the metalanguage of descriptive linguistics, there is no sense that the author makes a virtue of exhibiting the process of technical linguistic description. If critics feel inclined to question the details of Epstein's analysis, their attack will not be on the grounds of the irrelevance of the technical exposition, but in terms of the significance of the literary phenomena noticed: that is to say, it is natural to argue with this paper according to the normal canons of critical discourse, not in terms of that ancient red herring, the impertinence of linguistics *tout court*.

Epstein boldly confronts the age-old problem of the variability of literary form in relation to content. He assumes, as I believe one must, that it is possible to 'say the same thing' 'in different words'. His concern with this problem is not theoretical (as is Ohmann's),[10] that is to say, he does not set out to demonstrate the independent variability of form and content on the basis of the axioms of an advanced theory of language. Support for Epstein's stand on the variability of form derives from his observation that in some verse, arrangements of surface structure are quite arbitrary from the point of view of meaning, while in other examples surface structure is patterned in such a way as to suggest a determinate and valuable integration with meaning. Copious examples of these two states are given in his text. The particular kind of integration Epstein discusses occurs, or does not occur, or occurs to a certain degree, on a *mimetic* scale. Form may or may not

[10] See R. Fowler, 'Style and the Concept of Deep Structure', *Journal of Literary Semantics*, 1 (1972), 5–24.

mime content; when it does, different levels of language may
be utilized in the imitative process; different conceptual and
physical processes may be mimed by the language (Epstein
discusses only a limited range of 'imitands', and does not claim
to provide a complete discussion of the difficult theoretical
problem of what content-structures *can* be imitated by language); and our culture assigns varying values to different
kinds of mimesis. The main course of Epstein's argument is in
fact guided by a generous cultural-historical premiss: that in
post-Renaissance European literature mimesis of content by
form has been a favoured poetic technique, and, more specifically, that a conventional hierarchy of values is assigned to
different strategies of mimesis with, in the Romantic and post-
Romantic period (presumably), the highest score going to the
combined force of phonology and syntax operating to imitate
the poet's image of himself. Since Epstein can provide a formal
taxonomy of types of mimesis by tagging the varieties according
to solid categories drawn from linguistics, he is able to suggest
a regular scale of values in mimetic achievement, with their
linguistic correlates. Thus the ultimate aim of Epstein's paper
is to make linguistic methods and concepts serve a formal
demonstration of one aspect of value in literature. All of the
specific exercises in practical criticism within his paper are to be
regarded with that broad ambition in mind.

I will presume to comment briefly on my own contribution
to this volume. My point of departure is a consideration of the
technique of formalist analysis which has become familiar in
the writings of Roman Jakobson on sonnets and other short,
highly patterned, poems. Such poems are obviously very
accessible to linguistic description since their metrical format—
and often their rhetorico-logical structure—is extremely salient
and is also based on units closely matched in scale to the
primary units of linguistic analysis (sentences). The effect of
Jakobsonian analysis seems to be the transformation of the
literary object into a quasi-spatial structure, diagrammed by
linguistic categories; a construction apparently more complex
than the original (but not actually so), and certainly lifeless in

comparison with the original. Here I use the word 'lifeless' unashamedly impressionistically—but I believe that it is a fair term for the feeling that is produced by the results of this stylistic mode. The analysis is very distant from the interpretation; the poems become, paradoxically, meaningless when exposed to a technique which is supposed to reveal meaning. My attempt to provide an alternative technique, a technique which hopefully re-connects critical interpretation and linguistic analysis, is based on the assumption that it is legitimate to take account of the reader's response. I am not concerned with anything like the whole range of possible types of response, however—certainly not with shivers in the spine. Specifically, I try to show how the linear organization of syntax directs the reading process in the retrieval of meaning. This approach through syntax is an enlargement of Michael Riffaterre's method of analysis (which is based on the lexical rather than syntactic code); it might also be compared with the 'affective stylistics' recently advocated by Stephen Booth and Stanley Fish, but it differs from the work of those critics to the extent that its use of syntactic analysis is more explicit.[11]

The title of this book mentions the two complementary terms 'style' and 'structure'. Both terms, and likewise 'texture' which overlaps with 'style' and also balances with 'structure', have long been controversial in literary theory. There is no need to reopen the controversy here; the words are used only as familiar labels for aspects of literature selected for attention by different formalist approaches both of which, interestingly for our purposes, can be attached to a basically Saussurean model of language. Focus on 'style', either in the traditional sense found in historical and comparative stylistics, or in the extended usage whereby scholars such as Chatman, Halliday,

[11] Compare Michael Riffaterre, 'Describing Poetic Structures: Two Approaches to Baudelaire's *Les Chats*', in *Structuralism*, ed. Jacques Ehrmann (New York: Doubleday Anchor, 1970), pp. 188–230; Riffaterre, 'Interpretation and Descriptive Poetry: A Reading of Wordsworth's "Yew-Trees",' *New Literary History*, 4 (Winter, 1973), 229–56; Stanley Fish, 'Literature in the Reader: Affective Stylistics', *New Literary History*, 2 (Autumn, 1970), 123–62.

Jakobson, Leech, Levin, Ohmann, Sinclair, etc., have been called 'stylisticians', entails close attention to the surface structure of literary texts, and an assumption that phonology, syntax, everything which makes up rhetoric, are of paramount importance in determining the identity of the literary work and the nature of the audience's engagement with it. The first three papers in this volume might according to this extended characterization be said to be concerned with style.

On the other hand, a 'structuralist' approach to literature manifests a type of reading which subordinates aspects of surface structure in favour of an investigation of some deeper, more abstract patterns which govern the inner form of a work; this form can be related to that of other works, and ultimately perhaps to the general conventions of all literary discourse. 'Stylistics' emphasizes particularity, individuality, concreteness; 'structuralism' is more given to generalization and abstraction. Stylistics makes the individual work more recognizable, more discrete, its physiognomy more salient. In structuralist analyses, particular literary works tend to become less recognizable: they are transformed, as Barthes says, 'into a more schematic version'.[12] Barthes himself disavows interest in style. His analysis of Balzac's story *Sarrasine*[13] aims to render the work as a tissue of five cultural and literary 'codes' which presumably enjoy some form of existence independent of this particular story and which might be encountered in other works. No attention is given to rhetorical features except insofar as they carry connotations of the codes. The individual work is thus projected on to a system of conventions outside of itself: ultimately it is the system, not the particular work, which is the object of literary description. The same principle—priority of the abstract system over any individual manifestation of it in a particular literary text—governs the better-known French work on the structure of narrative. It is perhaps most vigorously stated by Tzvetan Todorov, for whom the individual work is interesting only to the extent that the analyst can derive from

[12] 'Style and its Image', in *Literary Style*, ed. Seymour Chatman, p. 5.
[13] *S/Z* (Paris: Seuil, 1970).

it regularities (very abstract and general schemata) which link
it to other works of its genre and ultimately to the universal
properties of literary discourse. Todorov's technique (strongly
influenced by that of the Russian formalist Vladimir Propp)[14]
is clearly illustrated in his monographs on *Les liaisons dangereuses*
and the *Decameron*: actions, character-relationships, situations
are expressed in an abstract metalanguage which can be
rendered in an alphabetic notation; so powerful generalizations
can be stated in rule-form and the rules invoked to capture
fundamental similarities and contrasts among narratives.[15]

The full quotation from Barthes, from which I excerpted one
phrase in the preceding paragraph, goes as follows: 'The
structural analysis of narrative, in its present accomplishment
and future promise, is based entirely on the conviction (and the
practical proof) that one can transform a given text into a more
schematic version, set it a metalanguage which is no longer the
language of the original text, without essentially changing its
narrative character.' Jonathan Culler's paper, which falls in the
area of narrative structure analysis mentioned by Barthes,
opens with an allusion to one kind of transformational process:
'telling a story in different ways'. To summarize the narrative
of a work is to present it in a more schematic version—and
such summaries are, of course, of great interest to the analyst
of narrative, since they display the basic constituents of a story,
and the relationships among those constituents, more nakedly
than the work itself does. In a sense a summary retelling *is* an
analysis of plot: it separates off a distinct level of plot in the
work, sorts the narrationally functional items of mention at the
surface of the story from those which are incidental, which have
to do with atmosphere, etc.; places these items in a simplified
but overt relationship with each other; and so on. Of course,

---

[14] Vladimir Propp, *Morphology of the Folktale*, trans. Laurence Scott,
second ed., rev. and ed. by Louis A. Wagner (Austin: University of Texas
Press, 1968).

[15] See Tzvetan Todorov, 'Poétique', in O. Ducrot *et al.*, *Qu'est-ce que le
structuralisme?* (Paris: Seuil, 1968), pp. 99–166; *Littérature et signification* (Paris:
Larousse, 1967); *Grammaire du Décaméron* (The Hague: Mouton, 1969).

a verbal plot-summary is merely the crudest form of narrative analysis—it is insufficiently abstract and will allow only clumsy comparisons with other plots—but it does point to the autonomy of a level of 'plot' and its availability for more systematic analysis.

Culler offers a related observation suggesting the systematicity and analysability of narrative: our *intuitions* about plot are generally reliable, accessible, for informed discussion of various aspects of the subject. We can check summaries in discussion with other people, agree on various kinds of borderline situation, assess whether a plot is adequately rendered in translation to another medium, etc. Presumably the bases of these judgements can be established through a descriptive science of narrative structure.

Such a science will resemble generative linguistics, while not actually being a part of linguistics. Culler's use of the term 'intuition' recalls Chomsky's 'intuition' in linguistics: the tacit knowledge which enables a speaker or reader to make certain judgements concerning utterances, or stories: knowledge which we have internalized of language, or narrative. It is natural, then, to introduce the idea of 'literary competence': so the study of narrative is ultimately (part of) the study of literary competence.

Culler observes that, though our intuitions of narrative structure are generally extremely powerful, that fact alone does not ensure that we have access through them to a valid theory of narrative structure. Not only is the range of narrative phenomena which would have to be accounted for by a theory of narrative bewilderingly large, but also the range of theoretical proposals is already considerable. Very different metalanguages, with distinct theoretical implications, have been offered; but little effort has been devoted to any attempt to *evaluate* these proposals. Culler points out that any scheme for isolating and labelling narrative units may 'work' pragmatically but nevertheless be totally arbitrary, vacuous. A valid scheme must generate descriptions which 'correspond with our intuitive sense' of particular plots and 'prohibit descriptions which are

manifestly wrong'. Through a description of Joyce's story
Eveline (which has the advantage of having already been
submitted by Chatman to the analytic categories of Barthes/
Todorov/Greimas),[16] Culler illustrates the kinds of facts which
an intuitively valid theory of plot structure must explicate,
and proceeds to examine some French and Russian formalist
proposals in this light.

I will not attempt to convey all the ramifications of the
complicated and ingenious argument of L. M. O'Toole's paper,
but may nevertheless indicate how it fits in with the historical
and conceptual frameworks implied by other contributors to the
book. The specific historical background appealed to is provided by early Russian formalism, in particular the work of
Viktor Shklovsky and Vladimir Propp,[17] and by the much
more recent, and less well known, Russian structuralists,
represented here by Alexander Zholkovsky and Yuri Scheglov.
O'Toole discusses the relationship between the approaches of
the formalists and the structuralists (the 'analytic' and 'synthetic' respectively, in his title) and compares it to stages in the
movement towards generative linguistics. The work of the early
pioneers can be likened to the 'finite-state grammar' which
Chomsky attributes to pre-transformational grammarians,
whereas the ideas of the more recent Soviet writers correspond
to those of generative linguists.[18] The formalists provide a

[16] Seymour Chatman, 'New Ways of Analyzing Narrative Structure',
Language and Style, 2 (1969), 3–36.

[17] On Russian formalism generally, see Viktor Erlich, *Russian Formalism*
(The Hague: Mouton, 1965). For representative selections see Lee T. Lemon
and Marion J. Reis, eds. and trans., *Russian Formalist Criticism* (Lincoln, Na.:
University of Nebraska Press, 1965); Ladislav Matejka and Krystyna
Pomorska, eds. and trans., *Readings in Russian Poetics* (Cambridge, Mass.:
MIT Press, 1971); T. Todorov, ed. and trans., *Théorie de la littérature: textes
des Formalistes russes* (Paris: Seuil, 1965).

[18] Here I should point out that the term 'kernel' introduced by O'Toole
in expounding this analogy is taken from Chomsky's *Syntactic Structures* (The
Hague: Mouton, 1957) where it means, roughly, 'basic sentence-type'.
'Kernel' in Culler's paper is used quite differently: it translates *noyau* in
Barthes' exposition of the units of narrative structure ('Introduction à
l'analyse structurale des récits', *Communications*, 8 (1966), 1–27).

useful, but static, analysis of the underlying components of a
work; the structuralists attempt to show how a text is generated
out of these elements (Scheglov seems to attach a literal meaning to 'synthesize'—construct new texts on the basis of our
knowledge of the derivational rules for a genre—but O'Toole
rejects this mechanistic venture). O'Toole demonstrates the
contrast between analysis and synthesis in a study of a Sherlock
Holmes story. He begins with an abstract theme for the story—a
fundamental semantic contrast between reason and the irrational—and shows how this is realized as a 'sequence of textual
elements'. This sequence of textual elements is in fact seen as
a many-dimensioned construct organized in such a way that
traditional literary categories apply to it: fable, plot, narrative
structure, point of view, character, setting, language. The
derivational techniques permit a description of the tale which
conveys a much richer impression of the work than would, say,
a Todorovian account limited to treatment of the events of the
story. Yet the synthesis remains generative in the required
sense: it is a controlled account of the way a text relates a
selection from the underlying elements of narrative.

O'Toole confesses that he has chosen for his demonstration a
highly stylized, almost parodic, example of an extremely
simple kind of narrative. But there is no reason why, in principle, the method should not be applied to more complex works
of fiction. Both the traditional and the structuralist approaches
and categories on which he relies are inclusive enough to
accommodate richer and less schematic narratives. In fact,
the paper which follows, that of John Rutherford, does undertake the analysis of a longer and more complicated narrative.

Rutherford's paper both comments on and illustrates the
methods and aims of structuralist-generative poetics. The
author enters into dialogue with both Culler and O'Toole:
he offers to submit his scheme for the analysis of story, character,
environment and narrative mode to the criteria for narrative
analysis demanded by Culler; and he welcomes O'Toole's
paper as a valuable contribution to the analysis of (particularly) character, showing how the ideas may be extended, and

how they may be given alternative symbolization on the plan
of a distinctive-feature matrix of the kind familiar in generative phonology.[19] (It might be added that the traditional
category of 'character' usually comes off worst in structuralist analyses. Following the practice of Propp, the structuralists tend to treat characters as functional elements within
the syntax of the action rather than as independent entities.
Both O'Toole and Rutherford assume that characters possess
some qualities which are not dictated by their functions in
plot.)[20] Attentive to the Anglo-Saxon objections of several
questioners at the Norwich conference, Rutherford points out
that the fashionable ideas of contemporary French structuralism
should not be regarded as a complete approach to the study of
narrative—the structuralists should not be dismissed for alleged
failure in a role they do not offer to undertake. The most
accessible, and most severely reductive, approach [my evalua-
tions, R.F.], e.g. Todorov's development of Russian formalism,
is intended as a contribution to only one section of the necessary
framework for the structural description of narrative. The
structuralists make a fundamental distinction between *histoire*
'story' and *discours* 'narration', and their work is largely concentrated on 'story'. Rutherford adjusts this framework to
include four primary categories, which he spells out in his title:
'story', 'character', 'environment' and 'narrative mode'. He
illustrates how analysis would work in relation to all four of
these, but goes into detail on two, 'story' and 'narrative mode'
(i.e. the major topics under *histoire* and *discours* respectively).
In an extended exposition of the story-structure of *El amigo
Manso* by Benito Pérez Galdós, he introduces, analyses critically
and develops the methods devised by Todorov for the generative description of story structure—in particular, the approach
utilized by Todorov in his *Grammaire du Décaméron*. Noteworthy
is the fact that the technique of structural analysis is here

[19] On distinctive feature analysis in phonology, see Sanford A. Schane,
Generative Phonology (Englewood Cliffs, N.J.: Prentice-Hall, 1973).
[20] Cf. Seymour Chatman, 'On the Formalist-Structuralist Theory of
Character', *Journal of Literary Semantics*, 1 (1972), 57–79.

demonstrated in relation to a full-length novel in the modern European realistic tradition: an implicit rebuttal of the Anglo-Saxon criticism that structuralist analysis 'works' only for exceptionally schematic narratives (detective stories, fairy-tales) or exceptionally short ones. Finally, Rutherford explores one aspect of narrative mode as it is organized in *El Amigo Manso*: the handling of enigma in the novel, its enunciation, compounding, false or ambiguous unfolding, its final, and aesthetically functional, equivocal divulgation. This is, of course, only one aspect of narrative mode: but as Roland Barthes has shown (cf. his exposition, in *S/Z*, of the workings of the 'hermeneutic code' in Balzac's story *Sarrasine*) it is a potent and crucial part of the strategies by which the presentation of narrative in modern fiction controls the reader's participation.

The final essay in this volume, 'The Structure of Narrative Transmission', is the work of Seymour Chatman, a pioneer in 'linguistic stylistics' who has written authoritatively on many topics in this field: metre, theory of style, semiology, practical stylistic criticism of both verse and prose. In the present paper he is concerned with narrative structure, at the level of *discours* rather than *histoire*. In terms of Rutherford's framework of four categories, Chatman's paper relates to 'narrative mode'; specifically, to the linguistic techniques associated with different kinds of narrative 'transmitters' in various situations of mimesis. The terms 'transmitter' and 'transmission' serve to remind us that narrative discourse, as discourse, has inalienably a particular origin within the fiction, a source of the encoding. To put it another way, narrative discourse is an activity under the control of some fictional speaker. There is inevitably a teller as well as a tale; language, necessarily mediating between the story and our experience of it, cannot possibly be a neutral or transparent medium—even a printed discourse, black and static on the page of an ostensibly 'realistic' novel, nevertheless implies the active presence of a teller, of someone articulating and governing the discourse. Since Wayne C. Booth's *The Rhetoric of Fiction* (Chicago: University of Chicago Press, 1961), this observation has been standard in Anglo-American literary theory: in Booth's formulation, a story can never be merely 'shown'—it is always 'told', though the activity of telling ('transmission' in Chatman) may be more or less explicitly signalled, more or less 'obtrusive'. Chatman reminds us of Booth's account, of the latter's distinction between authors real and implied, narrators reliable and unreliable. Now it might be charged that Booth's *The Rhetoric of Fiction* is not really a rhetoric because it lacks reference to conventions of verbal patterning. Chatman's aim is to supply this particular vacuum, to specify how the various acts of narration, the various states of the 'transmitter', are realized in distinct linguistic manifestations. In the first part of his discussion, Chatman links the characterization of narrative discourse with the theory of 'speech acts', a movement in philosophy originating with J. L. Austin and developed by John R. Searle, increasingly popular in linguistics and recently applied to literature by Richard Ohmann.[21] In the present paper Chatman restricts his attention to one class of narrational acts: 'structures with the least presumption of a narrator's presence—that is, "transcripts" ' (p. 233 below). He reviews the linguistic patternings conventionally employed for the transcription of speech in direct and indirect forms, and then discusses in sequence the linguistic conventions used for the narrative communication of written records (letters, journals), pure speech records and records of thought and feeling. Chatman's paper obviously contributes part to a more general and more ambitious treatment of the linguistic character of complex narrational presences in literature, a project on which he is currently engaged.

[21] J. L. Austin, *How to Do Things with Words*, ed. J. O. Urmson (London: Oxford University Press, 1962); John R. Searle, *Speech Acts* (London: Cambridge University Press, 1968); John Robert Ross, 'On Declarative Sentences', in *Readings in English Transformational Grammar*, ed. Roderick A. Jacobs and Peter S. Rosenbaum (Waltham, Mass.: Blaisdell, 1970), pp. 222–272; Richard Ohmann, 'Speech, Action, and Style', in *Literary Style*, ed. Seymour Chatman, pp. 241–54; Ohmann, 'Instrumental Style: Notes on the Theory of Speech as Action', in *Current Trends in Stylistics*, ed. Kachru and Stahlke, pp. 115–41.

CHAPTER ONE

THE STRATEGY OF FUSION: DYLAN THOMAS'S SYNTAX[1]

Donald C. Freeman

This paper starts from what might be called the Ohmann Hypothesis, most succinctly put in his landmark book on George Bernard Shaw: 'stylistic preferences reflect cognitive preferences'.[2] In a later, post-Chomskyan formulation, Ohmann held that 'style is in part a characteristic way of deploying the transformational apparatus of a language . . .'[3]

I want to extend this principle with reference to aspects of the grammar of poetry, a topic so far little studied from a transformational-generative point of view. One way in which poetic language differs from ordinary language, I hope to show,

[1] Research for this paper was supported in part by the Language Research Foundation, Cambridge, Massachusetts. Earlier versions were read at the 1971 meeting of the National Council of Teachers of English, the Linguistic Circle of the University of Lancaster, the Englisches Seminar of the University of Freiburg, and the Conference on Style and Structure in Literature at the University of East Anglia. For discussion of many points I am grateful to Professor Herbert Pilch of the University of Freiburg, Norman Fairclough and Anne Cluysenaar of the University of Lancaster, Roger Fowler, and Adrian Akmajian, Samuel Jay Keyser, and David Porter of the University of Massachusetts, Amherst. I am particularly indebted to my colleague Barbara Hall Partee for several helpful suggestions. Needless to say, probably no one of the foregoing would agree with everything said in the present version of this study.

[2] Richard Ohmann, *Shaw: The Style and the Man* (Middletown, Conn.: The Wesleyan University Press, 1962), p. 22.

[3] Ohmann, 'Generative Grammars and the Concept of Literary Style', *Word*, 20 (1964), 431.

is that a poet's deployment of his language's transformational apparatus, its syntactic patterns, not only reflects cognitive preferences, a way of seeing the world; perhaps more importantly, it reflects the fundamental principles of artistic design by which the poet orders the world that is the poem. If we can discover the strategies by which a poet manipulates these patterns, we will gain a deeper insight into the poem's inner form and aesthetic centre. Poetic design dictates linguistic strategy, for the poet; for the critic, the discovery of poetic design begins with the discovery of linguistic strategy.

Evidence supporting a theory of the relationship of poetic language and poetic form along the lines just sketched out must come, in the first instance, from cases where syntactic strategies can be shown to parallel and reinforce other strategies of design—metaphor, rhetoric, even meter—a design or set of abstract aesthetic organizing principles as difficult to inspect directly as the command of linguistic strategies which helps to achieve it.

Some earlier transformational analyses of poetic syntax[4] have concentrated on the writing of microgrammars.[5] For the purposes of stylistics, however, we need a more discriminating instrument than a microgrammar of an entire poem, or even

[4] J. P. Thorne, 'Stylistics and Generative Grammars', *Journal of Linguistics*, 1 (1965), 49–59; 'Generative Grammar and Stylistic Analysis', in *New Horizons in Linguistics*, ed. John Lyons (Harmondsworth: Penguin, 1970), pp. 185–97.

[5] By the term 'microgrammar' I mean a set of phrase-structure and transformational rules characterizing the syntactic patterns of the language of a particular poem, with only analogous reference to the rules of ordinary language. In a poem with a line such as 'Altarwise by owl-light', for example, there might exist a rule for making a particular subclass of nominal compounds involving -*light* which would say that nouns can compound with -*light* when they derive from a sentence 'Only Ns can see in this light' (where *N* is any animate noun). 'Owl-light' thus would derive very roughly from 'Only owls can seen in this light' → 'In this light only owls can see' → 'owl-light.' Ordinary English, on the other hand, has a different compounding rule for -*light*: most nominal compounds involving the mass sense of -*light* derive from 'N casts light' → 'light which is cast by N' → 'N-light' (e.g. 'firelight', 'candlelight', 'moonlight', etc.). A microgrammar of 'Altarwise

of a poet's whole corpus. One doesn't want to know every syntactic fact about a poem; one wants to know the significant ones, where 'significant' means 'essential to the poem's design'. An important part of poetic design is syntactic foregrounding, the exploitation by the poet, at points crucial to a poem's thematic structure, of rarely used rules of the language, or the creation of syntactic texture in a poem by motivated use of particular structures in a disproportionately high frequency compared with that encountered in non-poetic language.[6] A poet often bends the laws of ordinary language where his design most asks us to notice. In the poems to be discussed here, the poet bends the laws of the language a great deal, but stops just this side of breaking them. The 'bendings' form such a large part of each poem that in explaining them we go a good way toward explaining its fundamental organizing principles and the ordering of its world.

This paper will examine aspects of three poems by Dylan Thomas, a poet whose idiosyncratic language, along with that of e. e. cummings, has been a frequent subject of studies seeking to analyse patterns of syntax in poetry. Links between linguistic and poetic design will be proposed so that the method can provide a basis for similar studies of poets whose management of syntax is more subtle and less representational than in these poems.

Dylan Thomas was above all a poet of *fusion*: in many of his best-known poems he sought to fuse natural process and human physiology, the forces of nature and human mortality, and, as I shall argue, man's individual life and death with collective human and cosmic history. I want to examine three of Thomas's strategies of fusion in increasing order of importance and significance: fusion by contradiction, in 'Light

by owl-light', or, more generally, of Thomas's poetic works, would consist of a set of rules of this sort.

[6] The classic treatment of foregrounding is of course Jan Mukařovský, 'Standard Language and Poetic Language', in *A Prague School Reader on Esthetics, Literary Structure, and Style*, ed. Paul L. Garvin (Washington: Georgetown University Press, 1964), pp. 17–30.

Breaks Where No Sun Shines'; fusion by relation in 'The Force that Through the Green Fuse Drives the Flower', and fusion by preposing, in a more extended analysis of 'A Refusal to Mourn the Death, by Fire, of a Child in London'. Discussion of the first poem will exemplify Thomas's syntactic foregrounding; discussion of the second will show some of the consequences of a particular syntactic choice for a poem's design; in the third poem, I want to relate the way in which Thomas manipulates our perception of the poem to one of his major themes.

Light breaks where no sun shines

Light breaks where no sun shines;
Where no sea runs, the waters of the heart
Push in their tides;
And, broken ghosts with glow-worms in their heads,
The things of light
File through the flesh where no flesh decks the bones.

A candle in the thighs
Warms youth and seed and burns the seeds of age;
Where no seed stirs,
The fruit of man unwrinkles in the stars,
Bright as a fig;
Where no wax is, the candle shows its hairs.

Dawn breaks behind the eyes;
From poles of skull and toe the windy blood
Slides like a sea;
Nor fenced, nor staked, the gushers of the sky
Spout to the rod
Divining in a smile the oil of tears.

Night in the sockets rounds,
Like some pitch moon, the limit of the globes;
Day lights the bone;
Where no cold is, the skinning gales unpin
The winter's robes;
The film of spring is hanging from the lids.

Light breaks on secret lots,
On tips of thought where thoughts smell in the rain;
When logics die,
The secret of the soil grows through the eye,
And blood jumps in the sun;
Above the waste allotments the dawn halts.

The most striking linguistic feature of 'Light Breaks Where No
Sun Shines' is a series of six contradictions, found most densely
in the poem's first stanza and setting the dominant tone of the
work (typically, Thomas concentrates these devices at the
beginning of poems in which they appear, as if asking us to
notice them immediately). An adverbial clause undercuts each
main clause in 'Light breaks where no sun shines', 'the waters
of the heart push in their tides where no sea runs', 'the things
of light file through the flesh where no flesh decks the bones',
'the fruit of man unwrinkles in the stars where no seed stirs',
'the candle shows its hairs where no wax is', and 'the skinning
gales unpin the winter's robes where no cold is'.

All of these sentences are a slight but definite violation of the
natural-language rule that a sentence cannot contain embedded
sentences whose semantic interpretations taken together contradict that of the sentence as a whole.[7] 'Light breaks' is an idiom
applicable only to sunrise; light cannot break where no sun
shines. Only seas have tides; the waters of the heart cannot
push in their tides where no sea runs. Nothing can 'file through
the flesh were no flesh decks the bones'. Fruit cannot 'un-
wrinkle', i.e., mature, 'where no seed stirs'. All candles have
wax. Where there are winter's robes there must also be cold.

With these contradictions is paired a syntactic strategy that
brings them sharply into focus: the six adverbial clauses have
an identical, very compressed, and highly unusual form:
where no N V. All of the clauses derive from sentences which are
in some sense existential. Existential sentences, particularly
those using *to be*, usually make use of *there* ('Light breaks where

---

[7] See Jerrold J. Katz, 'Analyticity and Contradiction in Natural Language', in Jerry A. Fodor and Jerrold J. Katz, eds., *The Structure of Language*
(Englewood Cliffs, N.J.: Prentice-Hall, 1964), p. 450.

there is no sun shining'). Negative existential sentences normally involve the Negative-*any* construction so common in English:

(1) Where there isn't any sea running
(2) Where there isn't any seed stirring
(3) Where there isn't any wax
(4) Where there isn't any cold

And, if the *any*-construction is not used, the negative most often is expressed in the auxiliary system:

(5) Where flesh doesn't deck the bones

The use of the syntactic frame *Where no N V*, without adjectives, no adverbs, no auxiliaries, and, out of the six clauses, only one transitive verb with object, creates an astringent starkness which, taken together with the repetition of the clauses, further foregrounds the contradictions they express.

These contradictions are resolvable only if the light is some other kind of light than the sun; the tides part of some other body of water than the ocean; the flesh something other than the physical body, and so on—in other words, only if Thomas's meaning is metaphorical, not literal. And of course his meaning *is* metaphorical: at just these points of semantic contradiction, the poem's language asks to be noticed as language; it displays *maximum syntactic foregrounding*. At these semantic and syntactic cruces Thomas places the poem's most crucial metaphors, which underlie the design of the whole poem: the light breaking is the inspiriting of the human soul at the moment of conception; the tides the circulating blood impelled by the heart; the 'things of light' the inherited genes, imprinted in the foetus at the moment of conception before the flesh they shape is flesh; the fruit man's offspring, born not of a flowering seed—as is the fig—; the candle the phallus, symbolic of sexual force; the gales the forces of aging, stripping from the body its protection against oncoming senility and death. The metaphors achieved by the contradictions and the starkness of the syntax in which they are expressed constitute a fusion of natural forces with the progress of human life; the forces of the world are one with the forces inside every human, within the 'poles of skull and toe'. 'Man,' as Thomas wrote elsewhere, 'be my metaphor.' The poem is about contradiction and fusion—it says, in effect, the force which causes the sun to rise causes man to be conceived a spirited being, possessing a light which is not light. And the poem uses a strategy of contradiction and syntactic spareness to achieve that fusion.

The force that through the green fuse drives the flower

The force that through the green fuse drives the flower
Drives my green age; that blasts the roots of trees
Is my destroyer.
And I am dumb to tell the crooked rose
My youth is bent by the same wintry fever.

The force that drives the water through the rocks
Drives my red blood; that dries the mouthing streams
Turns mine to wax.
And I am dumb to mouth unto my veins
How at the mountain spring the same mouth sucks.

The hand that whirls the water in the pool
Stirs the quicksand; that ropes the blowing wind
Hauls my shroud sail.
And I am dumb to tell the hanging man
How of my clay is made the hangman's lime.

The lips of time leech to the fountain head;
Love drips and gathers, but the fallen blood
Shall calm her sores.
And I am dumb to tell a weather's wind
How time has ticked a heaven round the stars.

And I am dumb to tell the lover's tomb
How at my sheet goes the same crooked worm.

'The Force that Through the Green Fuse Drives the Flower' presents a different strategy of fusion: it seeks to identify the forces of man and of nature by syntactic relation. The dominant grammatical features of this poem are two: the repetition of the syntactic frame of the last two lines of each stanza—in which the operative word frequently is *same*—and the relative clauses of the first part of each of stanzas 1–3. Thomas's extensive use of the relative clause yields a highly subordinated or hypotactic style.

The two syntactic styles of hypotaxis and parataxis—basically, subordination and coordination—are different ways of relating, or linking, two or more propositions. While hypotaxis subordinates one proposition to the other, presenting a clear hierarchy, parataxis merely joins propositions serially with a coordinator of some sort, and leaves to the reader assessment of their relationship to one another. One reason why the relationship between the propositions is vaguer in a paratactic style is that the reader must process, in surface structure, two full sentence structures with only one grammatical link. If we were, for example, to recast the first lines of this poem's hypotactic syntax in a paratactic, coordinated style, the result would be: 'A force drives the flower through the green fuse and the same force drives my green age; it blasts the roots of trees and it is my destroyer.' We may roughly diagram these syntactic relations as in (6) (see p. 27).

The subordinated, hypotactic style (see (7), p. 28) which Thomas chooses instead has fewer major structural elements. Each of the two sentences (S_1 and S_2) constituting the coordinate structure that is the poem's first sentence (S_0) has fewer major structural elements than the paratactic version: one subject noun phrase (NP_1 and NP_2) instead of two, with two propositions clearly predicated of each subject noun phrase (VP_1 and S_3, for S_1; VP_2 and S_4, for S_2).

Thomas reinforces this strategy by using verbs in the two predications which semantically are either very closely related or identical: *drives* the flower, *drives* my green age; *blasts* the roots of trees, is my *destroyer* (which derives ultimately from *destroys* me); *drives* the water through the rocks, *drives* my red blood; *dries* the mouthing streams, *turns* mine *to wax* (from *turns-to-wax* my streams); *whirls* the water in the pool, *stirs* the quicksand; *ropes* the blowing wind, *hauls* my shroud sail. The noun phrases which are objects of these identical or similar verbs are being equated: flower = my green age; the roots of

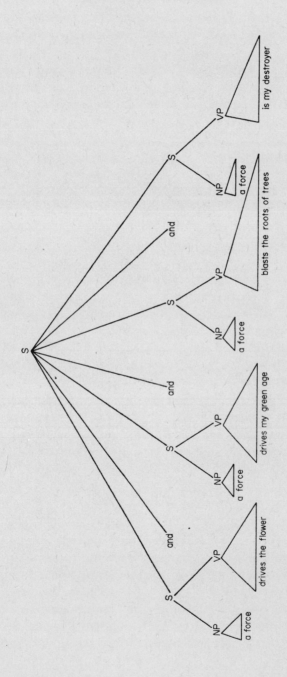

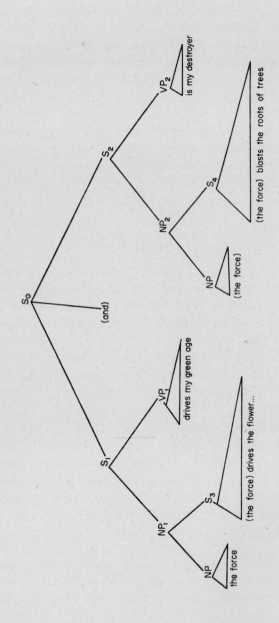

trees = me; the water = my red blood; the whirlpool = the quicksand; the mouthing streams = my streams, the blowing wind = my shroud sail. The same force which works in nature and in the world as a whole—the explosive force of growth and natural destruction, of wind and water—works within each individual human as the force of sexuality, of ageing, and of death. Thomas not only pushes the strategy of relation to its limit, but beyond it: in the second line of the first three stanzas he omits the required repetition of 'the force' before the second relative clause ('that blasts the roots of trees . . .') so that this coordinated sentence seems like another subordinated one, making the hypotaxis even stronger and the fusion more complete: one force drives, drives, blasts and destroys; one force drives, drives, dries and turns to wax; one force whirls, stirs, ropes, and hauls.[8]

Thomas's strategy of relation is the syntactic correlate of the oneness postulated in his repetition of the word *same* throughout the poem, and is at the centre of the poem's design—indeed, it is a near-perfect example of Roman Jakobson's famous statement that 'the poetic function projects the principle of equivalence from the axis of selection into the axis of combination':[9] to a considerable degree in 'The Force That Through The Green Fuse Drives the Flower', syntax is statement.

Let us now turn to a third strategy of fusion, in which Thomas orders the syntax of a poem so as to identify the life cycle of individual man with the cycle of human history. Here I want to pursue quite a bit further the method used in looking at the first two poems: a linguistic feature, crucial to a poet's deployment of the transformational apparatus of the language, is at

[8] Barbara Hall Partee has pointed out to me another set of parallels in these lines. At the start of each of the first three stanzas, positive and negative (or destroying, limiting) forces are yoked by this curious 'double hypotaxis': *drives, drives: blasts, destroys; drives, drives: dries, turns to wax; whirls, stirs: ropes, hauls.*

[9] Roman Jakobson, 'Closing Statement: Linguistics and Poetics', in *Style in Language*, ed. Thomas A. Sebeok (Cambridge, Mass., and New York: Technology Press and Wiley & Sons, 1960), p. 358.

the centre of a poem's artistic design. Here the important strategy is *preposing*: as I hope to show, Thomas orchestrates a complex variety of transformations which have the effect of moving crucially important semantic materials to the *left* of their ordinary syntactic positions.

A Refusal to Mourn the Death, by Fire, of a Child in London

Never until the mankind making
Bird beast and flower
Fathering and all humbling darkness
Tells with silence the last light breaking
And the still hour
Is come of the sea tumbling in harness

And I must enter again the round
Zion of the water bead
And the synagogue of the ear of corn
Shall I let pray the shadow of a sound
Or sow my salt seed
In the least valley of sackcloth to mourn

The majesty and burning of the child's death.
I shall not murder
The mankind of her going with a grave truth
Nor blaspheme down the stations of the breath
With any further
Elegy of innocence and youth.

Deep with the first dead lies London's daughter,
Robed in the long friends,
The grains beyond age, the dark veins of her mother,
Secret by the unmourning water
Of the riding Thames.
After the first death, there is no other.

This poem embodies the conventional paradox of the elegy— a poem whose occasion is to mark and mourn a passing, explicitly refuses to mourn, and finds an eternal life in death. In 'A Refusal to Mourn', I hope to show, this paradox is to be found in the poem's syntactic machinery itself.

The greatest interpretational difficulty in this poem is simply analysing the structure of its first sentence. Between the introductory negative adverb *never* and the inverted auxiliary element *shall* Thomas puts in our way as stumbling blocks a triple set of conjoined included sentences with three subjects and three predicates, two of which themselves contain conjoined structures: 'the darkness tells with silence', 'the still hour is come of the sea tumbling in harness', and 'I must enter again the round Zion of the water bead. . . .'

Never is one of a class of negative adverbs, phrases, and clauses which share an odd property in English. Adverbs and adverbial phrases normally appear between subject and verb (as in the preceding clause of this sentence) or between the auxiliary and the verb ('John can easily beat Bill at tennis'). They can in many cases be preposed to the front of the sentence ('Occasionally Mary travels by train'), and if a preposed adverb has a negative in it, the subject inverts with part of the auxiliary:

(8) I have never seen such a cold spring → Never have I seen such a cold spring

(9) Americans seldom drink tea → Seldom do Americans drink tea

This rule can be extended to cover cases where a prepositional phrase serving as sentence modifier intervenes between the negative element and the inverted auxiliary, even when this modifier is compounded:

(10) Wild animals rarely approach humans at any season → Rarely at any season do wild animals approach humans

(11) Wild animals rarely approach humans at any season, and then only when the pangs of hunger are particularly sharp → Rarely at any season, and then only when the pangs of hunger are particularly sharp, do wild animals approach humans

This rule generalizes to a wide range of cases in English. Any sentence using it ought to be easily decoded by a reader or listener, but this one at the beginning of 'A Refusal to Mourn' is not, because it forces us to hold in abeyance, uninterpreted and unrelated to the rest of the poem, so much syntactic material before we come to the subject and predicate of the sentence in the tenth line of the poem.

Thomas strongly foregrounds this material by exploiting a characteristic of the human language faculty: the limits on our ability to hold in storage syntactic structures which have not yet been resolved, which remain incomplete grammatical units.[10] Storage capacity can be illustrated as follows: there is a rule of English syntax which allows us to embed one sentence in another without a relative pronoun, creating a surface structure with two nouns followed by two verbs:

(12) The jet Sam boarded took off.

But there is a limit on our ability to decode such embeddings, although in theory such a rule should be able to function again and again:

(13) The jet the pilot Harry knew flew landed.

Here the embedding rule is 'pushed', straining beyond its limits our capacity to 'store' the subjects of these embedded sentences while we wait to pair them up with the verbs to which they are syntactically related. We very nearly have to work out the sentence with a pencil and paper.

Thomas is similarly 'pushing' the adverb-preposing rule, which allows us to place very complex sentence adverbs at the beginning of sentences. This sentence is so complicated that our processing or decoding capacity again is exceeded. The passage thus is syntactically foregrounded, thrust before us as an act of language.

The preposing of *never* along with a second preposing of the long *until*-clause (which normally would occur at the end of the sentence), themselves sharply foregrounded, also bring into focus an important paradox by juxtaposing the contrary entities *never* and *until*. One can't *never* do X *until* Y happens; that is, one can't say he will never do something and then immediately stipulate a time when he will do it. If *never* remains unpreposed, that paradox is muted.

[10] For a general discussion of performance limitations of this sort, see Noam Chomsky, *Aspects of the Theory of Syntax* (Cambridge, Mass.: The M.I.T. Press, 1965), pp. 12–13.

The preposing of *never* also has a consequence which makes it clear that Thomas is not merely indulging in syntactic obfuscation for its own sake. As we have pointed out, the presence of a negative element in the preposed adverb requires the inversion of part of the auxiliary with the subject, as we can see more clearly in the following partial, very rough derivation of the sentence:

(14) *Before adverb-preposing;* I shall never let pray the shadow of a sound until the mankind making . . . darkness tells with silence the last light breaking . . .

Adverb-preposing; Until the mankind making . . . darkness tells with silence the last light breaking . . . I shall never let pray the shadow of a sound . . .

Never-preposing; Never until the . . . darkness tells with silence the last light breaking . . . I shall let pray . . .

Auxiliary inversion; Never until the . . . darkness tells with silence the last light breaking . . . shall I let pray . . .

Thomas manages the syntactic patterns of this sentence so that while he has put up barriers to our decoding of the sentence, he has nevertheless given us a clear sign: after *never*, we know that the end of the material we are being asked to hold in suspension will be clearly signalled by an inverted auxiliary element. Notice that without this preposing of *never* and its necessarily consequent inversion, our way through the sentence is much less clear:

(15) Until the mankind making, bird, beast and flower fathering, and all humbling darkness tells with silence the last light breaking and the still hour is come of the sea tumbling in harness and I must enter again the round Zion of the water bead and the synagogue of the ear of corn I shall never let pray the shadow of a sound. . . .

The dislocations of the poem's syntax thus have both limits and a purpose. We are asked to suspend interpretation of certain semantic and syntactic material over nine lines of poetry.

But several problems remain. When we examine the embedded sentence beginning with 'the mankind' and ending with

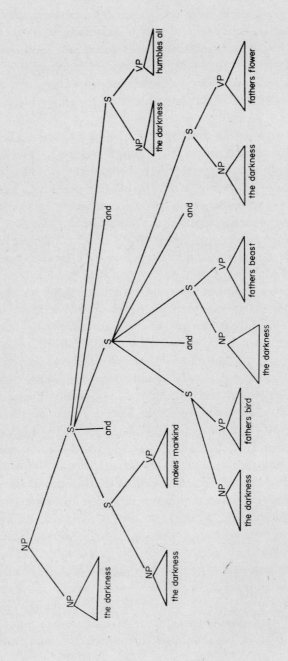

'breaking' we find more syntactic difficulties. In written English, a phrase containing a noun followed by a present participle verb normally is interpreted with the noun as subject of the participle:

(16) I saw a boy sleeping = I saw a boy who was sleeping.
A special case of these phrases is interpreted with the noun as *object* of the verb:

(17) I saw a man-eating tiger = I saw a tiger which ate men.
These special cases are marked in the written language with a hyphen, and in the spoken language with a special stress pattern.

The crude diagram (see (18), p. 34) of the underlying structure of the very complex noun phrase which is subject of *tells* shows graphically how a structure which in its 'unmarked' form[11] is heavily right-branching (notice that *darkness* is on the left, and the predications march off to the right) is changed by Thomas's exercise of particular transformations in English into a structure which is heavily loaded to the left of the noun head.

Notice, too, that one of the embedded sentences within the modifying structure—'the darkness fathers bird and the darkness fathers beast and the darkness fathers flower' (which normally would become a long relative clause, 'which . . . fathers bird, beast, and flower')—is itself converted into a left-heavy structure, 'bird, beast, and flower fathering (darkness).' At three levels, then—this embedded modifier, the subject noun phrase of *tells*, and the sentence adverb—Thomas's syntactic strategy is to shift very heavily to the left.

As we have observed, modifiers of *darkness* exploit this special case of Noun followed by Present Participle, where the noun is object, not subject. The nature of this pattern, with the direct object preposed to the verb and the subject postposed, 'mankind-making darkness', means that if several identical surface modifying structures of this form are conjoined, with the head they modify at the end, the object of the second structure will at

[11] i.e., the form in which its surface structure would emerge without application of what might be called 'marked' transformations permuting the order of certain modifying elements.

first be open to interpretation as at least two other syntactic entities. In this embedded sentence—'mankind making bird beast and flower fathering and all humbling darkness'—*bird* can at first glance be either object of *making* (with *mankind* as subject: 'mankind which makes birds') or subject of *making* ('bird which makes mankind'). These interpretations are possible because when we move the object in front of the verb the object position is left empty.

(19) After creation of Noun-Participle structures:

Mankind making   bird . . . fathering   darkness

←————Object   ←————Object

Language perception is temporally ordered. When we are presented with difficult syntax, we employ perceptual strategies to try to decode it—that is, to make sense of it—as it is presented to us. The foregoing discussion has sought to establish that Thomas syntactically foregrounds by creating difficulties, most of them within the rules of English syntax; here I want to suggest how an idealized reader (analogous to the idealized speaker-hearer) goes about solving them.

The first perceptual stratagem is to seek a plausible object for a transitive verb, *making*, which must have one.[12] The most likely candidate is the next following noun in the structure which remains, *bird*.

(20) mankind making bird . . . = 'mankind which makes birds'?

---

[12] In this discussion of perceptual strategies I am adopting some of the proposals of Thomas G. Bever's important article, 'The Cognitive Basis for Linguistic Structures', in *Cognition and the Development of Language*, ed. John R. Hayes (New York: John Wiley & Sons, 1970), pp. 279–362. The stratagem involved in seeking a plausible object for *making* arises first from Bever's Strategy A (p. 290): 'Segment together any sequence X . . . Y, in which the members could be related by primary internal structural relations, "actor action object . . . modifier".' Here the sequence 'mankind making bird' could be related as 'actor action object'. This stratagem is reinforced by Bever's Strategy D (p. 298): 'Any *Noun-Verb-Noun* (NVN) sequence within a potential internal unit in the surface structure corresponds to "*actor-action-object*".'

The second strategem is to invoke the special case of the preposed object, making *bird* the subject (as in 'man-eating
tiger').[13]

 (21) mankind making bird . . . = 'bird which makes mankind'?

Only when we reach the head noun *darkness* is the reader able
to make sense of the syntax and realize that the three participial
structures are conjoined equal modifiers.

 (22) mankind making bird . . . fathering and all humbling
   darkness.

The noun phrase finally is never ambiguous, but the reader,
on this analysis, goes through a number of false starts before he
finds that it is not; in the process, the phrase, as an act of language, is foregrounded, again as a consequence of the strategy
of preposing. The reader once again is forced to hold in abeyance his interpretation of this at first anomalous sentence, and
with it, the semantic material it contains. Again, as with the
preposed adverbial clause, the end of this holding in abeyance
is clearly signalled by the subject-finite verb sequence 'darkness
tells'. *Tells* is the inflected main verb, *darkness* is the subject, and
all of the previous participial structures modify *darkness*.

 This poem would have been much easier to comprehend had
Thomas written its first stanza without all of the left-ward
shifting. But its effect would have been very different, lacking
the intense buildup of tension and release which is the hallmark
of this poem.

 (23) I shall never let pray the shadow of a sound, or sow my
   salt seed in the least valley of sackcloth to mourn the
   majesty and burning of the child's death until the darkness, which makes mankind, fathers bird, beast, and
   flower, and humbles all, tells with silence the last light
   breaking, and the still hour is come of the sea tumbling
   in harness, and I must enter again the round Zion of the
   water bead and the synagogue of the ear of corn.

Of course Thomas did not write 'A Refusal to Mourn' this

---

[13] This strategem is invoked because *bird* appears to signal the end of a
noun phrase (see Bever's Strategy 'E', p. 323).

way. And in not writing it this way he exploited a number of devices in the rules of English syntax which make what are ordinarily last things in the sentence first, and first things last. These facts and the means of their achievement must necessarily engage the attention of the critic as well as that of the linguist.

For Thomas, as has been recently argued,[14] birth and death are not discrete events, but part of a never-ending cycle, a 'Biblical rhythm', of birth, life, death, decay, and regeneration, epitomized in the Biblical tales of the Garden of Eden, the Flood, the sacrifice of Isaac, and the life of Christ. An act of creation, for Thomas, must be viewed as leading to an act of destruction. Conversely, destruction and death must be viewed as containing in themselves the seeds of regeneration and rebirth. If birth is the beginning of a cycle culminating in the 'sundering ultimate kingdom of Genesis' thunder', as Thomas writes in 'Ceremony After a Fire Raid', then death, too, begins a cycle in which Thomas saw 'seed of sons in the loin of the black husk left. . . .' No death, therefore, can be seen apart from its context as the beginning of life.

In 'A Refusal to Mourn', Thomas's syntactic strategies do not allow us to see the individual death of the girl apart from its context in the entirety of human history. The poem's grammar first preposes from their natural word order modifying elements which speak of the first creation, the 'mankind-making, bird beast and flower-fathering and all-humbling darkness', and then syntactically fuses that creating and fructifying darkness with the darkness of the last day, which 'tells with silence the last light breaking', time far beyond this one death, when the speaker must enter the 'round Zion of the water bead and the synagogue of the ear of corn', themselves embodying the germs of a new creation which can follow even this final death.[15] For Thomas, both the Creation and the Day

[14] For discussion of this aspect of Dylan Thomas's poetics, see William T. Moynihan, *The Craft and Art of Dylan Thomas* (Ithaca, N.Y.: Cornell University Press, 1966), pp. 217–81.

[15] It is worth pointing out that Thomas's syntax here again makes use,

of Judgement are Apocalypses. Only after the poem's language forces us to perceive this death firmly embedded in its cosmic context, between the first creation and the last destruction—in each of which it forms so central a part—are we able to sort out the poem's syntax and discover all of these grammatical elements pointing to the death itself. With a strategy of fusion by preposition, Thomas identifies an individual human life with the entire history of the created world.

A brief summation is in order. Transformations can be viewed as formal models for ways in which we can express a given concept. I have sought to demonstrate that analysis of a poet's typical or idiosyncratic manipulations of these syntactic processes can lay bare the deep form of particular poems—the form controlling metaphor, theme, tone, imagery, and diction. I have tried to show how a number of syntactic strategies—first, the yoking of immediate syntactic constituents which are contradictory; second, intensive use of the relative clause formation and related transformations, and finally, various kinds of preposing transformations—have functioned with increasing force in three poems to help achieve the unity of man and natural process which is one of the central principles of Dylan Thomas's poetics.

---

in a much subtler way, of the strategies of contradiction and relation central to 'Light Breaks Where No Sun Shines' and 'The Force that Through the Green Fuse Drives the Flower.' In one sentence it is predicated of a darkness held, in its prenominal modifying structures, to be the source of creation, that it is the source of destruction. The modification which is to be undercut is built up in maximally reduced relative clauses—so reduced that, unlike all other relative clauses except those which transformational grammarians analyse as underlying one-word prenominal adjectives, they may be preposed in front of the head noun.

CHAPTER TWO

THE SELF-REFLEXIVE ARTEFACT: THE FUNCTION OF MIMESIS IN AN APPROACH TO A THEORY OF VALUE FOR LITERATURE

E. L. Epstein

The two pillars upon which a theory of criticism must rest are an account of value and an account of communication.

I. A. Richards, Principles of Literary Criticism[1]

It will, I imagine, seem ridiculous that things are made manifest through imitations in letters and syllables; nevertheless it cannot be otherwise.

Plato, Cratylus *425d*[2]

In the model of language-production that is assumed for the purposes of this paper, a speaker or writer first constructs a lexical constellation which mimes a state of affairs; this constellation is then realized in linear and segmental form syntactically, and then either phonologically or graphemically. This realization may be produced *automatically*, that is, with no principle of selection operating among its linear elements other than the style of the speaker or writer (and that style operating

---

[1] I. A. Richards, *Principles of Literary Criticism*, 2nd ed. (London: Routledge and Kegan Paul, 1926), p. 25.

[2] Plato, *Cratylus* 425d, trans. H. N. Fowler, Loeb Classical Lib. Ed., Vol. VI (London: Heinemann, and Cambridge, Mass.: Harvard U.P., 1953).

outside of awareness), in which case the final speech-act is casual prose. On the other hand, there may be *conscious* or *quasi-conscious* selection and arrangement of syntactic and phonological linear elements of form, in which case a 'poetic function' is operating.

In this paper, the second type of speech-act will be closely examined and analysed, to observe the relationship or lack of relationship between the principles of selection and arrangement operating on the elements of form to see whether they are determined or not determined by the particular state of affairs conveyed by the lexical constellation chosen, and also to suggest a reason for formal mimesis of content as part of a criterion of value for literature.

The relation of content to form in poetry is one of the perennial issues of criticism. Some critics deny the existence of the problem; 'meaning' for them is a term describing the global and indivisible effect of a work of verbal art. Others find in the 'poetic function' of language a degree of organization of form that in casual discourse usually operates only in the choice of expressions of content. However, even among these critics, descriptions of relationships between content and form in poetry are rare.

The clearest description of a possible reflection of content in form is to be found in Donald Davie's *Articulate Energy* (1955). Davie describes five types of organization of syntax in poetry, four of which bear a direct positive relationship to content: (1) *subjective*, whose 'function is to please us by the fidelity with which it follows the "form of thought" in the poet's mind'; (2) *dramatic*, whose 'function is to please us by the fidelity with which it follows the "form of thought" in some mind other than the poet's, which the poet imagines'; (3) *objective*, whose 'function is to please us by the fidelity with which it follows a form of action, a movement not through any mind, but in the world at large'; (4) *'syntax like music'*, whose 'function is to please us by the fidelity with which it follows a "form of thought" through the poet's mind *but without defining that thought*';

(5) '*syntax like mathematics*', '*when its function is to please us in and for itself.*'[3]

Davie recognizes that his 'mathematical syntax' is unlike the other four: 'it differs from other kinds of syntax only in this— that the pleasure it gives has nothing to do with mimesis' (94). This difference, however, should be given greater weight in his scale of effects than he gives it. I would suggest that there are basically only two types of formal relationship to content— *mimetic* and *non-mimetic*. With this scheme it is possible to des- cribe other sorts of reflection of content besides syntactic—there is the whole subtle problem of lexical mimesis, and the confused problem of sound-symbolism, the phonological contribution to the mimicking of content.

A. NON-MIMETIC FORMS OF EXPRESSION

Logically there are two types of non-mimetic forms of expres- sion—one type in which no recognizable schemata of formal organization can be discerned (and hence no mimetic forms), and another type in which recognizable forms exist but do not reflect any principle of organization from any level higher than the syntactic.

I. The first type, taken in its purest form, would lack any lexical ordering and hence would lack all informative power. There are few utterances of which this is true—even enigmatic grunts usually signal the presence of the grunter. A less pure form would acknowledge the mimetic function of lexis, but would only contain the most neutral possible syntactic and intonational structures. (In classical transformational terms, one utterance is more 'neutral' than another if it is derivable with fewer transformations.) There would indeed be mimesis between forms of syntax and such elements of organization of the non-linguistic universe as contiguity in time and space, and psychological processes of perception. Also, the sounds of such

[3] Donald Davie, *Articulate Energy: an Inquiry into the Syntax of English Poetry* (London: Routledge and Kegan Paul, 1955), pp. 68, 76, 79, 86, 92.

utterances could be shown to resemble sound-patterns other than those of speech. However, since these subordinate patterns are 'automatized' in presentation and reception, they do not reflect the non-automatic mimesis of the reality presented by the lexis of the utterance. This type of utterance entirely lacks the 'poetic function' of language, and besides gives rise to certain communicative difficulties even as casual prose. The description of such difficulties also helps to establish the necessity of mimetic subordinate forms within the utterance.

II. The second type would include utterances displaying Davie's 'syntax as mathematics', as well as phonological organization such as rhyme, meter, and alliteration, and various rhetorical figures—antithesis, isocolon, phonological chiasmus, and the like. These figures would not reflect lexical content, or might even actively contradict it.

Examples of this second type are easy to find, not only in 'older poetry' and especially in poetry of the English Augustan age, as Davie suggests (94), but among any poetry deriving from an aesthetic in which content may be indefinitely subordinated to form. English Augustan poetry, though it does generally conform to a style of content-decorum, contains many examples of organization of form independent of content or contradictory of it. For example, Pope in his early pastoral poetry often displays this non-mimetic degree of organization.

> But see, the Shepherds shun the Noon-day Heat,
> The lowing Herds to murm'ring Brooks retreat,
> To closer Shades the panting Flocks remove,
> Ye Gods! and is there no Relief for Love?
>
> (*Summer: The Second Pastoral*, ll. 85–8)

The syntactic chiasmus in the two middle lines is entirely gratuitous (unless the herds go one way and the flocks another!)

> Where-e'er you walk, cool Gales shall fan the Glade,
> Trees, where you sit, shall crowd into a Shade,
> Where-e'er you tread, the blushing Flow'rs shall rise,
> And all things flourish where you turn your eyes.
>
> (*Summer: The Second Pastoral*, ll. 73–6)

The peregrinations of the adverbial of place, from initial position to internal position to initial position to final position,[4] do not mime any such wandering on the part of the beloved. If they did, it would suggest she didn't know just where she was going. The motive for the dispersal of the adverbials is, of course, entirely decorative or 'mathematical'; the original version of these lines was all too symmetrical:

> Winds, where you walk, shall gently fann the Glade,
> Trees, where you sit, shall crowd into a Shade,
> Flow'rs, where you tread, in painted Pride shall rise,
> And all things flourish where you turn your Eyes!

There is a psychological value, however, to the final patterning of these adverbials. In the last line the adverbial is in 'normal' position—that is, according to most phrase-structure rules, the place for adverbials is at the end of utterances. By putting the adverbial first at the beginning of the utterance, then by moving it into the utterance (second line), then returning it to initial position (third line), and finally allowing it to appear in its canonical final position, Pope teases the reader at first and finally satisfies him. This effect is entirely dependent upon syntactic placement and has no lexical-mimetic value—the 'teasing' is inappropriate both to the tone of the passage and to the situation expressed by it.

> Lo Earth receives him from the bending Skies!
> Sink down ye Mountains, and ye Vallies rise:
> With Heads declin'd, ye Cedars, Homage pay;
> Be smooth ye Rocks, ye rapid Floods give way!
> The Savior comes! by ancient Bards foretold:
> Hear him ye Deaf, and all ye Blind behold!
>
>   (*Messiah*, ll. 33–8)

There is a mechanically operating pattern of chiastic syntax in this passage—every even line exhibits syntactic chiasmus. There is no reason for this elaborate symmetry in the situation expressed.

---

[4] See Winifred Nowottny, *The Language Poets Use* (London: Athlone Press, 1962), pp. 11–12.

Thou wert from Aetna's burning Entrails torn,
Got by fierce Whirlwinds, and in Thunder born!
> (*Autumn: The Third Pastoral*, ll. 91-2)

These lines exhibit a double chiasmus of Syntax:
(Subject-Auxiliary) Prepositional-Verb; Verb-
Prepositional; Prepositional-Verb.
There is no reason beyond the requirements of meter for this
chain of chiasmus.

> Adieu ye *Vales*, ye *Mountains*, *Streams* and *Groves*,
> Adieu ye Shepherd's rural *Lays* and *Loves*,
> Adieu my Flocks, farewell ye *Sylvan* Crew,
> Daphne farewell, and all the World adieu!
>> (*Winter: The Fourth Pastoral*, ll. 89-92)

There is a double grade of chiasmus expressed in the third and
fourth lines syntactically, and a (related) grade of phonological
chiasmus.

1. The *Adieu* clauses are in chiasmus:
   Exclamation—Nominal : *Nominal—Exclamation*
   Adieu   my flocks: all the   Adieu
                          world
2. The *farewell* clauses are in chiasmus:
   Exclamation—Nominal : *Nominal—Exclamation*
   farewell   ye *Sylvan* : Daphne   farewell
                Crew
3. The repetition of sounds is chiastic:
   Adieu   farewell   farewell   Adieu

Thus a double syntactic chiasmus is enclosed within a phonological chiasmus. This elegance of patterning, however, mimes
no aspect of the situation expressed. It seems to be motivated
rather by a formal aspect of the *Pastorals* themselves; Pope seems
to feel the need for a 'decorative' ending to provide a formal
climax to his structure—these lines end the last Pastoral. It
could perhaps be said that the complexity of these lines mimes a
craftsman's impulse in the poet, and therefore it is, in Davie's
terms, an example of 'subjective' mimesis. Davie's term 'form

of thought' would certainly comprehend conscious acts of
formal construction as well as more emotional impulses; when
a reader feels that a creator has risen to an occasion, when the
poet seems to acknowledge his own understanding of his
creation, by 'decorating' important structural points either
mimetically or non-mimetically, there is a certain degree of
dramatic excitement engendered as a result. This could be
illustrated from the works of so diverse a selection of writers as
Homer, Milton, Dante, James Joyce, and Henry James.

The last example of non-mimetic verse shows a case of
missed opportunity by the poet.

> Then sings by turns, by turns the Muses sing,
> Now Hawthorn blossom, now the Daisies spring,
> Now Leaves the Trees, and Flow'rs adorn the Ground;
> Begin, the Vales shall ev'ry Note rebound.
>
> (*Spring: The First Pastoral*, ll. 41–4)

The chiasmus in the first line represents an attempt to mime the
notion of alternate singing—an example of Davie's 'objective'
mimesis—but curiously it fails: alternate singing is chiastic only
when the second voice provides a mirror-strophe to the first
voice's strophe. As we see from the song actually produced,
each strophe is very like every other strophe. The odd fact about
this situation is that the poem that Pope is imitating in this
passage, Virgil's *Third Eclogue*, achieves an authentic example of
objective mimesis:

> Dicite, quandoquidem in molli consedimus herba,
> et nunc omnis ager, nunc omnis parturit arbos,
> nunc frondent silvae, nunc formonsissimus annus.
> Incipe Damoeta, tu deinde sequere, Menalca;
> alterna dicetis; amant alterna Camenae.
>
> (ll. 55–9)

The notion of 'alterna' in the Virgil passage is expressed in
lines 56 and 57, before the word actually appears. In these lines
the position of the governing verb does indeed alternate:

> nunc omnis ager, nunc omnis *parturit* arbos,
> nunc *frondent* silvae, nunc formonsissimus annus.

Then, when the chiasmus within line 59 occurs (*alterna*-Verb: Verb-*alterna*), it includes within itself the notion of alternation established in the previous lines, and is not simply a mirror-repetition, as it is in Pope. For some reason, a chiasmus *between* lines seems to convey alternation, whereas chiasmus *within* a line conveys only mirror-repetition. (C. Day Lewis in his translation of this eclogue also achieves only a single-line chiasmus: 'You begin, Damoetas, and you, Menalcas, follow.')

The presence in utterances of non-mimetic symmetrical or counter-symmetrical syntactic or phonological schemata does not seem to indicate a high degree of poetic value, at least in a post-Romantic age. Traditional craftsmanship as such is not the most highly valued element in an age which has come to expect a perceptible degree of emotional involvement of the writer in his work. If, therefore, the schemata in the utterances that make up the work are lower-level regularities without reference to the lexical level of the work, the judgment of the age is that the work exhibits only a low degree of value. Indeed, such low-level regularities are characteristic more of comic or ironic poetry than of more highly valued forms. The comic or ironic rhymes and rhythms of Eliot, for example, exhibit this preference of modern readers. The metrical perfection of Prufrock's 'I do not think that they will sing to me' contrasts ironically with its completely flat tone, to provide a moment of ironic anticlimax. Therefore, in modern poetry, non-mimetic forms are either automatized, or 'foregrounded' for comic or ironic effect.

B. GRADES OF MIMESIS

Davie provides four types of mimetic syntax (he does not discuss phonology), but the possibility of a ranking of value within these types is only suggested. I would like to propose such a possible ranking.

First, however, I would like to dispose of Davie's 'syntax as music', his fourth type of syntax. It seems to me that here Davie is not describing a mode of regarding syntax distinct from his other three types, but rather a type of modulation of attention which may be present during the reception of the other types. It would be to the other types of schemata as, for example, amplitude is to pitch in acoustics. The 'morphology' of an emotion, when the emotion itself cannot be named, could be recognized whether the mimesis is that of the writer himself, or of a *persona*, or even (within limits) of an objective situation described by the writer (or indeed described by a *persona*), with emotion or the absence of emotion substituted for the emotion of the human author or his humanoid *persona*. Indeed, Davie's examples of 'syntax as music' clearly seem to provide mimesis of psychological processes, or perceptions of objective processes in the world outside the consciousness, and therefore his musical syntax is reducible either to 'subjective/dramatic' mimesis, or 'objective' mimesis.

The word *mimesis* would here be reserved for the presence of analogous schemata in the lexical level and one or both of the lower levels of syntax or phonology (or graphemics). However I believe that while Davie correctly distinguished mimesis of entities other than human consciousnesses from mimesis of human consciousnesses (in his description of 'objective' syntax), I am not sure that his distinction between 'subjective' and 'dramatic' mimesis is of the same sort. A *persona* is not an object with an existence independent of the writer; its existence is entirely contingent upon his. I would rather class Davie's dramatic mimesis as a grade of subjective mimesis than as a class of its own. The creation of *personae* has traditionally formed part of the equipment for the expression of the writer's personality. A *persona* has one property that distinguishes it clearly from an objective phenomenon but which does not distinguish it from subjective portraits: neither the description of a fictional *persona* nor the description of the writer's *persona* can be debated, for completeness or for accuracy, with the describer of it. No observer ever sees exactly the same object or process as another, from precisely the same point in space and time, but relative coincidence of point of view may be achieved for an objective phenomenon, whereas points of view on subjective phenomena cannot even begin to be similar. Of course, as Davie remarks (79), even objective phenomena are not observed directly: each observer describes an *imago* of the object or process, not the phenomenon itself. However, subjective phenomena have, in addition to this 'automatic' criterion of subjectivity, a quite personal subjectivity which cancels the possibility of debate from the beginning.

Therefore I would suggest a schema as follows:
I. *Non-mimetic forms*
a. absolutely non-mimetic (not even lexical mimesis)
b. relatively non-mimetic (automatic lexical mimesis)
   1. non-mimetic phonological schemata
   2. non-mimetic syntactic schemata
   3. related combined but non-mimetic phonological and syntactic schemata
II. *Mimetic forms*
a. objective mimesis of lexis
   1. by phonological schemata
   2. by syntactic schemata
   3. by related combined phonological and syntactic schemata
b. subjective mimesis of lexis
   1. dramatic mimesis (mimesis of *personae*)
      a. phonological
      b. syntactic
      c. combined
   2. self-reflexive mimesis (mimesis of *imago* of self)
      a. phonological
      b. syntactic
      c. combined

(Graphemic mimesis is graded the same as the corresponding phonological class.) The farther down in the schema is the appropriate designation, the higher the 'value' of the utterance. The assignment of value is made on the principle that the more personal and therefore the less informative is the lexical constellation underlying the utterance, the more assistance it requires from mimetic forms of expression to be apprehended, and the more valuable it becomes when it *is* apprehended. Mimetic phonological and syntactic forms, therefore, provide a metaphor for lexis in the more highly valued forms. I assume that in this stage of history the communication of an intensely personal expressive constellation bears the highest value in a verbal work of art.

Of course, 'secondary' phenomena such as comic or ironic effects, or effects created by 'collage' techniques, pose special problems and would perhaps need to be graded on two scales—one, the scale above applied precisely, and two, the (presumed) gap between lexis and expression then re-evaluated as self-reflexive mimesis of the highest grade. Thus, for example, we can evaluate the self-mocking, Pierrotesque writing of Laforgue or Beckett or Donald Barthelme as mirroring the broken *persona* the writer perceives in himself, and the collage techniques of Joyce would first be graded as employing combined techniques for objective and dramatic mimesis of lexis, and would then be re-evaluated as the highest grade of value, a portrait of the artist 'writing the mystery of himsel in furniture', the 'zoantholitic furniture' of the 'hueful panepiphanal world' (*Finnegans Wake*, p. 184, lines 9–10; p. 611, lines 13–14).

1. Objective mimesis of lexis

The 'objective' phenomena to be mimed in literary discourse can be divided into objects and processes, but it seems clear that there is an inherent difficulty in miming objects in the linear stream of speech or writing, except as interruptions in flow (like a stone in a stream). This would tend to limit objective mimesis to imitations of processes; and indeed most examples of objective mimesis are of processes in time, psychological processes involved in the apprehension of phenomena external to the consciousness of the observer, as well as the linearly successive phenomena themselves—the flowing of water, waves, echoes, the ripening of vegetation, and the stream of speech itself.

Pope provides many examples of mimesis of objective phenomena. Echo-effects abound in his pastorals.

> Go gentle Gales, and bear my Sighs away!
> Come, Delia, come; ah why this long Delay?
> Thro' Rocks and Caves the name of *Delia* sounds,
> *Delia*, each Cave and ecchoing Rock rebounds.
> Autumn: The Third Pastoral, ll. 47–50)
> . . . . *Delia* sounds,
> *Delia*, ...

The echoing effect is, of course, deliberate; the name of the beloved originally was *Thyrsis*, but was altered to *Delia* to chime with *Delay* (as well as avoiding the suggestion of homosexuality in the Virgilian original). In addition to the repetitions of *Delia* and the chime with *Delay*, there are other repeated sounds— *Go-Gales, my-Signs, Gales-away, Come-come, Rocks-Caves-Cave-Rock* (this last perhaps not mimetic because chiastic—echoes do not repeat in reverse.)

> In hollow Caves sweet *Echo* silent lies,
> Silent, or only to her name replies,
> Her name with Pleasure once she taught the Shore,
> Now Daphne's dead, and Pleasure is no more.
> (Winter: The Fourth Pastoral, ll. 41–4)

There is much exact echoing: *silent-silent, her name-her name, pleasure-pleasure.* There is also sound-echoing: *silent-lies, taught-shore, Daphne's-dead.* There may be syntactic echoing between lines 41 and 42.

Another echo-effect appears in Pope's version of Virgil's *Fourth Eclogue*:

> Hark! a glad Voice the lonely Desert chears:
> Prepare the Way! a God, a God appears.
> A God, a God! the vocal Hills reply,
> The Rocks proclaim th'approaching Deity.
> (Messiah, ll. 29–32)

Natural processes are mimed syntactically in the first line of another couplet from *Messiah*, but falsified in the second:

To leaf-less Shrubs the flow'ring Palms succeed,
And od'rous Myrtle to the noisome Weed.

(ll. 75–6)

The syntactic inversion which places the two nominals together in l. 75, thus miming the change of vegetation from one state to a succeeding state ('leaf-less' → 'flow'ring'), is reversed in l. 76, becoming counter-mimetic, and consequently the two lines of the couplet would be of different values.

In a famous passage from *An Essay on Criticism*, ll. 337–73, Pope achieves a pyrotechnical display of mimetic ingenuity. All sixteen mimetic lines in this passage (ll. 345, 346, 347, 350, 351, 352, 353, 357, 365, 367, 368, 369, 370, 371, 372, 373) exhibit highly interesting linguistic features, mimetic of content.[5] However, they all derive their mimetic effect from phonological or syntactic structures (often semi-grammatical), or both. Line 347, for example, derives its mimetic effect from a combination of syntax and phonology.

And ten low Words oft creep in one dull Line.

Pope does indeed attempt to avoid lines composed entirely of monosyllabic words, but the mimetic effect of the line is only partly dependent upon the absence of polysyllabic words, with their 'normal transition' between syllables. One bisyllabic word in line 347, for example, would not by itself speed up the line appreciably. The effect depends partly upon the syntactic nature of the words in the line, and partly upon phonological transition-effects. Eight of the ten syllabic positions in the line are occupied by items from major syntactic classes—nouns, non-equational verbs, adjectives, numerals, adverbials—each demanding a major phonological stress. Only two of the syllables are occupied by members of minor classes—'and' and 'in'. In this sense, the 'Words' are not 'low', they are all too 'high' for a normal blank-verse matrix.

This stiffness of intonation forbids even the highly limited amount of transitional slurring between syllables (haplology)

---

[5] See E. L. Epstein, 'The Imitative Effects in Pope's *An Essay on Criticism* (forthcoming).

permitted in the performance of poetry. There are seven points out of the nine points of transition in the line where slurring would occur in casual speech, and where it now may not. This frustration of performance slows the performance of this line to a creep, which objectively mimes the 'lowness' and 'dullness' of a line so constituted.

1. *And-ten;* ordinarily (in casual conversation) a final alveolar plosive (/d/) would haplologized with an initial alveolar plosive (/t/). This is here avoided by an actual pause, a cessation of phonation.

2. *ten-low;* ordinarily an alveolar nasal (/n/) would move too quickly into an alveolar glide (/l/) for the preservation of the plus-juncture which prevents the sequence /ten + lʌw/) from becoming one bisyllabic word.

3. *low-words;* ordinarily the low glide (/w/) in *low* would be omitted before the initial consonantal /w/ in the following syllable.

4. *oft-creep;* in such a multi-consonantal environment the final alveolar plosive /t/ would be haplologized by an initial velar plosive /k/ in the following syllable.

5. *creep-in;* I find in my reading of these syllables a temptation towards the liaison of the final /p/ in *creep* with the initial vowel of *in,* which here is resisted by introducing a cessation of phonation.

6. *one-dull;* it is too easy to produce an initial alveolar plosive /d/ merely by releasing the previous final alveolar nasal /n/; this, like *ten-low,* would produce an unacceptable bisyllabic word, instead of two separate syllables, each of them entitled to a major stress.

7. *dull-line;* the final /l/ of *dull* must not be haplologized with the initial /l/ of *line.*
Since objective mimesis is effected by a combination of syntactic and phonological structures, the line would be entitled to a high grade of value.

The rest of Pope's mimetic lines would be entitled to lower or equal grades on a first approximation. However, there is a question about the nature of the mimesis effected. Each of the seventeen lines, in whole or in part, mimes an objective linear phenomenon—the performance of a line of verse—and therefore is entitled to a score reflecting some grade of objective mimesis. However, the lines do not all mime the *same* objective phenomenon, strictly regarded and viewed in context. The lines of verse they mime are all from forms different from that of the poem in which they are embedded. An *ars poetica*, which is the genre of *An Essay on Criticism*, need not contain imitative effects to be an *ars poetica*; though it usually contains examples of verse, the examples are usually clearly distinguished from the text, not embedded in the commentary. Therefore, these lines are not reflexive or mimetic of the work in which they appear. I would suggest that they must be judged as secondary comic or ironic phenomena, and achieve a value as a whole distinct from and higher than the values of the lines themselves. Here they achieve a high grade of value, since they are reflexive of the self-image of the creator, Pope himself, who takes obvious pleasure in his own virtuosity.

Milton also provides examples of mimesis of various sorts. An especially interesting example occurs in *Lycidas*, ll. 165-7:

> Weep no more, woful Shepherds, weep no more,
> For *Lycidas* your sorrow is not dead,
> Sunk though he be beneath the watry floar . . .

Line 167 accomplishes a remarkable degree of objective mimesis through a combination of syntactic and phonological structures. The movements of the tongue and lower jaw to accomplish the stressed vowels of this line mime a motion from *mid central* to *high front* to *back*:

Sunk though   he be beneath the   watry floar
/ sʌŋk+ðʌw+hi+biː | biniː:θ+ðə+wɔtri+flɔr |
mid central   high front   back

The motion mimes the relationship *low-high-low* expressed in the lexis—the body of Edward King on the sea floor (low) and the surface of the sea (high). The high front vowels mime the notion 'the watery floor' far beneath which King has sunk.

The unusual number of high front vowels—four in a row—flanked by mid or back vowels suggest that this phonological mimesis is deliberate. In this structure lexical 'high' and 'low' is expressed by phonological 'high-front' and 'low-back'. Note also that the mimetic pattern influences the line *as a whole*; 'beneath' is represented as part of the 'high' area, even though semantically it is 'low'; the reverse is true for 'watry floar'.

The vocalic mimesis is reinforced by the structure of stresses. Of the eight words in the line, only three are from major syntactic classes. The syntactic structure of the line could be represented as follows:

Perf Part—Subordinate Conjunction—*Pers Pron*—Copula—Prep—Art—*Adj (Modifier)*—*Noun*

(The major word classes are italicized.) Only representatives of major word-classes inherently receive major stress, all things being equal, and in this case the words receiving major lexical stress are also (with one exception—'be') those words centring around mid or back vowels. *Low* and *high* in this line, therefore, are mimed by a *stressed-mid-back—unstressed-high-front* polarization.

It hardly needs saying that the lexical situation is primary in the appreciation of the line and is reinforced by phonological and syntactic mimesis; if there were no polar situation to express, the phonology and syntax structures would be non-mimetic, and the value of the line would be low.

Interesting aspects of objective mimesis are revealed by an examination of French verse. A fragment from the work of the seventeenth-century poet Jean-François Sarasin (1604–54) demonstrates mimesis of an effect found often in poetry of the time, the periodic flow of water:

> Comme avec un grand bruit le Rhône plein de rage,
> Soulevé par les vents, ou grossi par l'orage,
> Vient et traine avec soi milles flots courroucés;
> L'onde flotte après l'onde, et de l'onde est suivie,

Ainsi passe la vie.
Ainsi coulent nos ans l'un sur l'autre entassés.[6]

The objective mimesis of periodic flow of water in the fourth
line is effected phonologically by the repetition of '*l'onde*'.
However, the simple phonological pattern contradicts lexis at an
important point. Whereas the three repetitions of *l'onde* mime
three successive wave-swells, in a 1-2-3 sound pattern, the
actual pattern of the swells of the Rhône, in context, is 2-1-3:
the first *onde* mentioned is actually preceded in time by the
second, and is succeeded by the third, in the objective situation
described. The complexity of the relationship between expression and form here is further complicated by a possible *third*
arrangement, a graphemic one: the three appearances of
l'onde on the page seem to me to suggest a 3-2-1 pattern—that
is, the rightmost swell seems to be the earliest. (This may be
conditioned by my right-handedness; perhaps a left-handed
person would perceive the reverse.)

Miming of flowing water was often attempted in the seven-
teenth century, both in France and in England. For example,
there is the *Plainte sur la mort de Sylvie* of Saint-Amant (1594–
1661):

Ruisseau qui cours après toi-même,
Et qui te fuis toi-même aussi,
Arrête un peu ton onde ici.[7]

Note that the effect remains when the pro-form 'toi-même' is
substituted for the repeating nominal element, 'Ruisseau'.
Martial Dumas de Brives (?–1656) accomplishes almost a
'metaphysical' effect within his mimesis (expressed by the word
coule), in his *Paraphrase sur le Cantique; Benedicite omnis opera
Domini Domino*:

Clairs amas des mers précieuses
Qui pendant sur le firmament,

[6] Text from André Blanchard, ed., *Trésor de la poésie baroque et précieuse*
(Paris: Seghers, 1969), pp. 155–6.
[7] Blanchard, p. 124.

Et coulant sans écoulement
Semblent être judicieuses. . . .[8]

Jean-Baptiste Chassignet (1571?–1635?) achieves an impressive
effect in much the same way as Sarasin, in his Fifth Sonnet:

Assieds-toi sur le bord d'une ondante rivière,
Tu la verras fluer d'un perpetuel cours,
Et flots sur flots roulant en mille et mille tours
Decharger par les prés son humide carrière.

Mais tu ne verras rien de cette onde première
Qui naguère coulait, l'eau change tous les jours,
Tous les jours elle passe, et la nommons toujours
Même fleuve et même eau, d'une même manière. . . .[9]

In this verse the effect of flowing water is achieved by the
repetition of words only the first pair of which is lexically
related to water: flots/flots. The other pairs mime the successive
swells by mere repetition: mille/mille, tous les jours/tous les
jours/toujours, même/même/même. This phenomenon demonstrates the mimesis to be truly phonological: once the lexis is
mimed by sound-repetition in *flots*, *any* sound-repetition there-
after reinforces the mimesis.

Ben Jonson, during the same period, accomplishes a remarkably successful mimesis of flowing water in his line
Slow, slow, fresh fount, keep time with my salt tears.
This line mimes the slow welling of the speaker's tears both
phonologically and syntactically, in ways similar to Pope's
slowing of line 347 from *An Essay on Criticism*.

(*a*) Phonologically, every syllable (with the exception of the
seventh—'with') contains either a consonant cluster or a 'long
vowel', a complex vocalic nucleus. Four syllables have both:
/slʌw/, /slʌw/, /fæwnt/, and /tiːrz/. There is, therefore, a
great deal of phonic material to get through relative to the
number of syllables. In addition, there is the obstructive final
t of '*salt*' and the initial *t* of '*tears*' to be pronounced carefully
and separately.

[8] Blanchard, p. 119.   [9] Blanchard, pp. 79–80.

(*b*) Syntactically, there are eight representatives from major syntactic classes out of ten. (The exceptions are the preposition *with* and the possessive pronoun *my*.) Eight out of ten syllables, therefore, are entitled to major stresses. In addition, however, each of the 'slow's' is in effect a sentence; in transformational terms each could be the reduced surface-representative of a structure dominated by ♯S♯. These 'imperative quasi-adverbials', as they may be called, are entitled to sentence intonation —that is, each may be followed by a major transitional juncture. These junctures slow the line still further.

The adjectival 'fresh fount' is succeeded by a major transition also, since it is in apposition to both of the imperative quasi-adverbials. This introduces another sentence-ending transition. Three 'sentences' intonationally, and four sentence-ending junctures, in a line of only ten syllables is unusual, and the movement of the performed line is correspondingly unusual.

A modern poet, Paul Valéry, imitates the action of water magnificently in the final section of *La Jeune Parque* (1917):

> Si l'âme intense souffle, et renfle furibonde
> L'onde abrupte sur l'onde abbatue, et si l'onde
> Au cap tonne, immolant un monstre de candeur . . .

The mimesis here, perhaps imitated from the Sarasin lines above,[10] is of a sea-swell breaking on a rocky coast. *L'onde* is not *wave*, in the normal English sense of the word; both for Valéry and for Sarasin the word *vague* expressed the normal physical meaning of *wave*. *L'onde* is here the sea itself, by synecdoche (as in 'England rules the wave'). Therefore, the three appearances of *l'onde*, both in Valéry and in Sarasin, do not mark the lexical recognition of three separate waves but of three manifestations of the same phenomenon or process. Thus it is the perception of three moments in time which is mimed, three stages in the continuous process of the sea breaking on the shore, or the Rhône flowing to the sea.

The modifiers of *l'onde* in the Valéry also mime the action, syntactically. *Abrupte*, while still retaining some of the force

10 Blanchard, pp. 16–17.

of the Latin participial form from which it was derived, is a 'true' adjective and represents a continuing attribute of the swell, while *abbatue* is a perfect participle and represents completed action. The passage from an attributive adjective to a true participle mimes the passage of time from the first perceived state of the swell, now simply a static attribute, to the second, still an active force. The third stage is represented by a finite verb (*tonne*); the complete action is mimed by a movement from static attribution through participial completed actions to dynamic verbal action.

Objective mimesis always has a tendency to seem trivial, a trick or, at any rate, a not particularly necessary part of poetic technique. Even when skillfully done, as it often is—by Pope, Jonson, and Valéry, for example—there is always a suggestion of a trick about it, an act of conscious craftsmanship. I would suggest that this impression is the result of the basically unnecessary nature of the act itself—the reader knows what slowly flowing tears, echoes, waves, and similar phenomena look, feel, or sound like without the assistance of sub-lexical mimetic techniques. Perhaps the true necessity of *subjective* mimesis conveys a factitious value to other types of mimesis.

2. Subjective mimesis

The subtlest, most valuable, and most difficult to achieve grades of mimesis are those that include imitation of personal sequences of emotion. The imitation is not that of the mind apprehending some external process or even of its own procedure in the gradual apprehension of some external phenomenon; it is rather an imitation of the observation of its own proper action. This is the act of the mind in observing the most private recesses of a private mind, its own (where there is no distinguishable *persona*), one in which individual conformations of character are so strong that communication of this component is under a severe inherent handicap. If, therefore, communication of this private component is assisted by elements in the message which mime these privacies by schemata of public syntactic or phonological codes of language, the resulting construct is of the highest value.

When this subjective reality is the content of a work of art to be conveyed, mimesis is extremely important. Here the reader and the author share no common knowledge, unlike the situation in objective mimesis. Both reader and author know what echoes, flowing water, the rhythms of speech, are like, but only the individual really knows what his own configurations of personality and memory are like.

I propose to analyse a work universally acknowledged as great, in which the element that is mimed in the work is derived from the self-image of a personalized creator—Blake's *Tyger*. The emotional situation mimed is extremely complex, compounded of fear and awe, combined with an overall feeling of universal comprehension, of *noesis*, a grasp of the secret of the energy of the universe. Close analysis of the syntax of the poem reveals complex mimetic schemata which reinforce and convey this subjective state to the reader.

The Tyger

Tyger Tyger, burning bright,
In the forests of the night:
What immortal hand or eye,
Could frame thy fearful symmetry?

In what distant deeps or skies,
Burnt the fire of thine eyes!
On what wings dare he aspire?
What the hand, dare seize the fire?

And what shoulder, & what art,
Could twist the sinews of thy heart?
And when thy heart began to beat,
What dread hand? & what dread feet?

What the hammer? what the chain,
In what furnace was thy brain?
What the anvil? what dread grasp,
Dare its deadly terrors clasp!

When the stars threw down their spears
And water'd heaven with their tears:
Did he smile his work to see?
Did he who made the Lamb make thee?

Tyger Tyger burning bright,
In the forests of the night:
What immortal hand or eye,
Dare frame thy fearful symmetry?

(Text from Blake, *Songs of Experience*, 1794)

What is here analysed is not a 'first reading' of *Tyger*, in the sense of a first scanning. Rather, it is the experience of a reader who encounters and understands *Tyger* completely for the first time, even though he may have scanned it before. After this 'first complete reading', as it could be called, all further readings contribute nothing new and become increasingly automatized scannings of a familiar linear pattern. In a certain sense, of course, a symbolic poem can never be exhausted of its meaning or completely linearized, and therefore can never have a 'complete' reading. However, in this analysis, a reader has experienced his 'first complete reading' when he realizes all the elements of mimesis in the poem.

There is a considerable amount of phonological structuring in *Tyger*, but it is all non-mimetic. For example, in each stanza there are three lines that exhibit alliteration and one that does not. (In lines two, six, and twenty-two, the alliteration is vocalic, in my idiolect: /farists//nait/:/fair//aiz/:/farists/ /nait/.) There is also phonological chiasmus in the first line: /taigər//bərniŋ//brait/. These regularities mime no objective or subjective entity mentioned or suggested in the poem. The commonplace metrical and rhyme schemes are certainly non-mimetic; they are those of 'Twinkle, Twinkle, Little Star.' Indeed, so automatized is the phonology that it seriously interferes with the correct intonation of the syntactic patterning, especially in the first and second lines, where syntactic subtleties are overridden by the insensitivity of the meter. Nor is there objective mimesis in *Tyger*, nothing that corresponds to claws, stripes, fire, roars, teeth, ferocity.

What Blake achieves in *Tyger* is a subjective mimesis, based on syntax, for a very high degree of value. It seems obvious from the poem that what Blake is conveying is his own awe at a complete mystical perception of the energy that drives the universe and the poet, a force here symbolized as a tiger, a power beyond good and evil.[11]

Energy, action, exuberance, excess, are for Blake the highest values in life and in art: 'All that is not action is not worth reading';[12] 'Energy is the only life and is from the Body and Reason is the Bound or outward circumference of Energy' (*Marriage of Heaven and Hell*). *Tyger* seems to record a moment of illumination, the moment when the nature of the fundamental energy of the universe became clear. There are, therefore, two aspects of this experience—memory of the sensation of mystic illumination, and awe before the object of perception. Both of these aspects are reflected in syntactic structures in *Tyger* that communicate this moment with great power to the reader. (Bertrand Russell is said to have fainted when he first heard *Tyger*, at Cambridge.)

In one way, *Tyger* is unusual in the works of Blake, and in another way it is unusual as compared to the works of any

[11] See Warren Stevenson, '*The Tyger* as Artefact', *Blake Studies* 2:1 (Fall, 1969), 5–19. The suggestion by H. Bloom in *The Oxford Anthology of English Literature*, eds. Kermode and Hollander (London and New York: Oxford University Press, 1973), Vol. II, p. 28 n., that the *persona* in the poem is not that of Blake himself but that of a limited perceiver of reality resembling Cowper, one overwhelmed by an essentially incomplete perception of reality, seems to me to be unlikely, based as it is upon Blake's drawing of a tiger that accompanies the poem. Blake's engraved tiger *is* rather a toy beast, but then Blake had never seen a real tiger, and the tiger of Stubbs's painting, that he *did* see, is lying down—Blake had no way of knowing how long a tiger's legs really were, so his beast suffers in consequence. I find no difficulty in seeing the poem as a direct reflection of Blake's own growing perception of the energy of the universe and its potentialities for good and evil.

[12] David V. Erdman, ed., *The Poetry and Prose of William Blake* (New York: Doubleday, 1965), p. 534.

author. It is the only poem Blake ever wrote in which the first stanza is repeated as the last stanza (with one word changed). In addition, it is composed entirely of unanswered questions; the only comparable stretch of questioning in literature occurs in the Book of Job, undoubtedly one of Blake's sources. It is by these two departures, from his own practice and from almost anyone's, that he communicates the two highly unusual psychological aspects of the content of *The Tyger*.

A. MAJOR FRAME

The clarity of his mystic perception is conveyed by a movement from ambiguity of syntactic structure to single structures, from the first stanza to the last. Eight different syntactic structures can be derived from the first two lines of the first stanza—that is, the first two lines contain three points at which two different syntactic structures can be discerned.

1. 'burning bright'

(*a*) This expression may be a combination of a present participle and a 'Quasi-predicative', i.e., a phrase like 'the moon was *shining bright*' or the 'candle was *burning blue*', or 'He tried *jumping clear* of the ship'.[13] In this reading, a reading which many readers automatically adopt, it is the Tyger that is 'burning', and it is becoming 'bright' only because of the burning. Hence the main activity of the Tyger is 'burning', and the brightness is ancillary and entirely dependent upon the burning. Another, related, syntactic interpretation would have 'bright' an adverb, even though it is adjectival in form; adverbial forms in Old English and later were frequently adjectival. In this interpretation again it would be the Tyger which is burning, but it would be the *burning* which is bright; this interpretation would require tolerance of a form which by our time, and

[13] Otto Jespersen. *A Modern English Grammar on Historical Principles* (Copenhagen: Ejnar Munksgaard, 1927), Vol. II, 17.1–17.3.

perhaps by Blake's, would be regarded as dialectal and substandard. This interpretation would make 'burning bright' equivalent in meaning to 'burning brightly'.

(*b*) The expression may have the structure 'Intensifier (Vb) —Adjective subjunct'—that is, it could be an expression like 'boiling hot', and related to forms like 'stony cold', and 'ashy pale'.[14] The Intensifier may take a number of forms; in 'boiling hot', 'shocking bad', and 'burning bright' the forms are verbal, and have the significance respectively of 'very hot, hot enough to boil my hand, were I to put it in', 'very bad, bad enough to shock me,' 'very bright, bright enough to burn my eyes.' This form has the curious property of defining the intensity of the adjective-subjunct it modifies by reference to some perception of an observer. In the case of 'burning bright', it is the *Tyger* which is bright, and the *observer's eyes* which are burning—quite a different interpretation from the interpretations in (*a*) above, which are entirely limited to attributes of the Tyger.

Therefore, the two main syntactic interpretations of the first ambiguous expression could be diagrammed as follows (the brackets indicate a choice; either the top alternative or the bottom must be chosen):

$$\text{The Tyger is} \left\{ \begin{array}{c} \text{burning} \\ or \\ \text{very bright} \end{array} \right\}$$

2. The second point of syntactic ambiguity occurs after 'bright'. Is the Tyger burning (or bright) *against* the background of 'the forests of the night', or is he merely *within* 'the forests of the night' in addition to burning or being bright? In other words, is 'burning bright, / In the forests of the night' one compound adjectival appositive to 'Tyger', or two separate ones? Blake's punctuation suggests the second interpretation, but his punctuation is a risky guide, especially at line endings (every line in the poem ends with a mark of punctuation, with the exception of

---

[14] Jespersen, op. cit., 15.21.

line seventeen, where there *should* be one). This second point of ambiguity may be diagrammed as follows:

$$\text{The Tyger is} \left\{ \begin{array}{c} \text{burning} \\ or \\ \text{very bright} \end{array} \right\} + \left\{ \begin{array}{c} \text{, and is in the forests} \\ \text{of the night} \\ or \\ \text{within the forests} \\ \text{of the night} \end{array} \right\}$$

3. The third point of syntactic ambiguity comes with the phrase 'the forests of the night'. This expression turns upon the preposition 'of', notoriously one of the most ambiguous particles in the English language, inheriting as it does the combined functions of an Old English preposition and the French genitive *de* (itself the heir of a complex situation from Latin). Here the problem is not to find ambiguities but to weed out the unlikeliest ones.

(*a*) The possessive interpretation of 'of' gives the expression the meaning 'the night possesses forests'—this would seem to mean that the night is of a forest-like thickness. 'The forests of the night' would then be equivalent to 'thick, tangled night.'

(*b*) On the other hand, it could be the characterizing 'of' which is employed, as in 'the knight of the woeful countenance', 'the house of the seven gables', or 'the inn of the sword'. This form is much more French than the first, i.e., 'Rue de la Goutte-d'Or', 'Place de la Concorde', and so on. It is more or less equivalent to 'with', and therefore 'the forests of the night' would mean 'the forests with (or characterized by) night', that is, 'dark forests'.

With a phrase turning on 'of', it is difficult to be able to decide which part of the phrase is metaphorical. (Indeed, the whole phrase may be a metaphor for a third entity.)[15] The semantic structure of the first stanza is no help, since the Tyger could just as easily be in forests or (since he is, after all, a cosmic

---

[15] See Christine Brooke-Rose, *A Grammar of Metaphor* (London: Secker, 1958), pp. 93 ff.

symbol) interstellar night.[16] This situation can be diagrammed as follows:

$$\text{The Tyger is in} \begin{Bmatrix} \text{thick night} \\ or \\ \text{dark forests} \end{Bmatrix}$$

The complete diagram of this octuply ambiguous expression is as follows:

The Tyger is

$$\begin{Bmatrix} \text{burning} \\ or \\ \text{very bright} \end{Bmatrix} + \begin{Bmatrix} \text{, and is in} \\ or \\ \text{against the} \\ (or \\ \text{within the}) \end{Bmatrix} + \begin{Bmatrix} \text{thick night} \\ or \\ \text{dark forests} \end{Bmatrix}$$

This complex ambiguity is resolved by the time the stanza is repeated at the end of *Tyger*, and the resolution provides the major formal frame for the poem. In the second, third, and fourth stanzas it is made clear that the Tyger has been forged in a cosmic smithy, or perhaps in a cannon-foundry, one of Blake's dark, Satanic mills.[17] This information immediately resolves the first point of ambiguity, and leads to the resolution of the other two. Artefacts in the process of being forged by a smith or a founder are often extremely 'bright' as they come from the furnace or smithy fire, but although flames sometimes flicker along the edges of red-hot or white-hot metal, it cannot really be said that they are normally ever literally 'burning'. Therefore, the Tyger is not burning but rather is 'very bright'. Since 'brightness' requires contrast more strongly than does 'burning', the Tyger is *within* or *against* 'the forests of the night'. Then finally the more 'English' of the two possibilities for 'the

[16] Blake could have imagined the Tyger as a constellation; he had been apprenticed to the engraver for the Royal Society, who provided diagrams for the astronomical reports of Herschel; see William S. Doxey, 'William Blake and William Herschel: the Poet, the Astronomer, and THE TYGER', *Blake Studies* 2:2 (Spring, 1970), 5–13.

[17] David V. Erdman, *Blake: Prophet against Empire*, rev. ed. (Princeton, N.J.: Princeton U.P., 1969), p. 203.

forests of the night', the one employing the possessive 'of', is also the more semantically likely. Hence, the syntactic structure of the last stanza is different from that of the first in being completely unambiguous. The first two lines of this stanza are also unambiguous (syntactically); they can be paraphrased

The Tyger is very bright, burning to the beholder's eye, against thick tangled darkness.

Although the resolution is effected by semantic means, the effect is gained by the reduction of syntactic possibilities. Lexical ambiguity is never in question here except as deriving entirely from syntactic ambiguity; there are a great many different possible meanings for 'Tyger', or for 'forests', or 'night'. Exploration of these lexical ambiguities, on top of the syntactic ones, would expand the interpretation of the poem to immense lengths, and would not ever be resolvable to the same degree of explicitness as its syntactic complexities.

The movement from eightfold syntactic ambiguity to single structure provides syntactic mimesis for the feeling of universal understanding with which the reader finishes the poem, and also reveals the structural reason for the repetition, unique in Blake's poetry, of the first stanza as the last. Beethoven, Blake's almost exact contemporary, accomplishes the same effect in some of his late sonatas and quartets, in which a simple melody is explored through all its manifestations until all of its structural elements are expanded and developed and its meaning and nature thoroughly understood by the listener, at which point the melody is brought back again in its simple form to be fully appreciated in all its parts. It could be said that the only alteration in Blake's repeated stanza, from 'could frame' to 'dare frame', a move from a neutral auxiliary to a more intense verbal particle, is an acknowledgement of the movement from confusion to clarity, from a multiple vision of the energy of the universe to a clear, more awed view of the same phenomenon.

This movement of understanding provides the large frame for the poem, a frame of revelation. Within this major frame there is a minor frame, one which provides a much more moderate degree of enlightenment, less of a definitive revelation. The question-forms in *Tyger* move from peculiar forms of 'what'-questions which, as we will see, cannot even begin to be answered, to 'yes/no' questions, in the penultimate stanza, which one can at least *begin* to answer, confident that the answer to them will be either 'yes' or 'no'.

There are, then, two frames of revelation in 'The Tyger':

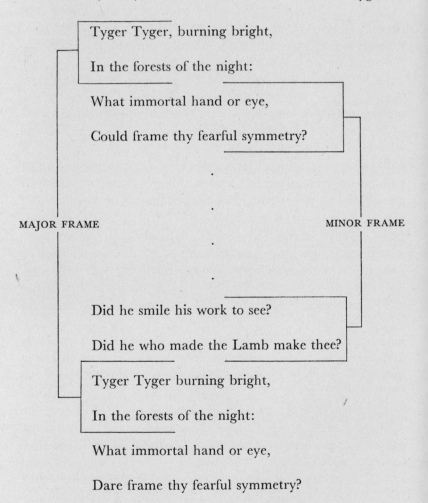

Tyger Tyger, burning bright,

In the forests of the night:

What immortal hand or eye,

Could frame thy fearful symmetry?

MAJOR FRAME   MINOR FRAME

Did he smile his work to see?

Did he who made the Lamb make thee?

Tyger Tyger burning bright,

In the forests of the night:

What immortal hand or eye,

Dare frame thy fearful symmetry?

B. MINOR FRAME

The form of the 'what-questions' in the poem contribute the second psychological effect of the poem—the awe unmixed with ignorance before the phenomenon of the Tyger. The fact that the form of the questions reinforces a feeling of awe with remarkable subtlety helps to clarify the apparent paradox of an act of mystic revelation expressed partly by questions—forms usually associated with lack of knowledge, not with complete understanding.

In two ways, Blake weakens the illocutionary force of his 'questions' by reducing what could be called the 'ignorance motive' normally operative in the creation of questions.[18] First of all, the fact that the questions in *Tyger* are *written* questions weakens them considerably as questions. All written questions, with the exception of those in printed plays, personal letters, and government forms, are 'rhetorical' questions, or as Robinson calls them, 'exclamatory' questions.[19] They are exclamatory

[18] For a description of the question of illocutionary force, see J. L. Austin, *How to Do Things with Words* (Oxford: Clarendon Press, 1962); William P. Alston, *Philosophy of Language* (Englewood Cliffs, N.J.: Prentice-Hall, 1964); John R. Searle, *Speech Acts* (London: Cambridge University Press, 1969). However, Richard Ohmann believes that illocutionary forces normally associated with utterances are lost, except as mimesis, in all literary works; see Monroe Beardsley's discussion of this point in 'The Concept of Literature', in *Literary Theory and Structure*, eds. Brady, Palmer, and Price (New Haven, Conn.: Yale Univ. Press, 1973), pp. 30 ff. In my opinion, whatever the merit of Ohmann's argument, utterances that would otherwise possess illocutionary force may lose it by other means than by being included in a literary artefact—by, for example, being subtly incorrect in form, as in the analysis above—and this loss is different in kind from the inherent literary loss of illocutionary force, and logically precedent to it.

[19] Fred Robinson, 'Verb Tense in Blake's "The Tyger",' *PMLA*, 79, 5, 666–9. Bloom (see note 9 above) refers to the 'increasingly rhetorical questions' in the poem without really describing how the rhetoricity of the Tyger questions 'increases'. See also Eli Pfefferkorn, 'The Question of the Leviathan and the Tiger', *Blake Studies*, 3:1 (Fall, 1970), 53–60, for an interpretation of the poem based upon the 'rhetorical' nature of the questions. None of the

questions in the sense that no answer is required, since no
answer is possible in such a form. (In a trivial sense, of course,
no answer can be expected from a tiger, not even a cosmic one,
and especially no answers about his own process of manufac-
ture.) Blake employs graphemic/discoursal expectations to keep
part of the illocutionary force of questioning without the
substance of it—the confession of ignorance that a true question-
situation almost inevitably reveals.

The second reason, more complex but also more powerfully
effective, why Blake's questions in stanzas one through four of
the poem are only the husks of questions, is that they are
questions of a highly unusual type. There are two sorts of
questions in English. First, there are 'yes/no' questions, characterized by word-order inverted from that of the normal
indicative sentence, and answerable, at least in theory, by a
simple assent or negation. (There are some more complex
forms of this type of question, but they play no part in the poem.)
Second, there are what Jespersen calls 'x-questions', questions
to which the answer cannot be 'yes' or 'no' but which must be a
phrase, a substitute for an interrogative pronominal, and whose
syntactic class is strictly governed by the choice of interrogative
pronominal.[20] For example, in a 'where'-question the only non-
evasive or non-irrelevant answer would be in the form of an
adverbial of place; a 'when'-question is answerable only by
an adverbial of time; and so on. In English the interrogatives
'where', 'when', 'why', 'who' only possess a *simple* form in
questions—that is, nothing but a verbal auxiliary may appear
immediately after the interrogative in a question: 'Where *did*
you go?' 'When *could* he go?' (the only apparent exception to
this rule is the so-called 'echo-question'—'Why a horse? Why
not a cow?') Other interrogatives—'how' and 'what'—may
appear either in *simple* or *complex* form—either 'How *do* you

above, however, pursues the problem of what a rhetorical question is, or
how we can tell one from a non-rhetorical question.
[20] Otto Jespersen, *A Modern English Grammar on Historical Principles*
(Copenhagen: Ejnar Munksgaard, 1940), Vol. IV, 480–1.

feel?' and 'What *do* you want?' or 'How *long* did it take?' and 'What *man* did you want to see?' In these complex forms the interrogative pronoun may be followed by adjectives, or nouns, or both. 'Which' and 'whose' may appear only in *complex* forms—'Which *button* do I press?' or 'Whose *hat* is missing?' This last is true, unless the following nominal has been deleted, either because it has just been mentioned in some previous sentence or because it has been indicated in some non-verbal manner:

Man A; Look at the row of buttons.

Man B; Which do I press?

Or Man B may simply point to the array of buttons without waiting for Man A to introduce them to him, and say, pointing, 'Which do I press?' This does not alter the rule that 'Which'- and 'Whose'-questions must be either explicitly or implicitly complex in form.

With this situation in mind, for the language as a whole, let us examine the Blake questions. All but four of Blake's x-questions are complex in form; they either begin with 'What + Noun' or 'What + Modifier + Noun'. (One of them begins with a preposition, 'in', a situation which does not alter the analysis.)

There are rules, as yet unformulated, for the use of complex interrogatives in discourse that Blake subtly infringes. The emotional effect of this infringement is a reinforcement of the awe of the lexical level; the 'ignorance-factor', which is one of the 'constitutive conditions' of an utterance with the complete illocutionary force of a question, is hereby reduced, without affecting other emotive factors concomitant with the asking of questions.

A tentative approach to the description of these rules can be made by considering why 'which' and 'whose' are always complex interrogatives (subject to the reservations above). We then may be able to ascertain why 'what' is more flexible, in that it can appear in both simple and complex form. A man who asks another man, 'Which button do I press?' seems to have 'ordered' his immediate situation, i.e., before a panel of buttons the dimensions and characteristics of which are well known to

him. The use of 'which' is, therefore, a sign of an advanced
comprehension of a situation, and the question-form is based
upon this understanding. Hence the nominal which by rule
follows 'which'; attention has already been focussed on the
entity expressed by the nominal, an array of buttons, one of
which is to be pressed. The same description would apply for
'whose'; the situation is clear enough to the questioner to
allow him to ask for an assignment of possession of an entity
already sufficiently analysed to deserve such an 'advanced'
interrogative. In simple 'what'-questions, however, the questioner's attention has *not* been so focussed, and the perception
of the situation is far less advanced than in the 'which' and
'whose' situations. An ordering of the situation still remains to
be done, and this is accomplished by a discourse pattern com-
mencing with a simple 'what'-question and proceeding to more
and more complex ones, each complex 'what'-question demanding a further modifier of the nominal until the situation is
sufficiently ordered:

Q.1:	What do I press?	(*Primary question*)
A.1:	The button.	(*Primary answer*)
Q.2:	What button.	(*Secondary question*)
A.2:	The réd button.	(*Secondary answer*)
Q.3:	Whát red button?	(*Tertiary question*)
A.3:	The red button	
	marked 'Stárt'.	(*Tertiary answer*)

And so on; there is no reason why there should not be complex
questioning of a higher order than tertiary. It will be noted,
first, that while the primary question elicits a nominal answer,
the secondary and higher grades of question elicit the primary
nominal qualified by the appropriate number of modifiers, and
second, that every grade of question and answer higher than the
first, in a 'normal' discourse-frame such as the above, is characterized by contrastive stress and pitch patterning, on the
secondary and tertiary interrogatives and on the modifiers supplied. If the process is abbreviated—that is, if the first question
in a discourse is tertiary in form, i.e., Q: 'What red button

marked "Start" do I press?', or if the answer to a primary question, 'What do I press?' is tertiary, 'The red button marked "Start" ', the situation for contrastive stress is not present, since either the questioner or the answerer has already advanced beyond the point of confronting an unordered situation. The canonical ordering of questions as demonstrated above has as its purpose the ordering of a situation such as the 'which' or 'whose'-questioner has already ordered.

Blake violates this rule of question-precedence in *Tyger*. All of his questions in the poem that begin with 'what' are, with four exceptions, either secondary or tertiary questions, none of them preceded by the appropriate primary question. The effect of this violation is to rob the questions of the power to elicit information of which the questioner is ignorant—that is, these 'questions' are semi-grammatical, not really questions at all, but disguised exclamations. Blake's situation, it is implied by this practice, is not really unordered, and his information is therefore much more complete than his questioning pose would suggest. Therefore, while his utterances look like questions and sound like questions, they lack the illocutionary force of questions. In cognitive terms they are awed exclamations—'awed' because of the question-flavour still clinging to these husks, but 'exclamations' rather than questions because of the high degree of information that Blake cannot conceal he possesses.[21]

This highly skilful and unprecedented violation of norms of syntax in discourse (see Appendix) provides the right tone for the core of the poem: the reader is uneasily aware that exclamations are disguised as questions which cannot even begin to be answered, since their form in discourse is incorrect and the syntactic form of the answer expected is not clear. When the 'yes/no' questions in stanza five appear, they come as a great relief, since they are in perfect canonical form, and the construction of an answer can at least begin for them. Thus the 'true' questions in stanza five act to release tension previously created by the asking of questions subtly false in form. This

[21] See Robinson, p. 669, and E. Kruisinga, *A Handbook of Present-Day English*, 5th ed. (Groningen: P. Noordhoff, 1932), pt. 3, pp. 319–20.

movement from high tension to much lower tension provides
the dynamic for the minor frame of the poem. A similar structure is to be found in music, of a slightly later period, in Schu-
mann's song 'Im Wunderschönen Monat Mai'. In this song,
famous in the history of harmony, the ending is a dominant
seventh chord in one of the main keys of the song. A dominant
seventh ordinarily demands resolution to the tonic in imperious
terms, but the hearer of this song is content with the unresolved
dominant seventh, since the body of the song is so chromatic
and its modulations so volatile that a reference to a main key,
even in the form of a dominant seventh, is accepted almost
with composure. The 'composure' is not complete, because the
dominant seventh still keeps a fragment of its restless power
even in this context, just as the 'questions' in *Tyger* retain
enough of their illocutionary force as questions to produce the
requisite feeling of awe, but are robbed of their power of
demanding cognitive resolution, and do not interfere with the
main psychological mood of complete understanding provided
by the major frame.

In the description of some structures in *Tyger* we have seen
how two subtle, complex, and apparently contradictory
emotional states, complete knowledge and questioning awe,
are mimed, reinforced, and finally reconciled by the satisfaction
and frustration of syntactic expectations in the reader. Not only
does this entitle the poem to a very high grade of value; it
actually makes the poem possible. It is difficult to see how just
this highly subjective proportion of differing elements, awe and
illumination, could otherwise have been conveyed.

CONCLUSION

The procedure of critical analysis employed in this paper relies
upon linguistic techniques of description. Applied with some
caution, this approach has the virtue of accounting for certain judgements of value, now made on an intuitive basis,

of literary artefacts by a comparatively objective procedure.

However, the comments in this paper on sub-lexical mimesis as an indicator of value are obviously incomplete in a number of respects. For one thing, it should be clear from the examples chosen to illustrate the thesis that this standard of value applies mainly to varieties of Renaissance and post-Renaissance poetry from the technologically advanced countries of Western Europe and America. Other sorts of poetry would be measured by other standards. For example, classical Welsh and Irish poetry, skaldic verse, and similar medieval forms seem to derive their value from their approximation to abstract phonological schemata, not from their degrees of mimetic approximation to their content. It is an open question whether the need for mimesis of an increasingly heterogeneous lexical situation from medieval periods to our own caused the abandonment of the medieval scale of valued schemata in favour of our own more loose schemes of metrical and rhyming alliterative patterns, or whether the most highly valued forms of poetry were *always* those that demonstrated mimesis beneath the lexical level, and that it was the gradual realization of this that caused the general abstract paradigms of verse-making to crumble.

Another question to be explored involves judgement of a work in which there exist several grades of value as measured by sub-lexical mimesis. Is the work *as a whole* to receive a value related to the value of its parts, and if so, what value should it receive? Or perhaps the assignment of value to a work of literature is ultimately an assignment of value to the (putative) author of it, so the rule for assignment of value for a whole work might be that it receives the value as a whole which is equal to the highest value *any part* of it displays; the author has demonstrated an ability to 'rise to the occasion' which is the mark of an outstanding craftsman. Then the further question arises, is a work by one author in which the highest grade of value is assigned to *one* of its parts only half as valuable (in some other sense) than a work by another author in which the highest grade of value is assigned to *two* of its parts? Can a *whole work* be mimetic on several levels? How is 'part of a work' to be defined?

These and other questions remain to be answered. However, investigations along this line eventually might enable us to answer the ultimate critical questions, 'What are works of art, and why are they *necessary*?'

APPENDIX

Secondary and tertiary questions, prepared or unprepared, are comparatively rare in most types of literature. For example, there are none in the Book of Job, one of Blake's major sources for *The Tyger*, and not very many in the King James Bible as a whole; there are a number of 'What + Noun' and 'What + Adjective' questions, mostly in the books of Genesis and I Kings, and a fair number of archaic 'What manner + of + Noun' questions. There are only two 'What + Modifier + Noun' questions, both unprepared and both obviously 'exclamatory':

And what one nation in the earth is like thy people . . .?
(II Samuel 8:23   I Chr. 17:21)
What further need was there . . .? (Hebrews 7:11)

In all of the works of another of Blake's primary sources, Shakespeare, except for an archaic use of 'what time' as a substitute for the relative pronoun 'when', there is only one secondary question and no tertiary ones:

What news on the Rialto? (M Ven 1.3.39)

Even this secondary question is archaic; a modern version would not be in secondary form: 'What is the news on the Rialto?'

They are rather more common in the works of another of Blake's primary influences, Milton, who may have provided Blake a model for the use of these sentences. In the table below there is tabulated the primary, secondary, and tertiary questions, all of them 'unprepared', in the poetry in English of Milton, in the *Tyger* and all the other writings of Blake, and in the poetry and plays of a modern poet much influenced by Blake, W. B. Yeats, this last as a 'control'.

What-questions in the works of Blake, Milton, and Yeats

	Primary (incl. archaic 'What + the + Noun' forms, and forms intro. by a preposition	*Secondary* (incl. forms intro. by a preposition	*Tertiary* (incl. forms intro. by a preposition
BLAKE			
Tyger	3	1	5
Other	*106*	*17*	4
Total	109	18	9
MILTON			
poetry in English	104	58	15
YEATS			
complete poems and plays	92	24	10
AVERAGE	102	34	12

It seems clear that the unprepared tertiary form is statistically unusual in written utterances, at least in those examined by me, and that they all seem to be reserved for the purpose Blake employs them for in *Tyger*—as pseudo-questions, exclamations of awe.

Another source besides Milton is possible for the use of these forms—the preachings and meditations of Hervey and Augustus Toplady, in which these exclamatory questions are very common. Blake knew the works of these popular preachers very well; he even did a water-colour illustration for Hervey's *Meditations*; see David Erdman, *Blake: Prophet against Empire* (rev. ed. New York, 1969), p. 113.

One of the Yeats' examples of an unprepared tertiary questions seems to show a link, not only to Blake but specifically to *The Tyger*. As the table above shows, there are more tertiary questions in *Tyger* than in all the rest of Blake. (What the table does *not* show is that there are actually more tertiary questions in *Tyger* than in any single work of Milton; there are only three in all of *Paradise Lost* and only three in *Samson Agonistes*.)

> The darkness drops again: but now I know
> That twenty centuries of stony sleep
> Were vexed to nightmare by a rocking cradle,
> And what rough beast, its hour come round at last,
> Slouches towards Bethlehem to be born?
>
>   ('The Second Coming')

It is tempting to find in the Yeats poem a great coincidence of syntax, theme, and mood with that of *The Tyger*; may we not answer Yeats's unanswerable question, 'What rough beast . . .?' with 'The Tyger'? (However, see A. M. Gibbs, 'The "Rough Beasts" of Yeats and Shakespeare', *Notes and Queries* N.S. 17:2 (February 1950), 48–9, for a Shakespearian source for the 'rough beast'.)

CHAPTER THREE

LANGUAGE AND THE READER: SHAKESPEARE'S SONNET 73

Roger Fowler

The pros and cons of linguistics in practical criticism have recently become sharply delineated in discussions of the sonnet form.[1] The sonnet is one of the most highly formalized, strictly conventionalized, genres in European literature, and is certainly the most familiar and long-lived of all the formal genres. Its design is rigidly prescribed: there are very few variants, and those are summed up in a terse set of rules. The most common type of English sonnet was defined (in fewer words than a sonnet itself) by George Gascoigne in 1575:

I can best allow to call those Sonnets whiche are of fouretene lynes, euery line conteyning tenne syllables. The firste twelue do ryme in staues of foure lines by crosse meetre, and the last two ryming togither do conclude the whole.[2]

---

[1] In the writing of this paper I have enjoyed the benefit of comments and advice from Michael Hollington, University of East Anglia, and Sears Jayne, Brown University. An early version was delivered as a seminar presentation at the University of Wisconsin, Milwaukee.

[2] George Gascoigne, *Certayne Notes of Instruction* (1575) in *Elizabethan Critical Essays*, ed. G. Gregory Smith (Oxford: O.U.P., 1904), I, 55. On the adaptation of the Italian sonnet to the demands of the English language, see Jiří Levý, 'On the Relations of Language and Stanza Pattern in the English Sonnet', in *Worte und Werte, Bruno Markwardt zum 60. Geburtstag*, ed. Gustav Erdmann and Alfons Eichstaedt (Berlin: Walter de Gruyter & Co., 1961), pp. 214–31.

A stern recipe: evidently, the sonnet offers a formidable technical challenge to its practitioners. Those who possess the craftsmanship to shape a poem according to this demanding formula (or its variants) have access to rich rewards: in reading Shakespeare, Milton, Wordsworth, we experience the infinite resources of language tensed variously against a constricting, repetitive format. Successful sonneteers can at once override the rigid metrical structure and at the same time exploit it for rhetorical force. Sonnets lend themselves to intense ratiocination, argumentation driving towards the logical consummation in the couplet, but their simple formal structure will not allow the poet to deprive his readers of the consolation of solid, very square, stability.

Similar opportunities present themselves to the analyst as to the poet and reader. Formal patterns in the sonnet leap to the eye, and the 'linguistic critic' has the outline framework of his diagrammatic analysis drawn already for him: the rhyme scheme dividing the poem into neat sections, the syntax adjusted to the requirements of the metrical divisions, the rhythm either easily congruent or (as, e.g., in Donne) violently straining against the conventional bounds. Often, too, the semantic emphases of the poem are clearly displayed, the prominent rhymes inviting the poet to place words in obviously significant relationships, and making these relationships salient to the analyst's eye.

The combination of brevity and rigid structure has made it seem that a sonnet could be exhaustively analysed, or at least exhaustively analysed at one level of linguistic structure. The latter approach is illustrated by two notorious articles by James J. Lynch and by Dell Hymes, exploring the sound-structure of sonnets by Keats and Wordsworth.[3] The former, the attempt at total analysis on metrical, phonetic, syntactic and semantic levels, finds its most celebrated and controversial expression in

[3] James J. Lynch, 'The Tonality of Lyric Poetry: An Experiment in Method', *Word*, 9 (1953), 211–24; Dell Hymes, 'Phonological Aspects of Style: Some English Sonnets', in *Style in Language*, ed. T. A. Sebeok (Cambridge, Mass.: MIT Press, 1960), pp. 109–31.

the work of Roman Jakobson.[4] The objections to such endeavours, now generally acknowledged, are objections which might be made to any 'ultra-structuralist' analysis, of any phenomenon, linguistic or not; indeed, they are the standard objections to all professedly empiricist versions of inductive method in science. Suppose the object of analysis (a poem, a social group, etc.) is ordered according to many and complex principles working in several dimensions. If you select one level and explore it systematically, you run the risk of vacuity or misinterpretation through neglect of interpenetrating factors on other levels. For instance, metrical analysis makes no sense unless one pays attention to syntax: there is certainly an abstraction 'metre' separable for a particular verse tradition, but the texture of its realization in any one poem depends on the syntax which carries it. The unique metrical 'feel' of a specific poem or poet is determined by the way the sentences he constructs play against the reader's more schematic expectations.[5] The Lynch-Hymes type of analysis is similarly unrevealing through concentrating on only one level. A count is made to determine what are the most frequent phonemes in a sonnet.

---

[4] See Roman Jakobson and Claude Lévi-Strauss, 'Les Chats de Charles Baudelaire', L'Homme, 2 (1962), 5–21: English trans. by Katie Furness-Lane in Structuralism: A Reader, ed. Michael Lane (London: Jonathan Cape, 1970), pp. 202–26; Roman Jakobson and Lawrence G. Jones, Shakespeare's Verbal Art in 'Th'Expence of Spirit' (The Hague: Mouton, 1970); Roman Jakobson, 'Une microscopie du dernier Spleen dans les Fleurs du Mal', Tel Quel, 29 (1967), pp. 12–24. (The last Spleen 'Quand le ciel bas et lourd . . .' is of course not a sonnet.) Samuel R. Levin's analysis of Shakespeare's Sonnet 30 in Linguistic Structures in Poetry (The Hague: Mouton, 1962), ch. vi, though it does not employ the exhaustive technique of full 'Jakobsonian' analysis, is based on the central theoretical principle as announced in Jakobson's 'Closing Statement: Linguistics and Poetics', in Style in Language, p. 358: 'The poetic function projects the principle of equivalence from the axis of selection into the axis of combination.'

[5] See the distinction between 'verse design' and 'verse instance' sketched in Jakobson, 'Closing Statement: Linguistics and Poetics', in Style in Language, p. 364, and elaborated in my 'What is Metrical Analysis?', Anglia, 86 (1968), 280–320: rept. in The Languages of Literature (London: Routledge and Kegan Paul, 1971), pp. 219–37.

The scores are weighted, taking account of the expected frequency of phonemes in an ordinary text of the language. The analyst then looks for places where the most frequent phonemes cluster together: the assumption seems to be that if there are such places they may be thematically significant. For instance, Lynch and Hymes find that in Keats' 'On First Looking into Chapman's Homer' the two most frequent vowels, and four of the five most frequent consonants, are collected in the word 'Silent'; they decide that this word is 'summative. for the sonnet. Since no guide is given as to the method for arriving at the theme which this word allegedly sums up, the procedure seems arbitrary as interpretation and incomplete as formal analysis.

A 'total' analysis at all levels might seem to obviate the above dangers. The practical critic can provide a systematic explication of structure at every distinct level of language, therefore no fact at one level which might make sense of an observation at another level can be overlooked. But Jakobsonian analysis is undermined by the very thoroughness which seems to be its prime virtue. A complete analysis provides *too much* detail; it is unselective in that it fails to distinguish between those structural facts (patterns, numerical distributions) which are significant and those which are not. All characteristics of a text are reduced, by being displayed, to the same level of detailed but banal observation. This fault is the basis of Riffaterre's scrupulous dismantling of the Jakobson-Lévi-Strauss analysis.[6] (It is a particular version of the deficiency which Noam Chomsky finds in structuralist grammars of whole languages—that such grammars are adequate *only* observationally, providing no more than a re-ordered rehearsing of the structures of sentences, without explaining those structures.)[7] The classic Jakobsonian

[6] Michael Riffaterre, 'Describing Poetic Structures: Two Approaches to Baudelaire's *Les Chats*', in *Structuralism*, ed. Jacques Ehrmann (New York: Doubleday Anchor, 1970), pp. 188–230. (*Structuralism* is a reprint of *Yale French Studies*, 36–7, 1966.)

[7] Noam Chomsky, *Current Issues in Linguistic Theory* (The Hague: Mouton, 1964), ch. ii.

analysis, however, does not merely re-arrange the poem as a catalogue of linguistic observations. It uses these observations to figure the poem as a set of diagrammatic structures, allegedly simultaneously perceived. If (to construct a hypothetical example) the first eight lines of the poem are all in the past tense, the last six in the present, the poem has the structure 8:6 (octave against sestet); if the first and third quatrains contain animate nouns, the second quatrain and the couplet inanimates, the structure is 4 (4) 4 (2); if the seventh and eighth lines consist entirely of monosyllables and no other lines do so, the centre of the poem is foregrounded against its edges; and so on. The thesis is that a poem consists of a set of simultaneously existing, linguistically based, frameworks, structures, or matrices. These are additional to the matrix provided by the metrical scheme. The complexity of this approach, in its further extension, is self-evident, and its weakness should be, too: because language contains so many features which may be noticed and invoked in justifying a division of the poem, the number of competing frames, or frames in tension with one another, becomes uncontrollably large. Jonathan Culler has demonstrated, for one poem analysed by Jakobson ('Quand le ciel bas et lourd . . .'), that more structures can be proposed than Jakobson discovers.[8] There is no way of deciding which of them are the most significant, nor which tensions between pairs of frames are the most vital; and as Riffaterre has pointed out, some of the features Jakobson appeals to in building these frames are below the threshold of perception.

Jakobson's poetic structures are 'diagrams' in only a figurative sense: he does not actually commit them to visual form. However, they have powerful spatial connotations, and can without violence be reduced to pictures. I draw below six frameworks which Jakobson and Jones discover in Shakespeare's sonnet 129 ('Th'expence of spirit . . .'); the sectionaliz-ation (a) is based on metre, the other five largely on syntactic *differentiae*:

[8] Jonathan Culler, 'Jakobson and the Analysis of Literary Texts', *Language and Style*, 5 (1971), 53–66.

(a) Metre

(b) Odd against even

(c) Outer against inner

(d) Anterior against
posterior

(e) Couplet against
quatrains

(f) Centre against
marginals

In addition to these six structures, there is also the unity of the poem as a whole established by 'pervasive features'.[9] Not all frames are considered to be equally important: e.g. (d), 'anterior against posterior', the first eight lines against the last six, is said to play 'a subaltern, third-rate role' (p. 24);[10] but finally all frames are granted some relevance: 'amazing external and internal structuration palpable to any responsive and unprejudiced reader' (p. 31). The final sentence of Jakobson and Jones's monograph invites us to inspect 'text' and 'poetic texture' 'in all its interlaced facets'. Jakobson and Jones have attempted to show that this is a complex, highly organized poem, and, even if some of their frames are suspect, this is a reasonable motive; at least, they have forced themselves and their readers to scan and rescan a sonnet with such intense attention that no arbitrary dismissal such as John Crowe Ransom's can seem adequate.[11]

If Jakobsonian analysis does no more than make us read minutely, however, its critical value is extremely questionable. It is not clear what these analysts claim for their technique (other than that, in this case, it confronts Ransom's judgement that Shakespeare was a poor craftsman as far as his sonnets are concerned—but that challenge has been much more subtly offered by Arthur Mizener and by Stephen Booth).[12] The very brief Ch. 4 of *Shakespeare's Verbal Art*, 'Interpretation', is no more than a paraphrase of the cognitive content of the poem and a few notes on sexual *doubles ententes*. That the authors are not interested in any richer or more extended paraphrase is made obvious by their deprecation (pp. 31–2) of the permissive rewordings of Laura Riding and Robert Graves; and they

[9] *Shakespeare's Verbal Art*, ch. v.

[10] It is interesting that a very simple reason for the relative unimportance of this pattern is not mentioned: that this is not a petrarchan sonnet and thus any division into octave and sestet is likely to be weakly reinforced.

[11] John Crowe Ransom, 'Shakespeare at Sonnets', *The Southern Review*, 3 (1938), 531–53.

[12] Arthur Mizener, 'The Structure of Figurative Language in Shakespeare's Sonnets', *The Southern Review*, 5 (1940), 730–47; Stephen Booth, *An Essay on Shakespeare's Sonnets* (New Haven: Yale University Press, 1969).

presumably would not tolerate the graceful paraphrases of William Empson.[13] Apparently Jakobson and Jones rest their case for the worth of sonnet 129 purely on the demonstration of complexity, of 'amazing . . . structuration'. This 'structuration' apparently justifies the simplistically laudatory *Shakespeare's Verbal Art* in the title of the monograph: we are asked to accept the habitual formalist premiss that what is complex must be aesthetically excellent. It is clear enough that the merits of Shakespeare's 'Th'expence of spirit . . .' reside largely in its linguistic and rhetorical complexity, and in particular in its dense word-play tormenting the reader with a paradoxical logic: chiasmus (*lust in action, and till action, lust; well knows . . . knows well*), antitheses (*Enjoy'd . . . despised; bliss . . . woe; heaven . . . hell*); word-repetition (*mad/Mad*); puns (*proof . . . prov'd*), etc. The effect of this rhetorical battering is to pitch the reader into just the category of love's fools described in the couplet: the quatrains have rigorously instructed him so that he 'well knows' the paradox of bliss and grief in sex, but the reiteration of the irrationality in the *heaven . . . hell* of the last line ('it *is* heaven but it leads to hell'; 'it *can't be* heaven because it leads to hell'; it *can't be* hell because it is heaven') produces a violent Catch-22 effect: the reader is trapped within the insane logic of this sonnet, which has become his own logic.[14] Thus the worth of this poem can be directly related to its structural complexity, but Jakobson and Jones make no attempt to argue this relationship. Their assumption that complexity results in excellence, automatically—rather than that, in some cases including this one, specific aesthetic effects may be shown to issue from certain kinds of linguistic complexity—is an exceedingly dangerous one. It hardly needs pointing out that there are many highly artful poems of the utmost mediocrity. On the other hand, there are lots of simple poems which are astonish-

[13] Laura Riding and Robert Graves, *A Survey of Modernist Poetry* (1928; rpt. New York: Haskell House, 1969), ch. iii; William Empson, *Seven Types of Ambiguity*, 2nd ed. (London: Chatto and Windus, 1947), e.g. pp. 50–1.

[14] Joseph Heller, *Catch-22* (1955; rpt. London: Corgi Books, 1966); for some nice examples of the application of the catch, see pp. 54, 172–3.

ingly powerful and which Jakobsonian analysis might reject, or, worse still, render irrelevantly complicated.

In his critique of Jakobson and Lévi-Strauss' analysis of 'Les chats', Michael Riffaterre claims that the analysis makes use of 'constituents that cannot possibly be perceived by the reader' ('Describing Poetic Structures', p. 195). This criticism invites immediate assent, and I think it is a justified criticism. Of course, Riffaterre's point does not relate merely to *physical* perceptibility, to the inadequate realization of a part of the poem considered as physical object; the failure of Jakobson and Lévi-Strauss is a failure to assign *significance* to the structures they posit, hence a failure to identify correctly the patterns that are artistically foregrounded. The gravest consequence of these shortcomings is that critical interpretation is impossible, at least, it cannot follow from Jakobsonian analysis as that technique is practised by its originator. Riffaterre's answer to Jakobson is to introduce as a 'tool of analysis' his famous 'super-reader', a development of the heuristic 'Average Reader' device proposed in his own earlier work.[15] The super-reader is equipped with a body of appropriate linguistic and literary-historical knowledge, and he works through the text sniffing out places which can be shown to be particularly significant in terms of the specified knowledge which he possesses. One area of the super-reader's knowledge in which Riffaterre has consistently interested himself is the lexical code: the system of regular paradigmatic correspondences and oppositions between vocabulary items. This system of lexical relationships is part of our ordinary linguistic competence; but in poetry, the relationships holding between items in the system are projected into the linear orderings of the syntagm. (E.g. antonyms in the system produce oxymoron when concatenated in the syntagm: 'dearest enemy',

---

[15] 'Describing Poetic Structures', pp. 203–4. For the original 'Average Reader', see 'Criteria for Style Analysis', *Word*, 15 (1959), 154–74. In the recent French translation of his essays, Riffaterre renders 'Average Reader' as 'archilecteur' and comments on the misleading nature of the original term. See *Essais de stylistique structurale*, trans. Daniel Delas (Paris: Flammarion, 1971), pp. 46–7.

'black as snow', etc.) Riffaterre's most recent paper shows how a study of some English lexical structures, from the viewpoint of the Jakobsonian poetic principle, can serve the interpretation of a specific poem.[16] One of my aims in the present paper is to extend Riffaterre's procedure, to show how the reader's linguistic competence determines his engagement with the literary text at other levels of organization than the lexical. I will be attempting to demonstrate what Jakobson and Lévi-Strauss, and Jakobson and Jones, fail to demonstrate: how significant literary structures are coded, for the informed reader, in his knowledge of the conventional regularities of language, and how they are 'realized' in the sequential experience of reading.

The 'super-reader' section of Riffaterre's 'Describing Poetic Structures' is headed 'The Poem as Response' (p. 202). The range of responses entertained by Riffaterre is strictly limited: for the most part they are responses which are controlled by the reader's normal linguistic competence, that is to say, responses which can be predicted on the basis of observed linguistic regularities in texts; and in effect the restriction is even closer than that, since Riffaterre is concerned almost exclusively with foregrounded lexical patterns. However, despite these precise and salutory cautions, Riffaterre's section-heading is apt to be read as a slogan. Compare it with two other recent formulae which might be regarded as announcing a similar sentiment:

'The Poem as Response' (Riffaterre)

'le lecteur comme producteur du texte' (Roland Barthes)[17]

'Literature in the Reader: Affective Stylistics' (Stanley Fish)[18]

[16] Riffaterre, 'Interpretation and Descriptive Poetry', *New Literary History*, 4 (Winter, 1973), 229–56. The 'Jakobsonian Poetic Principle' is quoted in note 4 above.

[17] *S/Z* (Paris: Seuil, 1970), p. 265.

[18] Title of article in *New Literary History*, 2 (Autumn, 1970), 123–62; shortened version rpt. as Appendix in Fish's book *Self-Consuming Artifacts* (Berkeley and Los Angeles: University of California Press, 1972), pp. 383–427.

Extremely diverse specific motives underlie these 'pronounce-
ments'. At the risk of doing violence to the views of the critics
in question, I would venture a collective generalization: all of
these remarks stem from a general, and growing, dissatisfaction
with the reader-excluding premisses of classic formalist criticism
in both the Anglo-American and Russian/Prague/French traditions. I cannot here digress to a full discussion of the faults
in formalist theory which have led critics of such different
persuasions to argue for the reintroduction of the reader into
literary theory: but see pp. 9–10 above, pp. 120–2 below, and
further references cited at those points. Here it will be convenient simply to quote the views of Professor Fish, whose paper
is an overt attack on the dogmas of American formalist criticism
of the post-Wimsatt and Beardsley era.[19] Fish's views are particularly relevant to the present context, for several reasons. He
stresses the importance to criticism of a description of the linear
experience of reading, and in this respect his attack on American
formalism chimes with one of my complaints against Jakobsonian analysis: its presentation of poems as spatial (rather than
temporal) and static (rather than engagingly kinetic) constructs.
Fish proposes '*an analysis of the developing responses of the reader in
relation to the words as they succeed one another in time*' ('Literature in
the Reader', pp. 126–7; Fish's emphasis). Later, a 'description
of the reader's experience is an analysis of the sentence's
meaning' (p. 130); 'a method of analysis which focusses on the
reader rather than on the artefact' (p. 139): and then come two
passages which summarize Fish's assumptions and programme:

in the category of response I include not only 'tears, prickles', and
'other psychological symptoms', but all the precise mental operations
involved in reading, including the formulation of complete thoughts,
the performing (and regretting) of acts of judgement, the following
and making of logical sequences; and . . . my insistence on the
cumulative pressures of the reading experience puts restrictions
on the possible responses to a word or phrase. (p. 140)

[19] W. K. Wimsatt, Jr., and Monroe C. Beardsley, 'The Intentional
Fallacy' and 'The Affective Fallacy', rpt. in Wimsatt, *The Verbal Icon*
(Lexington, Ky: University of Kentucky Press, 1954), pp. 3–18 and 21–39.

Who is *the* reader? Obviously, my reader is a construct, an ideal or idealized reader; somewhat like Wardhaugh's 'mature reader' or Milton's 'fit' reader, or to use a term of my own, *the* reader is the *informed* reader. The informed reader is someone who

(1) is a competent speaker of the language out of which the text is built up.

(2) is in full possession of 'the semantic knowledge that a mature . . . listener brings to his task of comprehension'. This includes the knowledge (that is, the experience, both as a producer and comprehender) of lexical sets, collocation probabilities, idioms, professional and other dialects, etc.

(3) has *literary* competence.

That is, he is sufficiently experienced as a reader to have internalized the properties of literary discourses, including everything from the most local of devices (figures of speech, etc.) to whole genres. (p. 145)

I find myself in agreement with a good part of Fish's pro gramme, and with some of his principles. His appeal to the analogy of generative linguistics, very evident in the wording of the three conditions listed in the immediately preceding quotation, seems to me a useful point of departure in the pro gress towards a new stylistics. However, I cannot detect much evidence to suggest that Fish takes the analogy of generative grammar seriously, and it does not appear that his analyses, where they involve syntactic considerations, make any specific use of the delicate metalanguage of syntactic description which has been developed by Chomsky and by his recent successors (e.g. Lees, Rosenbaum, Lakoff, Jackendoff and the contributors to anthologies such as those of Reibel and Schane, and Jacobs and Rosenbaum—to cite only descriptive work in the syntactic compartment of generative grammar, research which would naturally nourish a critical programme such as that outlined by Fish.[20] Fish's theory lacks just the control which is exercised in

[20] Robert B. Lees, *The Grammar of English Nominalizations* (The Hague: Mouton, 1960); Peter S. Rosenbaum, *The Grammar of English Predicate Complement Constructions* (Cambridge, Mass.: MIT Press, 1967); George Lakoff, *Irregularity in Syntax* (New York: Holt, Rinehart, and Winston, 1971); Ray S. Jackendoff, *Semantic Interpretation in Generative Grammar*, Studies in Linguistics No. 2 (Cambridge, Mass.: MIT Press, 1972); David

Riffaterre's scrupulous (but cautious) appeal to the facts of language: we are invited to witness the reader responding sequentially to language in literature, but the reader cannot be kept in decent communal order because he is not controlled by the constraints of precise communal syntax. The reader is not the 'ideal reader' we might expect in a generative stylistics based on generative grammar, but a less organized, regrettably substantial, actual reader—'a real reader (me) who does everything within his power to make himself informed' (Fish, op. cit., p. 145). Naturally, the practitioner of stylistic criticism, as a fallible mortal, could enjoy no less fleshly a specification; yet Fish's article focusses on stylistic *theory*, and at that level of critical abstraction we could benefit from a conception of an ideal reader of Chomskian mould.

One of Stanley Fish's colleagues at Berkeley, Stephen Booth, has applied a technique of affective criticism to Shakespeare's sonnets (see note 12); here are some general remarks from his book:

Where Shakespeare presents a formal pattern, a logical pattern, and a syntactical pattern that run simultaneously but not concurrently, he forces a reader subject to them all to give the poem some of its energy by the act of reading it. (p. 51)

. . . as one reads through a Shakespeare sonnet, the different patterning factors come into focus and out of it constantly, rapidly, and almost imperceptibly, 'each changing place with that which goes before'. The mind of the reader is kept in constant motion; it is kept uneasy as it is made constantly aware of relationships among parts of the poem that are clear and firm but in an equally constant state of flux. (p. 84)

Booth's strategy is essentially a response to the fundamental and classic interpretative problem of Shakespeare's sonnets: taken all together, the 154 are difficult to make sense of as a sequence, or even as a set of sequences; to compound the problem, the

A. Reibel and Sanford A. Schane, eds., *Modern Studies in English* (Englewood Cliffs, N.J.: Prentice-Hall, 1969); Roderick A. Jacobs and Peter S. Rosenbaum, eds., *Readings in English Transformational Grammar* (Waltham, Mass.: Blaisdell, 1970).

individual sonnets themselves are very often hard to figure out.
Booth rejects traditional attempts to solve 'the problem of
Shakespeare's Sonnets' by mechanical imposition of an interpretation: textual emendation and repunctuation, re-arrange-
ment of the sequence, provision of an autobiographical 'key',
etc. Booth leaves the text and the sequence as they are in the
first printing, and he eschews biographical speculations. His
analyses attempt to show how the reader, responding to patterns of syntactic, logical, rhetorical and metrical organization,
constructs interpretative frameworks for individual sonnets or
for groups of sonnets. Some of these frameworks are incompat-
ible one with another, but Booth is not disturbed by this fact:
he considers this variability and switching of meanings a central
aspect of the aesthetic design of the Shakespearian sonnet
corpus. Booth's attitude to the general problem of interpretation
might be regarded as indecisive or evasive. On the other hand,
there is no denying that his approach produces readings which
are uninhibited, ingenious and energetic. Booth's work illustrates how criticism can be refreshed if the reader is liberated
from the bounds placed on him by formalist doctrine as it
issues from Wimsatt and Beardsley.

Inevitably, affective criticism as practised by Booth raises
questions of validity, generalizability, control. How can we
assure ourselves that the reader Booth employs to lead us
through the Sonnets is the right kind of reader? that he is like
ourselves in ways in which he ought to approximate us? that he
is superior to us in possessing some areas of knowledge which
are expressly relevant to the elucidation of the Sonnets? The
qualifications for a super-reader or ideal reader become an issue
here, as with the other stylistic approaches I have mentioned
in this essay.

Jakobsonian analysis is intimately in contact with the
structure of language, but produces the paradoxical outcome
that the language, reduced to spatial pattern, loses both meaning and movement. Fish and Booth ask us to reinstate the
temporality of the reading experience, but provide no guarantee
that in following their technique we do not absolutely throw

caution to the winds. Riffaterre's 'lexical code' supplies a method for controlling the superreader and for ensuring the validity of the results of analysis—the lexical code being part of the formal linguistic knowledge of readers and thus subject to the Chomskian principle of idealization.[21] However, it could be argued that Riffaterre's lexical code is too cautious: certainly the reader possesses areas of coded knowledge, mediated through the structure of language, which are more abstract and of broader range than the lexical code. Conscious of the limitations of all the above approaches, I will try to avoid them in the analysis below, which is an attempt to read a poem as close to the language as possible, while regarding language structure as mediating larger, and interpretatively significant, formal structures; these structures being validated in the 'ideal reader's' experience because they reflect culturally coded knowledge activated in the process of reading.

My demonstration is an analysis of Shakespeare's 73rd sonnet, which has been much admired and so has attracted a good deal of discussion. In an analysis of this kind it would be foolish to decline the insights of other critics—as I would have done if I had chosen a less familiar poem. (The linguist might choose a virgin poem and claim to use his analytic tools to 'discover' its meaning and value for the first time, but that would be to adopt a perverse posture.) This particular sonnet has also commanded my interest for a number of years: Winifred Nowottny, one of my tutors at University College, London fifteen years ago, displayed the attractions of the Sonnets—and of a 'syntactic' technique of critical reading—to my generation of undergraduates, and since then I have several times used this sonnet, and her published analysis of it, in my own teaching.[22] It is, as she says, 'a promising case' for analysis. At first reading it is simple, popular and accessible; the formal/metrical pattern very clear, the general sentiment and the drift of the metaphors

[21] Noam Chomsky, *Aspects of the Theory of Syntax* (Cambridge, Mass.: MIT Press, 1965), p. 3.

[22] Winifred Nowottny, *The Language Poets Use* (London: Athlone Press, 1962), pp. 76–83.

pretty transparent; the whole argument graspable and pointed. As usual in such cases, however, close inspection reveals a complicated internal mechanism: the more one re-reads this sonnet the more one experiences a nagging sense that the argument and the figurative structure are not quite as straightforward as the early readings suggest.

I quote the sonnet in the conservatively edited Penguin text:

> That time of year thou mayst in me behold,
> When yellow leaves, or none, or few do hang
> Upon those boughs which shake against the cold,
> Bare ruin'd choirs, where late the sweet birds sang.
> In me thou seest the twilight of such day,
> As after sunset fadeth in the West,
> Which by and by black night doth take away,
> Death's second self that seals up all in rest.
> In me thou seest the glowing of such fire,
> That on the ashes of his youth doth lie,
> As the death-bed, whereon it must expire,
> Consum'd with that which it was nourish'd by.
>   This thou perceiv'st, which makes thy love more strong,
>   To love that well, which thou must leave ere long.

Some initial impressions from early readings of this sonnet are very strong, and they are confirmed by more mature consideration. Under the heading of initial impressions I shall mention the metrical structure, the phonetic texture and what might, not too loosely, be called 'imagery'. Most immediately striking is Shakespeare's open acceptance of the formal possibilities offered by the metrical structure of the ABAB CDCD EFEF GG sonnet form, that is, his evident decision to make this formal division into three quatrains and a couplet work in symmetry with his syntactic and rhetorical structure. Each quatrain is dominated by one metaphor: the fall season, twilight, dying fire; the metaphors are semantically connected and alike in stature. The vehicle of each metaphor is highlighted by the related predicates 'mayst . . . behold' (1), 'seest' (5), 'seest' (9), and these words occur in the first line of each quatrain; this lexical pattern is continued at the start of the couplet with 'perceiv'st', so the four verbs of perception (drawn from a tight lexical paradigm) mark and link the beginnings of the four sections. At the same time, these verbs form the nuclei of parallel syntactic frames. Each quatrain consists of one sentence; the main clause in each case, based on the verb of perception, occupies and is coterminous with the first line of the quatrain. The remainder of each quatrain consists of a sequence of comparative, relative and appositive clauses, each one devoted to narrowing the definition of some noun in the previous clause. The couplet, though distinct from the quatrains in lacking a dominant metaphor or even a clear noun-phrase object for its verb, echoes their syntax in its loose string of a relative, a nominal and a relative clause. Other parallelisms abound. The objects of the main verbs in the quatrains are introduced by the similar yet elegantly varied phrases 'That time . . . /When,' 'such day, /As,' 'such fire, /That,' the second part of the formula every time falling in the first syllable of the second line of the quatrain. The main verbs recall one another by the phonetic parallelism in /st/: 'mayst' (1), 'seest' (5), 'seest' (9), 'perceiv'st' (13). Lines 5 and 9 are virtually identical, and even the words which vary are metrically similar, bearing in mind the positions they occupy: 'twilight-glowing', 'day-fire'. The phrases 'Bare ruin'd choirs' (4) and 'Death's second self' (8) are metrically alike—the juxtaposition of lexically stressed vowels levels out the metrical accents and slows the rhythm—and occur in identical positions in the first and second quatrains.

Correspondences and oppositions such as those I have mentioned in the last paragraph conspire to make the metrical, syntactic, metaphoric and logical plans of this sonnet isomorphic. The overall structure of the poem, at each linguistic level, could be pictured in a simple diagram such as (a) above (p. 84) with no competing structures such as those shown in (b)–(f).[23]

---

[23] I suppose that a most ingenious Jakobsonian analysis would be capable of uncovering linguistic minutiae to demonstrate multiple structures similar to those I have diagrammed above; but I feel that those features which are indisputably perceptible so strongly enforce the quatrain-quatrain-quatrain-

It fulfils John Crowe Ransom's criterion for congruence of metre and meaning (though Ransom disapproves of sonnet 73 for other reasons):

The metrical pattern of any sonnet is directive. If the English sonnet exhibits the rhyme-scheme ABAB CDCD EFEF GG, it imposes on the poet the following requirement: that he write three coordinate quatrains and then a couplet which will relate to the series collectively.[24]

According to Ransom, 'about a third' of the sonnets have this structure. Ransom finds fault with those which do not observe the pattern, but frequently Shakespeare makes brilliant use of other schemes. For instance, sonnet 64 ('When I have seen by Time's fell hand defaced . . .') consists of five two-line exempla followed by a two-line reflection on their significance and then a final couplet expanding the reflection at one logical remove. In 66 ('Tir'd with all these for restful death I cry . . .') every one of lines 2–12 is a distinct exemplum of injustice, so the quatrain-structure is totally effaced. Sonnet 76 ('Why is my verse so barren of new pride?') is almost petrarchan: a series of rhetorical questions, of varying lengths, carries the reader straight through to the end of line 8, and the last six lines are a quasi-reply, with only a minor logical break between lines 12 and 13. These are virtuoso pieces, salient in structure, no less 'workmanlike' than the poems Ransom admires. I would agree with Booth (pp. 24 ff.) that Ransom's assumption of automatic merit in 'congruent' sonnets and automatic demerit in non-congruent ones is preposterous. Reversing these values would bring us at least closer to modern taste and perhaps nearer to an appreciation of Shakespeare's greatest achievements in this genre.

However, sonnet 73 is a 'congruent' poem: it does not obviously play syntax or logic or figurative language against the given metrical format; rather, it quite ostentatiously upholds that format. Now part of the pleasure given by this

---

couplet structure that it would be a misrepresentation to plead for a multiple scheme for this poem.

[24] Ransom, op. cit. (note 11 above), p. 533.

poem derives from its comfortable symmetry. It invites the reader to contemplate three exempla figuring the state of a man subject to Time; each exemplum is a distinct metaphor contained within its individual quatrain; the vehicles of the metaphors come from connectable semantic fields (natural time, light, fire) and so the separate quatrains in one way compose a twelve-line whole; to this whole is opposed an a-metaphoric couplet, which invites the reader to interpret the set of exempla in a particular way. This sense of formal unity remains after many re-readings. But it does not explain the greatness of the poem. As the most careful commentators have argued, there is much more complexity within this scheme, a lot of activity which troubles the mind of the reader as he moves through the fourteen lines.

Let us go back to first impressions. If the poem strikes us instantly, and reliably, with its formal symmetry, it also impresses with the concreteness and density of its texture. The promise of the sense-perception verb 'behold' is fulfilled by a parade of nouns with concrete referents: 'leaves', 'boughs', 'choirs', 'birds'; these are associated with verbs and adjectives indicating physical states and actions: 'yellow', 'hang', 'shake', 'bare', 'ruin'd', 'sang'; 'cold' is a physical sensation, 'sweet' has sensual connotations. Although the second and third quatrains are less insistently physical, the nuclear metaphors of light and fire, and other hints of sensual processes, allow the richness of the first quatrain to be sustained in the others. 'Twilight', 'day', 'sunset' catch some light from 'yellow'; 'fadeth' keeps the reader's eye alert ('thou seest') for the impact of 'black night'. 'Glowing' (metrically linked with 'twilight' and offered visually by the repeated 'seest') sustains the light-imagery, as does 'fire'. 'Fire' recalls 'cold'. 'Ashes' are physical, as is 'bed'; 'lie' is a state like 'hang' (and is metrically parallel) and has, like 'youth', sexual suggestions. 'Death' can hardly escape its standard renaissance undertone; 'consum'd' and 'nourish'd' relate sex and feeding, and pick up some of the associations of 'sweet'.

The imaged concretion of physical reference is matched by a

literal concreteness in phonetic texture. Vowel patterns are especially prominent: unreduced vowels (i.e. all long vowels and diphthongs, and short vowels with the exception of /ə/ and lightly stressed /ɪ/) demand our attention. There is a metrical reason for the prominence of vowel sounds, and that is a relative lack of words more than one syllable long. There are only eighteen[25] words of two syllables (excluding the compound 'death-bed') and none of more than two syllables. In English iambic verse, polysyllables have the effect of reducing the number of strong metrical stresses in a line, and increasing the number of light syllables (chiefly /ə/ and /ɪ/): this is because English polysyllables carry only one heavily stressed syllable— *redúcing, métrical, incréasing, pólysyllables* (in my pronunciation). By the same rule, all 'lexical' words of one syllable *must* carry a primary stress—*mán, fíre, líght, cáke,* etc.—while 'syntactic' words—*in, that, of, can, it,* etc.—do not usually, but may in certain circumstances, take strong stress. Thus verse with many polysyllables cannot enjoy a profusion of strong vowels; Wordsworth's line

Unfolded transitory qualities

has, in an ordinary performance, only three vowels which are not /ə/ or /ɪ/.[26] On the other hand, concatenated monosyllables place their vowels on display, as Pope has (incidentally) demonstrated:

And ten low words oft creep in one dull line.

[25] I do not attach any absolute statistical significance to such figures. 18 seems an exceptionally low score for Shakespeare's sonnets (the first ten score 28, 22, 22, 30, 30, 24, 30, 29, 24, 25), but the difference in effect between scores of, say, 18 and 22 is difficult to assess in such short texts. Other factors are involved, also, such as the positioning of polysyllables, the syntactic functions of monosyllables, the vowels which occur at the nuclei of monosyllables, etc. However, as a general principle a low count of polysyllables makes available to the poet phonetic patterning of the kind I describe.

[26] For further discussion of polysyllables and metrical style, see my 'Three Blank Verse Textures' in *The Languages of Literature,* pp. 193–4.

Sonnet 73 tends to the latter extreme, without the dullness. Long vowels, diphthongs and short vowels with strong word-stress are extremely frequent. Some measure of the saturation with strong vowels can be indicated by an examination of the weak ones. In the first quatrain only seven of twenty possible weak metrical positions are filled by /ə/: *of*, *or*, *or*, *up*(*on*), *a*(*gainst*), *the*, *the*. Of these, the two *or*'s are, in view of the syntax of separated phrases, likely to be pronounced /ɔ/. A few other metrically unaccented places are filled by /ɪ/: *in*, *be*(*hold*), *which*, (*ru*)*in'd*; but the first syllable of *behold* probably attracts some of the /i/ quality from *me*, and the /ɪ/ of *ruin'd* is metrically 'promoted' by the fact that it is immediately adjacent to /u/ and that the word crosses a foot-boundary.[27] The remaining metrically unaccented places are occupied by strong vowels, some by highly sonorous vowels, e.g. *thou* in line 1, *do* in 1.2, *birds* in 1.4. Of the 40 syllables in the first quatrain, 29 have sonorous vowels at their nuclei—31 if we assume the two *or*'s are pronounced /ɔ/, 33 if the first syllable of *behold* is pronounced /i/ and if the /ɪ/ of *ruin'd* is granted metrical heightening by its context. It would be hazardous to attach any particular significance to these numbers, so I will say only that at least they may confirm one's immediate impression of the phonetic richness of the poem. As well as this general denseness of texture, there are some obvious specific places where sound is used decoratively: the massive sequence of sonorous vowels in 'Bare ruin'd choirs', balanced against 'sweet birds sang' at the end of the same line; the array of heavily stressed /e/'s in l. 8, and the filigree of fricative sounds in the same line (five /s/'s, one /θ/, one /f/, one /z/); the rhyming consonantal sequence /l . . . v . . . r . . ./ in the final words of each line of the couplet.

It would be easy enough to enjoy or condemn sonnet 73 as a poem with an artfully and correctly constructed formal framework containing richly figurative and euphonious language. Ransom finds Shakespeare self-indulgent in his development of the vehicles of metaphors, and dismisses the poem as romantic:

[27] See my ' "Prose Rhythm" and Metre', in *Essays on Style and Language* (London: Routledge and Kegan Paul, 1966), pp. 98–9.

It is one thing to have the boughs shaking against the cold, and in that capacity they carry very well the fact of the old rejected lover; it is another thing to represent them as ruined choirs where the birds no longer sing. The latter is a just representation of the lover too, and indeed a subtler and richer one, but the two images cannot, in logical rigor, co-exist. Therefore I deprecate *shake against the cold*. And I believe everybody will deprecate *sweet*. . . . It is a pure sentimentality. (1938: 550)

Other critics have tried harder. Arthur Mizener, replying to Ransom, pleads that such metaphors are not subject to the rigour of logical consistency. He speaks of 'compound metaphors', 'coexist', 'fusion', 'soft focus', i.e. he admits and approves of the romanticism of the poem.[28] (I may hint here that it is essential to admit the poem's romanticism, because that element is functional for the meaning of the poem: that is why I have made such a fuss about concreteness of imagery and fullness of sound-texture.) Empson produces a wealth of associations, including stained glass windows, choirboys, the destruction of the monasteries, to justify the comparison offered by line 4, and speaks warmly of 'richness and heightening of effect'.[29] Krieger refers to the 'rich and melancholy imagery' of this sonnet, but seems to find it unanalysable, for elsewhere he says 'we can only marvel at the developing interchange of properties between the natural and the human as we watch it become total' and proceeds to quote the first twelve lines of 73 and the first twelve of 60 ('Like as the waves . . .').[30]

Krieger's omission of the couplet is interesting. The couplets are generally ratiocinative rather than figurative. We must remind ourselves that Shakespeare's sonnets are argumentative as well as pretty: there are strong lines enough. Other critics,

[28] Mizener, op. cit. (note 12 above), p. 732.

[29] *Seven Types of Ambiguity*, pp. 2–3. It is strange that he finds 'no pun, double syntax, or dubiety of feeling' in the line, since the association of 'boughs' and 'choirs' depends on a double meaning for 'birds': literal birds sat on the boughs and sang, metaphorical birds sat in the choirs and sang.

[30] Murray Krieger, *A Window to Criticism: Shakespeare's Sonnets and Modern Poetics* (Princeton: Princeton University Press, 1964), pp. 123, 98.

recognizing this fact, have related imagery to theme and argument. Hallett Smith declares that the 'professed subject is the poet's age, which is contrasted with the youth of the young man' and proceeds with an extended paraphrase of the poem showing how the separate metaphors elaborate and develop this theme, 'bringing the metaphorical point closer to the subject as the poem progresses'; 'the relationship of the figures to each other is also a metaphorical one: the year and the day are both metaphors for a lifetime; the fire has to do both with the heat and life of summer and noonday as well as the vital essence of life'.[31] Nowottny (pp. 76–7) quotes Hallett Smith, seemingly accepting his interpretation ('The three quatrains . . . proceed from the declining of the year to the declining of the day to a declining of the fire,' p. 185), and then gives an extremely detailed account of the development of metaphors and their relationships with each other, admiring especially the way metaphors are built on one another (which is just what Ransom objected to)—'extra figuration', 'so highly figured as to attain the status of the metaphysical' (p. 79). Her thesis is that the poem's 'ground-plan' ('a reiteration of a common idea of declining') is, through this metaphorical elaboration or 'involution' (Hallett Smith's term, which she adopts) made more valuable than a prose restatement of it would be. Nowottny esteems concreteness of imagery and 'corporeality' of words, and so is able to respond sensitively and relevantly to sonnet 73.

Stephen Booth presents another minute analysis of this sonnet.[32] Like the other commentators, he assumes that the subject of the poem is human mutability—'mortality' (p. 126), 'the threat of mortality' (p. 130). As he does throughout his book, he stresses the demands the sonnet makes on the mental agility of the reader: 'the reader's mind is required constantly

[31] Hallett Smith, *Elizabethan Poetry: A Study in Conventions, Meaning and Expression* (Cambridge, Mass.: Harvard University Press, 1952), pp. 182–5. The alleged contrast between 'the poet's age' and 'the youth of the young man' doesn't seem to be evidenced in 73.

[32] *An Essay on Shakespeare's Sonnets*, pp. 118–30.

to act' (p. 120); 'The mind of a reader of line 2 of sonnet 73 is
in motion' (p. 124); 'intellectual gymnastics' (p. 127). He
develops Mizener's hint at analysis countering Ransom,[33]
showing the kinds of shifts of context the reader must work
through to make sense of the compound metaphors. For Booth,
the experience of the poem is disquieting, dramatic, partici-
patory: his ideal reader does not draw a sense of richness from
fuzzy transitions between metaphors, but *works* at the transitions
to make sense of them. Because the reader's mind has been
forced to such a delicate and energetic wrestling with the poem,
the poem cannot end up as the conventional mush that Ransom
arrives at: according to Booth, the successful reader has been
forced to experience the terrors of mortality. Booth's critical
position acknowledges the fact that a good reader's mind is very
active as he goes through a poem and in a very complex state
of tension when he has possessed it. His method encourages us
to look for those features of a work which *change* a reader; and
it does so by insisting on a tough and exhausting (I have typed
exhausting for exhaustive, but the error seems interesting
enough to stand) analysis of the language of the text. Ideally,
a technique of the kind practised by Booth ought to assume that
a poem does not permit just any old response that the reader's
ignorance/knowledge or the state of his metabolism might
encourage. One must assume that there is a set of permissible
readings *controlled by the verbal structure of the poem*; I believe that
my interpretative technique takes this notion of linguistic
control more seriously than does that of Booth.

Although Booth's interpretation of 73 rests on the most alert
and acute analysis yet seen, it assumes, like all the earlier
criticism of this poem that I have cited, that the poem's meaning
is clear, known in advance. Commentators usually regard this
sonnet as a dramatization, through 'rich and melancholy
imagery', of the horror of mortality; the poet reflects on his own
imminent death,[34] prettily figures it, and entreats his lover to

[33] Mizener, op. cit., p. 732, note 4.
[34] Cf. J. B. Leishman, *Themes and Variations in Shakespeare's Sonnets* (London: Hutchinson, 1961), p. 141: 'Before he wrote it, Shakespeare must have

love him the more for the inevitability of their impending severance; thereby the general reader is drawn in to a depressing recognition of the fact of human transience. An optional extra to this interpretation is the opinion that the power of the poem derives from the sincerity of the author: 'Shakespeare is contemplating . . . his own transience' (Leishman, op. cit., p. 32). There are substantial grounds for agreeing that the poem has as its major object the lamenting of mortality: much of its language is indeed melancholy in its connotations (e.g. 'cold', 'bare', 'ruin'd', 'ashes', 'death-bed', 'consum'd', 'leave' in the diction); the second quatrain evokes a fearful and threatening finality; the couplet terminates (itself, and the whole poem) with a matter-of-fact prognosis of separation by death. Then there is the context provided by sonnet 74, which is obviously a companion-piece[35] and which is even syntactically connected with 73 by its first word, which presupposes linkage with a preceding linguistic context:

> But be contented when that fell arrest,
> Without all bail shall carry me away,
> My life hath in this line some interest,
> Which for memorial still with thee shall stay.

74 is quite different in tone from 73; it is more depressing, moves further away from any glimmerings of life. It does not pick up the prevailing metaphors of 73, but that fact is immaterial: the couplet of 73, unfigurative and apparently unequivocal as it is, allows us to read through to 74 as a natural sequel, and thus to read *back* to 73 the plain sentiment ('I am going to die, but . . .') of 74. I will return to 74 later; for the moment, we will agree that it supports the fatalistic interpretation of its companion.

---

been, at most, in his early forties, although an uninstructed foreign reader, meeting with this sonnet in an anthology, might pardonably suppose that the author of it must have been at least in his late nineties.'

[35] Krieger, p. 123, speaks of 'the two-sonnet sequence' 73–4; Edward Hubler pronounces that 'Sonnets 73 and 74 comprise one poem'—see his 'Shakespeare's Sonnets and their Commentators', in Hubler *et al.*, *The Riddle of Shakespeare's Sonnets* (London: Routledge and Kegan Paul, 1962), p. 8.

As we have seen, most commentators have concentrated on the complex metaphoric structure of this sonnet; probably, they have done so for two reasons—because the metaphors are so spectacular, and the syntax and logic appear so straightforward (the latter view is encouraged by the neat 'stanzaic' structure). The syntax has an ostentatious air of exactitude about it. Each quatrain opens by isolating a noun phrase and announcing that it will proceed to tell us exactly what member of the class of referents designated by this noun phrase we are to contemplate: 'That time of year . . . When'; 'the twilight of such day /As';[36] 'the glowing of such fire /That'. The 'definition' proceeds by a sequence of qualifying clauses as if to make the focus ever more precise: the time of year is first expressed by a picture of leaf-fall; the leaves hang on boughs; the boughs shake against the cold; the boughs are like choirs; the boughs and the choirs were both recently occupied by songsters. This apparently meticulous signposting is duplicated in quatrains two and three: hardly a noun escapes further characterization by piled-up relative or appositive clauses. And since the imagery introduced by these clauses is extraordinarily particularized, it is wholly reasonable of us to believe that the promised definition gets fulfilled. This impression—that the objects of 'behold', 'seest' and 'seest' have been defined as promised—is apparently confirmed by the assertive 'This thou perceiv'st' at the opening of the couplet. A 'this' logically presupposes a 'something', and 'perceiv'st', echoing 'mayst behold', 'seest' and 'seest' semantically and even phonetically, leads us to assume that this particular 'something' must be the defined objects of perception in the three quatrains—more accurately, the united significance of these objects. Our conviction that there is a solid antecedent for the word 'This' can only be strengthened by its marked metrical position; it appears to invite very strong stress, for it seems to occupy the first metrical place in the one indisputable reversed first foot in the sonnet.

Commentators have, in general, agreed that the argument

[36] A copula or predicate has to be understood between 'As' and 'after' to complete the sense: 'is' or 'exists' or 'thou seest'.

of this poem is straightforward, that the focus of attention must be the metaphoric structure, and that the metaphoric content, and the relationships between metaphors, serve to bring home to the lover the imminence of the poet's death. The analytic energies of critics have been devoted almost exclusively to the figurative dimension of the poem. Since it has proved extremely difficult to work out the way some of the metaphors function, and the ways in which the metaphors relate to one another, it is surprising that the critics have not been tempted to question the trustworthiness of the syntax and thus to entertain the suspicion that the poem is conceptually more complicated than the staidness of the metre and the ostensive gestures of the argument initially suggest. Although we are bound to accept that the poem is primarily 'about' the waning life of the persona and the effect on the lover of realizing that his beloved is nearing his end, we may yet suspect that this statement is communicated in a slightly equivocal language. As we shall see, the syntax admits some interesting qualifications; and the metaphors, though figuring the approach of death, are complex enough to accommodate connotations of vitality (the metaphors are not only 'vital' in terms of their poetic technique, but semantically their vehicles also connote life while they figure death). The overall effect is the withholding of a final statement of inevitable, unqualified, loss. To be more specific, I am not saying that the persona offers any conventional comforts to soften the blow— blissful rebirth of the soul, reunion of the lovers in another world, Yeatsian wisdom of old age, recollection of shared joys in the past, or whatever. His prediction of the inevitability of his death is phrased in such a way as to cause a reinterpretation of the present state: the friend treasures what he is soon going to miss, treasuring it the more dearly because it will soon be no more, and he is brought to contemplate the object of his affections as a person who still has signs of vitality about him. The love spoken of in the couplet is realistic, present-tense, love, not the sentimental, recollective, appreciation of past happiness.

The couplet is syntactically ambiguous, although not with any profoundly disturbing effect:

> This thou perceiv'st, which makes thy love more strong,
> To love that well, which thou must leave ere long.

In one possible arrangement of its clauses, 'which makes thy love more strong' is parenthetical, and we read the noun clause 'To love that well' with its dependent clause 'which thou must leave ere long' as an appositive, loosely linked, complement to 'This.' On this analysis, the two lines might be paraphrased 'You realise that one loves well that which one must leave before long, and this realization strengthens your love.'[37] This interpretation treats the couplet as an aphoristic rephrasing of the 'lesson' of the quatrains; and it could be argued that the order of clauses in the couplet (changed necessarily in my paraphrase) places 'leave ere long' at the end for the sake of natural transition to the more frankly dismal Sonnet 74. This is a syntactically possible interpretation—as we shall see, it is paralleled elsewhere in the Sonnets—but it is not very interesting. By supplying a reference for 'This' (l. 13) from within the couplet itself, the interpretation makes the couplet grammatically self-enclosed and cuts it off from the metaphoric power of the main part of the poem.

The alternative analysis, and the one which is to be preferred (though the first cannot be absolutely excluded), assumes that there is an antecedent for 'This' outside of the couplet. Thus, 'You realize this [sc. something in the preceding context] and your realization strengthens your love in order to [or, so that you] love well that which you must leave before long.' On this syntactic analysis, the sequence of clauses 'To love that well, which thou must leave ere long' qualifies 'more strong'; it lacks the aphoristic quality it had on the first interpretation, though by its very position the sequence must remain summative in

---

[37] In both of my paraphrases I preserve 'leave', assuming that it carries more or less its literal modern meaning. According to English burial custom the mourners depart from the grave-side after the funeral, literally *leaving* the body of the deceased behind; 'leave' need not suggest the soul of the dead man leaving the earth, thus there is no need to explain away the reference to the lover 'leaving' the persona as an inversion of any expected process. I owe this explanation to Professor Sears Jayne.

function. The principal consequence of this second interpretation of the syntax is to throw the word 'This' into a semantic
prominence which suits its metrical prominence. The couplet
fails to explain 'This,' and at the same time foregrounds the
word metrically, thus directing attention to the lack of explanation. Now it is characteristic of the sentence-initial usage of the
word 'this,' when it is not followed by a head noun, to be
ambivalent in its reference—it is for this reason that students
are advised to avoid this construction. So, in such a case, if we
determine that 'this' refers back to the preceding linguistic
context, we have to make an interpretative decision as to the
content of the exact reference of the word. I do not wish to
formulate this decision before we have examined the body of the
poem in greater detail, but it can be said in advance that this
particular usage of 'this' bestows on us the prerogative of
proposing double reference for the pronoun.

(I have found that the word 'this'—in one case, 'these'—
appears in twenty other sonnets by Shakespeare in usages which
are pertinent to the present discussion. Only two of these
instances (33 and 129) involve syntactic ambiguity of the kind
proposed for 73, and these are doubtful cases, particularly 129).
In seven of the remaining eighteen (14, 50, 69, 80, 91, 104 and
123) 'this' is further specified by the kind of loose appositive
complement which I invoked in my first paraphrase of the
couplet of 73; compare 50

> For that same groan doth put this in my mind,
> My grief lies onward, and my joy behind.

or 123

> This I do vow and this shall ever be,
> . I will be true despite thy scythe and thee.

This syntactic structure is in fact more common that my count
of seven strict parallels would suggest, however: I have counted
only cases where the word 'this' appears as a whole NP,
without a noun. There are several other sonnets in which the
clause[s] of the final line are tacked on to a complete noun-
phrase including 'this'—e.g. 'this glutton' (1), 'this miracle'

(65). In the remaining eleven examples (2, 18, 45, 55, 66, 74, 107, 116, 124, 128 and 144) the word 'this' points back to the preceding text or to part of it, as it does in my second paraphrase of the couplet of 73; compare 2

> This were to be new made when thou art old,
> And see thy blood warm when thou feel'st it cold.

or 55

> So till the judgement that your self arise,
> You live in this, and dwell in lovers' eyes.

I will comment later on the reference and meaning of 'this' in some of these cases.)

We return to the beginning of the sonnet. For ease of reference, I give the complete poem once more:

> That time of year thou mayst in me behold,
> When yellow leaves, or none, or few do hang
> Upon those boughs which shake against the cold,
> Bare ruin'd choirs, where late the sweet birds sang.
> In me thou seest the twilight of such day,
> As after sunset fadeth in the West,
> Which by and by black night doth take away,
> Death's second self that seals up all in rest.
> In me thou seest the glowing of such fire,
> That on the ashes of his youth doth lie,
> As the death-bed, whereon it must expire,
> Consum'd with that which it was nourished by.
> This thou perceiv'st, which makes thy love more strong,
> To love that well, which thou must leave ere long.

Two complexities must be noted from the outset: one having to do with the mode of address to the reader or lover, one concerning the precise content of the statement carried by the metaphors of the quatrains. The second is the more relevant to our major task of determining the referent for line 13's 'This'; the first complexity relates to the appropriate behaviour in the lover once the 'statement' has been perceived. The modal verb 'mayst' in the first line hints that the speaker may have chosen an indirect linguistic strategy. For the persona, the attributes he goes on to metaphorize are real and inherent: they *can* be seen. But 'mayst' also carries a hypothetical note: 'you can, if you choose to,' 'you can, if you are perceptive enough'. In the other three sections of the poem, the main verbs are all simple indicative if we go by their surface structure, but the shadow of 'mayst', suggesting a potentiality dependent on the quality of the observer's vision and volition, is carried on to the other three verbs of perception. If the final predicate, 'perceiv'st' in line 13, can be read as alternatively 'perceive' or 'may perceive', the syntactic, semantic and rhetorical possibilities directed by the structure of the couplet are permuted.

Let us turn to the 'statement' communicated by the metaphors of the three quatrains. Critics agree that 'the bulk of each of the quatrains is devoted to metaphoric statements of the impending departure of the speaker' (Booth, p. 129). The poem predicts imminent death under the influence of devouring Time. Certainly; but the prediction is not voiced in an unequivocally despondent or final manner. For a start, the season of the opening quatrain is not an entirely straightforward symbol. Differences of nomenclature among the critics are interesting. Booth (pp. 121–2) calls it 'autumn', Nowottny 'the onset of winter' (p. 77) and 'a cold, bare, ruined season' (p. 78); Hallett Smith has 'early winter or late fall' (p. 183) and 'winter boughs' (p. 184). In a sense it doesn't matter what one calls this season (except that 'autumn', prosaically apparently the most neutral term, may well, for the reader competent in modern poetry, supply misleading Keatsian overtones); and in a sense too, it is rather important that one does *not* label this season. Shakespeare does not name it, though elsewhere (e.g. Sonnet 104) he is liberal with the names of the seasons. Hallett Smith's phrase 'early winter or late fall' is perhaps the most satisfactory nomination: this is an ambiguous season, connoting both fruition and decay; and in this poem, it appears more equivocal because it is at the same time precise and, like all transitions, uncertain. The variable responses of the critics are indicative of the ambivalence of this metaphorical season; turning this variety to use as an aid in stating the tenor of the metaphor, we may suggest that the productive, and ultimately kinetic, ambivalence here involves our evaluation of whether the persona is utterly drained of vitality, or whether the vitality lingers, enchanced and made more intense by its context of unquestionable decline.

In line 2, the a-chronological sequence 'yellow leaves, or none, or few' has been noticed (Hallett Smith, p. 183; Booth, pp. 121–4). The order is slightly unexpected; trying to quote from memory, people transpose 'none' and 'few', restoring the natural sequence of fall. Booth, preoccupied with his thesis of the reader's mind in action, appeals to this phrase as evidence of the unsettling effect of the language of the poem, tries out a naturalistic explanation—at a given moment in the fall some branches of a tree, some trees, will retain full yellowed foliage, some will be denuded, some will have a few leaves—and with perhaps excessive vehemence rejects the literalism of the suggestion. Hallett Smith finds a 'deliberate uncertainty' here, but makes nothing of it, branding it simply as a 'curious effect'. The uncertainty, I take it, is a miniature of a broader uncertainty about the state of the season, the fine edge between ripeness and decay. The wording of the line maintains a nice balance between negative and positive values: 'yellow' implies 'some' and is from some connotational perspectives a bright, attractive colour;[38] 'few' also implies 'some', so 'yellow' and 'few' together out-vote 'none' two to one in favour of the presence of leaves; but 'few' implies some only in strict logic—it also connotes near-loss; since the sequence leads through to 'few', it must finally be a negative sequence; however, because the positioning of the phrases 'or none' and 'or few' is metrically immaterial, the reader's mind is free to supply the natural and strict logical order—'yellow leaves, or few, or none' which is more negative still than the existing sequence, and so serves to remind us that the line might well have been even more fatalistic and final than it actually is. All in all, we are left with the

[38] But for rival connotations, contrast Macbeth's 'My way of life is fall'n into the sere, the yellow leaf' or 'my papers (yellowed with their age)' in Sonnet 17.

impression that though things are bad, they could be worse—
and have been better, in fact were better just a little while ago.

As the principal metaphor of the first quatrain is elaborated,
it becomes increasingly unreliable pictorially. The leaves might
suggest thinning hair; the boughs the thin arms of an old man;
when the boughs are metamorphosed into the ruined choirs of
derelict churches, the anatomical analogy can be sustained no
longer. We have to respond detail by detail, being unable to
construct the overall picture which was initially promised.
'Bare' (which simultaneously refers back to 'boughs' and for-
ward to 'choirs', making the transition possible) has been denied
by the suggestions of remaining leaves in line 2: the suggestion
of utter devastation carried by 'bare' fits the overt sentiment
of the quatrain, but the absoluteness implied by the word is
undermined by the connotations elsewhere of persisting vitality.
The locative clause 'where late the sweet birds sang' modifies
both 'boughs' and 'choirs', so the birds are first literal and then
metaphorical. The metaphorical sense 'choristers', given of
course by the context 'choirs', is important in introducing the
notion of man-made music. Having arrived at this point, we
can supply a metaphoric meaning for 'sang', taking it to refer
to the poet's faculty, his 'songcraft'. Now the leaves of l. 2 may
well carry a secondary meaning of the leaves of books of poetry,
and verses hanging in trees are warranted by Elizabethan practice as well as by Act III of *As You Like It*. Since the speaker in
these sonnets characterizes himself as a poet who is very self-
conscious about his practice of poetry, it is fair to suppose that
the state of life presented in 73 embraces the state of his art as
well as the state of his body. The clause ends the quatrain not
with a mood of unqualified gloom: ostensibly the birds, but
actually their singing, were 'sweet',[39] and they sang 'late', i.e.
'lately', 'just recently'. Perhaps one may still hear the echoes
in the word-music of the quatrain that I analysed earlier. If so,
the persona states the decline of his powers, hints that they are

---

[39] The adjective has been transferred to the surrogate head-noun 'birds'
according to the rhetorical device of hypallage. Thus we may discount
Ransom's accusation of sentimentality in 'sweet birds' (see p. 100 above).

not yet disappeared, and affirms the hint by putting them on display.

Quatrain 1 manages to connote lingering vitality in the same breath as it denotes bareness and ruin. Quatrain 2 more straightforwardly dramatizes the coming of death, but begins with the figure of 'twilight', which is logically equivalent to the season of the first quatrain, occupying the same place in the scheme of the day as the approach of winter occupies in the scheme of the year, and to some degree open to the same variety of interpretations: it is fading light, light about to be extinguished, but light nevertheless, testimony to the fact that day has existed. Moreover, it is light of a particular quality, the sky being brighter than the earth and therefore seemingly very intense. However, I must not exaggerate suggestions of vitality in the second quatrain, for this is the most unequivocally fatalistic section of the poem. Booth (p. 127) has pointed out that the syntax of 'twilight of such day' is curious, but it is not, I believe, significantly so. The focus is on 'twilight', not 'day': 'day' is there for semantic symmetry with 'year' in the first quatrain (time of year: time of day) and for syntactic symmetry with 'fire' in the third (twilight of such day: glowing of such fire). The second line of the quatrain (l. 6) makes the visual image more precise: the sun has vanished from sight and only its afterglow remains. 'Which' in l. 7 has as its antecedent 'twilight' as specified in ll. 5–6. The twilight does not fade, disappear of its own accord, but is the object or patient of an external action: the personified 'black night' (the phrase metrically charged through the juxtaposed strong monosyllables) 'takes it away', abducts the remaining light. There is a powerful sense of menace here, reinforced in the next line where night is further characterized as 'death's second self'. Finally, the threat is made universal ('all') and inescapable (the generic present tense of the verb 'seals'). 'Rest' provides no comfort or relief: the terrifying conventional associations of sleep and night are driven home. The last line of this quatrain, with its almost self-parodic semi-onomatopoeic sound-patterning, is insistently final. 'Seals up' might mean many things in Shakespearean English, but the overpowering sense here is of forcible suppression of life or unbreachable closure of the tomb.[40]

Critics have attempted to postulate some structuring principle for the sequence of metaphors in the three quatrains. Hallett Smith and Nowottny assume an orderly (perhaps, by implication, progressive) train of images of decline. But Nowottny notices that a statement of the poem's theme as a 'common ideogram of decline'

leaves out other movements going on within the particulars of the metaphors, moving as they do from a cold, bare, ruined season to a glowing fire, from a time of year to a crucial moment, from what has gone to what is imminent, from the separate perceptions and simple reference in the first quatrain . . . to the one complex image, highly figurative in expression and irradiated with intellection, in the last quatrain.

(*The Language Poets Use*, p. 78)

And Booth also observes that the implications of the metaphors do not conduce to one unified impression:

Moreover, there are several coexistent progressions in the quatrains. Time is measured in progressively smaller units: a season of a year, a part of a day, and the last moments of the hour or so that a fire burns. Color grows increasingly intense: yellow leaves, twilight after sunset, fire. Light grows dimmer: daylight (presumably) in quatrain one, twilight, night; space constricts from the cold windy first quatrain to the hot suffocating grave of ashes in the third. . . . The progressions are consistent with one another and with the nature of the three metaphors, but they are not mechanically parallel and do not lump together in the mind: the time units get smaller; the speaker

[40] Hallett Smith (op. cit., p. 184) cites T. G. Tucker, ed., *The Sonnets of Shakespeare* (London: Cambridge University Press, 1924), p. 149 for a meaning of 'seals up' as 'putting cattle away for the night'. This suggestion of rural domesticity gratuitously softens the harsh blow dealt by the quatrain. Likewise, in view of the clear pessimism of the second quatrain, Mizener's comment that the 'autumnal decline of nature' figured in the first quatrain suggests 'perhaps, only the prelude to a winter sleep rather than death' seems peculiarly inappropriate (see Mizener, 'The Structure of Figurative Language in Shakespeare's Sonnets', p. 732.)

looms larger; the color gets brighter; the light gets dimmer; the temperature gets hotter.

(An Essay on Shakespeare's Sonnets, pp. 125–6, 127)

Some of the details of this analysis are a bit fanciful, but the general point is salutary: though it is natural to read this sonnet as figuring a continuous decline or enfeebling towards the grave, in fact we are not presented with that exact slide. The resurgence of energy as the third quatrain takes over from the second should alert us to an indirectness in the poem's logical plan. Nowottny's and Booth's analyses both suggest a 'crescendo' effect as we reach the third quatrain. Certainly the third quatrain is in many ways more intense than the second: it contains a more intricate metaphor; the vehicle of that metaphor introduces heat and thus life; and so on. But I do not think that, considering the overall movement of the first twelve lines, there is a smooth progressive rhetorical crescendo to a climax in the third quatrain. (Just as the 'statement' of the poem does not lead straightforwardly and inexorably towards any absolute prognosis of death at the end.) Rather, quatrain three unexpectedly delivers connotations of vitality hard on the heels of the fatalistic quatrain two.

The disjunctive sequence 'yellow leaves, or none, or few' of l. 2, the arrangement of which prevents our coming away with a clear impression of devastation, is mirrored in the sequence of quatrains: the first is energetic in its imagery (and sound-patterns, etc.) and suggests potency not yet wholly stifled by the onset of age ('yellow leaves'); the second quatrain states utter universal loss ('none'); the third evokes a complex or in-between state in which potency is evidenced directly ('glowing') and paradoxically ('ashes' indicating past fire)—the third quatrain parallels 'few' of l. 2, for as we saw, 'few' implies 'some', 'not-none'. In a linear reading of the sonnet, two different responses are possible in the transition from the second to the third quatrain. The more immediate is the recognition that l. 9 ('In me thou seest the glowing of such fire') repeats structurally l. 5 ('In me thou seest the twilight of such day'), a repetition which raises the expectation that the third quatrain will re-state the content of the second. This expectation is fulfilled: 'ashes', 'death-bed' and 'consum'd' recall the vocabulary of mortality, and the phrase 'it must expire' reflects the determinism of the second quatrain. On one level the third quatrain is consistent with the others in being about the necessary dying of a fire where the first is about the declining of the year and the second about the supercession of day by night. The power of the quatrain comes from the subtle but energetic challenge to this statement of decline: our second realization on moving from l. 8 to l. 9 is a feeling that the gloom of the second quatrain is repudiated (or, visually, dispersed) by the glowing fire of l. 9. A glowing fire, even a fire which is on the point of extinction, evidences heat, life, vitality. This fire is presented with the particularity characteristic of the poem, and the mode of its dying is meticulously specified: it is choked by the ashes of the fuel which formerly fed it—'Consum'd with that which it was nourished by'. The ashes are concretely presented to us in l. 10, and of course the existence of embers bears witness to earlier, more intense, burning. 'Earlier' is given explicitly in the qualifying phrase 'of his [its] youth', but this phrase also serves to bring the metaphoric vehicle close to its human tenor, for the 'youth' of the fire suggests the younger days of the persona, and then the ashes hint at the physical ravages caused by a passionate early life. It is possible that there are also some traces of sexual innuendo here (perhaps in the 'consum'd/nourished' paradox of l. 12) but if so they are weakly reinforced and do not fit well with the meaning of the glowing coal metaphor. But even without sexual reference, the vigour of the final quatrain can be readily explained in terms of the specific vehicle chosen —which, let it be noted, is not only more concentrated in itself but also less diffusely handled than the fall metaphor of the first quatrain—and in terms of the complex and economical syntax which guides us from the glowing embers to the forceful, paradoxical proposition of line 12.

To recapitulate: Shakespeare's Sonnet 73 is a poem in which the denotative level of meaning, the 'paraphraseable content', is itself straightforward, but receives a superstructure of complication through several distinct but co-operating linguistic factors. The most palpable complication arises from the connotations of both the vehicles of the nuclear metaphors themselves (fall season, light, fire) and the incidentals which attend the development of these metaphors ('yellow', 'choirs', 'sang', 'sunset', 'glowing', 'youth', 'nourished'): although the poem states, and figures, the prognosis that the persona is on the brink of death, the lexical constituents which perform the figuring carry suggestions which discourage the reader from apprehending that fact without perceiving at the same time signs of vitality even in the persona's present deteriorating state. The character and interpretation of these signs will occupy us shortly. Second, there is a delicate suggestion of optionality in the mood of the verbs of perception which are credited to the addressee: the modally qualified 'mayst ... behold' might influence our apprehension of the extension of its vertical paradigm in 'seest', 'seest' and 'perceiv'st' so that we suspect all these predicates of carrying an implication of only hypothetical fulfilment. The signs are displayed, but the addressee may or may not interpret them in their complex fulness. Third, the order in which the statements and signs are presented is not directed towards a conclusion of inexorable, unconditional, extinction of life: the sequencing of the three quatrains contrives to displace the most pessimistic of the three figures of decline from a predictable, commonplace, third (final) position to a penultimate situation which serves to highlight the vital connotations of the third quatrain. If we add together the statement of decrepitude and the suggestions of remaining, unvanquished, potency, we may arrive at an interpretation which ascribes an increase in the lover's affection to his sense of the preciousness of the departing beloved, a sense heightened by the hint at a persistence of energy offered by what I have called the linguistic superstructure.[41] This interpretation says rather more than my first syntactic reading of the couplet does, but is nevertheless compatible with it: 'You realize that one

[41] For an earlier statement of this interpretation, see p. 105 above, the sentence beginning 'His prediction ...'

loves well that which one must leave before long, and this realization strengthens your love.' Over and above the reason spelled out in the couplet, an additional motive for the strengthening of love is provided by the evident, not just sentimental, value of the persona as communicated by the superstructure of connotations.

As we have seen, an interpretation of the poem which uses the first syntactic description of the couplet (with line 14 in apposition to 'This') is intelligible and not inappropriate; it is also compatible with the interpretation of the companion-sonnet 74; but it is a weak interpretation compared with the one which is available if we allow the pronoun 'This' to point back to an antecedent in the main part of the sonnet. In four of the eleven sonnets listed earlier (p. 108) in which a 'this' in the couplet is not amplified within the couplet itself, the word refers to the actual poem: these are 18, 55, 74 and 107. These four sonnets are among those which affirm the power of the poet's art to provide immutable monuments surviving and commemorating either the lover or the poet himself. The four (as if proving their own argument) are all popular or at least familiar—18 is 'Shall I compare thee to a summer's day?', 55 'Not marble, nor the gilded monuments'; 107 'Not mine own fears, nor the prophetic soul'; 74 is of course the companion to 73: 'But be contented when that fell arrest'. These four sonnets have as their explicit theme the perpetuating power of verse; 73 does not, but that is not to say that the theme is not circumstantially relevant—particularly in the light of the context provided by 74.

The remaining seven cases (2, 45, 66, 116, 124, 128 and 144) provide, as might be expected, a variety of references for the 'this' of the couplet. In a majority of instances 'this' relates precisely to some specific fact or question announced toward the end of the poem (see, e.g., 2, 45, 144). Elsewhere the 'this' refers to the content of a larger segment of the poem—in 128 it points to one aspect of the situation described in quatrains 2–3; in 116 and 124 it appears to sum the whole statement of quatrains 1–3 (124 is a most obscure poem and it is difficult to

be confident about exactly what is going on). In 66 the word
'these' refers unambiguously to an enumeration of discrete
observations in lines 2–12. Sonnet 116 is perhaps the closest
parallel to 73: 'this' means 'the gist of what I have just spoken
above.' In both 73 and 116 (and perhaps 124) the reference of
'this' is necessarily diffuse: that is an inevitable consequence of
this particular syntactic use of the word in a context which does
not supply a proximate nominal as antecedent; contrast 144,
which furnishes its 'this' with a precise semantic focus:

> And whether that my angel be turned fiend,
> Suspect I may, yet not directly tell,
> But being both from me both to each friend,
> I guess one angel in another's hell.
> Yet this shall I ne'er know but live in doubt,
> Till my bad angel fire my good one out.

Although sonnet 116 does not provide such an explicit antecedent for 'this' as does 144, it is however less dependent on the
decipherment of metaphor than is 73. The metaphors in 116
are built upon a direct statement constituting a 'definition of
love': 'love is not love/ Which alters . . . /O no, it is . . . It is',
etc. The assertions about the character of love clearly form the
reference of the 'this' of the couplet: 'If this be error . . .' But in
73 there is no direct statement preceding the metaphoric level
of utterance. The reader cannot discover the referent of 'This'
in l. 13 except through a decoding of metaphoric structure.
Of course, the last line of the poem constitutes a summary of
the poem's theme; but the syntactic and metrical positioning
of the word 'This' lets us know that we should check the content
of this summary against the preceding text, and in performing that operation we are obliged to come to terms with the
secondary connotations of the metaphors as well as the concepts
they primarily signify. In a linear reading, the two other
linguistic complications which I mentioned also become
effective in guiding our determination of the theme of the poem:
the modality of the verbs and the sequence of the metaphors.
All these factors co-operate, I believe, to supply a richly

qualified thematic referent for 'This'—a statement of decline expressed in language which resists the full implications of senescence. And the syntax of 'This' permits, even validates, an unstraightforward reference.

A final dimension to the theme of Sonnet 73 may be suggested by Sonnets 18, 55, 74 and 107 (where a comparable 'this' indicates the poem itself) and the other Sonnets which discuss, and often demonstrate, the perpetuating value of poetry. Sonnet 74 is usually regarded as a close companion to 73; it continues the theme of the imminence of the poet's death, though in a different, more gloomy, tone and with a fresh metaphoric system; and the first word, 'But', suggests that it is syntactically connected with 73:

> But be contented when that fell arrest,
> Without all bail shall carry me away,
> My life hath in this line some interest,
> Which for memorial still with thee shall stay.
> When thou reviewest this, thou dost review,
> The very part was consecrate to thee,
> The earth can have but earth, which is his due,
> My spirit is thine the better part of me,
> So then thou hast but lost the dregs of life,
> The prey of worms, my body being dead,
> The coward conquest of a wretch's knife,
> Too base of thee to be remembered.
>   The worth of that, is that which it contains,
>   And that this is, and this with thee remains.

The phrase 'this line' in l. 3 refers to the whole poem, of course; likewise 'this' in l. 5; then the body-spirit dichotomy foregrounds the spirit, of which the poem is the materially surviving expression; the couplet encapsulates the complete series of transformations: the body is worthy only through the spirit which it contains, and the spirit can be seen in the poem, which remains with the person to whom the poet's spirit was devoted.

Although 73 can be read independently of 74, the latter poem is evidently an extension of the theme of the former. An interesting connection between the two is provided by the word 'this',

pivotal to the argument of 73 and subject of a good deal of
linguistic play in 74. Notice 'When thou reviewest this' in l. 5:
'reviewest' is a member of the same lexical set as the main
predicates in 73—verbs of visual perception. One might
legitimately compare the phrase with 'This thou perceiv'st' in
73, and although 'perceive' cannot (unlike 'review') be understood to mean primarily 'read', it does mean 'consider, and
recognize the significance of', and the material to be considered
is an argument in virtuoso poetic form. As we have seen, the
'perception' referred to in l. 13 necessarily involves an awareness
of a flamboyant poetic technique, and it seems to me not
entirely implausible to suppose that the poet-persona overtly
displays the survival (against encroaching senescence) of his
poetic energies as evidence of his worth in the present-tense
time-scheme of 73, a worth which is transformed into a poetic
memorial in the future-time prediction of 74, a poem which
faces squarely the inevitability of death and affirms the power
of verse to bring about the survival of the spirit after the
collapse of the body.

I will add only a brief comment about the technique of
analysis employed in this paper. During the last ten years or so
I have been writing about the relationship between linguistics
and literary criticism, and about the necessity for criticism to
embrace a linguistic method, to repair the damage done to
literary studies by its unnatural divorce from philology. In
writing on these topics, I have made it clear that contemporary
linguistics (which in fact bears little resemblance to the old
philology of England and Germany) cannot be absorbed into
criticism without real modification; that linguistic analysis is
not at all the same thing as critical description; and that there
cannot be a 'linguistic criticism' in the naïve sense in which that
idea has sometimes been interpreted (mechanical discovery
procedure for poetic structure). My analysis of Shakespeare's
Sonnet 73 is not offered as a demonstration of 'linguistic
criticism', but as an attempt to provide a critical reading which
stays as close to language structure as is possible without com-
promising the licence of interpretative insight allowed to

criticism. Roman Jakobson's mode of concentration on the structure of the linguistic message is obviously inimical to critical interpretation. Even though his famous definition of the 'poetic function of language' is a profound elucidation of the operation of verbal artifice, the application of the principle in his own published analyses so completely ignores the referential dimension that language ceases to be recognizable as communicative discourse—ceases to be meaningful. Michael Riffaterre's riposte to Jakobson and Lévi-Strauss (countering their analysis with a technique enriched in his more recent work) re-semanticizes poetic language while retaining that sharp sensitivity to significant pattern which distinguishes the best of formalist criticism. Riffaterre's linguistic preoccupation is with lexical structure; yet his notion of 'code' can be extended to other levels of linguistic structure, and in the present paper I have tried to show how literary significance can be coded in syntactic patterning.

A syntactic reading (practised brilliantly, but without a formal linguistic technique or metalanguage, by Mrs. Nowottny) naturally requires the critic to pay attention to the linear, extensional, directional, character of the literary text—an aspect of structure which is scandalously neglected in American formalist criticism of the Wimsatt-Beardsley-Brooks stamp, and equally so in the linguistic formalism of Jakobson. My interpretation of Sonnet 73 has bestowed unusual prominence on the order in which statements and metaphoric, rhetorical and metrical constructs are arranged, in the belief that these arrangements (both 'micro', as the order of words in line 2, and 'macro', as the sequence of quatrains) are of crucial importance to the way the theme of the poem is apprehended, and thus to the precise theme that is apprehended. In choosing this emphasis on linearity, my approach in this paper comes close to the 'affective stylistics' of Stephen Booth and Stanley Fish (cf. pp. 89–91 above): that is, my approach necessarily invokes the idea of an experiencing reader who is active sequentially. This reader is opposed to the generally assumed reader of formalist criticism, a reader whose experience of the poem is supposedly restricted to an instantaneous apprehension, a 'click' of structural recognition occurring when the reading has been successful. Restoring the linearity of the reading experience is, I believe, a necessary corrective to the rather static creations of the New Criticism and its descendants. But the reader's experience, linear or not, raises a more general question which stylistics must confront in the next phase of its development: the exact theoretical nature of the 'superreader' or 'ideal reader', mentioned by stylisticians as diverse as Fish and Riffaterre, a natural constituent of any generative poetics and greatly in need of clarification. The syntactic, lexical and other linguistic knowledge which an educated reader brings to the experience of literature is only part of the knowledge making up 'literary competence'. An urgent priority for contemporary stylistics is to determine just what additional fields of knowledge are relevant to literary competence, how they vary according to the types of literary discourse, how they relate to the diversification of language outside of literature and, perhaps most fascinating of all to the linguistics-inclined critic, how these systems of literary knowledge are coded in the structure of language.

CHAPTER FOUR

DEFINING NARRATIVE UNITS

Jonathan Culler

It seems an elementary and intuitively given fact that a story can be told in different ways and remain, in an important sense, the same story. One can even transfer a story from one medium to another: a novel and a film, perhaps even a pantomime, can have the same plot. And therefore it seems not unreasonable to ask of literary theory that it explicate and provide some justification for these concepts whose appropriateness seems unquestioned and which we use without difficulty. We might expect, that is to say, that it provide an account of our notion of plot and indicate how it is that we identify and summarize plots.

The first step we must take—one on which all analysts of plot would seem to agree—is to postulate the existence of an autonomous level of plot structure underlying actual linguistic manifestations. A study of plot cannot be a study of ways in which sentences are combined, for two versions of the same plot need have no sentences in common, nor need they even have any linguistic deep-structures in common. But as soon as we state the matter in these terms the enormity of the task becomes obvious. To explain how sentences combine to form coherent discourse is already an extremely difficult enterprise, and there the units with which one is working are at least given in advance. Difficulties are multiplied in the study of plot structure because the analyst must both determine what shall count as the elementary units of narrative and investigate the ways in which they combine. No wonder Roland Barthes once observed that devant l'infini des récits, la multiplicité des points de vue auxquels on peut en parler (historique, psychologique, sociologique, ethnologique, esthétique, etc.), l'analyste se trouve à peu près dans la même situation que Saussure, placé devant l'hétéroclite du langage et cherchant à dégager de l'anarchie apparente des messages un principe de classement et un foyer de description.[1]

It is nonetheless apparent that the analysis of plot structure must be theoretically possible, for if it were not we should have to admit that plot and our impressions of it were random, idiosyncratic phenomena. And this clearly is not the case: we can, with some confidence, discuss whether the summary of a plot is accurate, whether a film adheres to the plot of the novel on which it is based, whether or not a particular incident or stretch of discourse is important for the plot and if so what function it serves, whether a plot is simple or complex, coherent or incoherent. To be sure, such notions are not explicitly defined. They have, shall we say, the vagueness appropriate to their function. We may often hesitate to say whether a particular item plays a significant role in the plot or whether a plot summary is really correct, but our ability to recognize borderline cases, to predict when and where disagreements are likely to occur, shows precisely that we do know what we are talking about: that we are operating with concepts whose interpersonal value we understand perfectly well. The fact that we can engage in discussion and verify statements about plots provides a strong presumption that plot structure is in principle analysable.

But when one looks into the matter one is baffled: not only, as Barthes suggests, by the heterogeneity of plots and the lack of obvious analytical starting points, but also by the variety of analytical approaches that have been proposed. Leaving aside

[1] 'faced with the infinitude of plots, the multiplicity of points of view from which one can talk about them (historical, psychological, sociological, ethnological, aesthetic, etc.), the analyst is in much the same position as Saussure, confronted by the diversity of linguistic phenomena and attempting to extract from this apparent anarchy a principle of classification and a focal point for description.' 'Introduction à l'analyse structurale des récits.' *Communications*, 8 (1966), pp. 1–2. All translations from the French are my own.

attempts to 'synthesize' plots which are fashionable in Germany and Russia,[2] and looking only at theories that have been propounded and discussed by French structuralists, one finds at least three approaches which are radically different in conception and each of which exists in a number of versions. Just to compare these theories and their variants would be a substantial and thankless task, but I am not, in any case, concerned with the exposition of conflicting theories.[3] The fundamental problem, the problem which must be brought to the fore if discussion of theories is to have any point, is that we have little sense of how to evaluate competing approaches. Each theory, constrained to define for itself the basic units of narrative, becomes a coherent and self-contained system in terms of which practically any plot can be described, and consequently they are difficult to compare. If any progress is to be made it will not be by erecting yet another system but by thinking seriously about the criteria to be used in evaluating competing approaches and hence about the goals of an analysis of plot structure.

There has been surprisingly little discussion of this problem, and I believe this is due, at least in part, to the prestige of linguistics and the fascination it exercized over structuralists. In the days before Chomsky's work brought such discussions to the fore, there was little explicit theoretical debate about the conditions which a linguistic analysis must meet. Linguists devoted much of their time to the development of procedures of segmentation and classification which were supposed to yield descriptions of the basic elements and their rules of combination; but, as Chomsky says, the belief that rigour was the hallmark of success in linguistics appears to have led to the widespread view that to justify a description one need only show that it is the result of some explicit procedure.[4] Analysts

[2] For Russian proposals see L. M. O'Toole, below. For German proposals see *Poetics*, 3 (1972).

[3] For further discussion see my *Structuralist Poetics* (London: Routledge and Kegan Paul, 1974), chapter ix.

[4] 'A Transformational Approach to Syntax', in *The Structure of Language*,

of plot structure, citing linguistics as a model, seem to have assumed that if their descriptions were the result of a 'coherent' metalanguage and if this set of categories enabled them to describe any plot, then perforce their descriptions and hence their theory must be valid.

This is quite incorrect, for a number of reasons. First of all, there are an infinite number of metalanguages which have a certain logical coherence and in terms of which any text could be described, but most of them are vacuous. Let me construct a few by way of example. Theory A says that plots consist of three classes of elements: situations, thoughts, and actions. To analyse the plot is to go through the tale and identify these elements. Theory B says that all plots can be described in terms of three categories: actions which succeed, actions which fail, and actions which neither succeed or fail but maintain the story. Plots can be differentiated according to their relative proportions of these three elements. Theory C says that plots consist of actions which destroy equilibrium, actions which restore equilibrium, actions which seek to destroy equilibrium, and actions which seek to restore equilibrium. Every action can be put into one or another of these classes, and thus any plot can be analysed in these terms.

Each of these theories has a certain logic to it (the various categories are not, that is to say, random choices), and each could be used to produce a description for any story. But precisely because a story can be described in any of these terms, the fact that a particular system enables the analyst to describe a range of stories does not count as evidence in favour of that system. To say that one's metalanguage enables one to describe the plot of any story is not a significant claim. Support for one's theory must be of another kind.

It is apparent, however, that what we need is not evidence about the general validity of the presuppositions on which each theory might be thought to be based. That is to say, if psycholo-

eds. J. Fodor and J. Katz (Englewood Cliffs, N.J.: Prentice-Hall, 1964), p. 241.

gists, sociologists, and philosophers were to argue that man is most fundamentally motivated by a desire to maintain states of equilibrium rather than by a desire to pursue what he does not possess, it would not follow that C was necessarily a better theory of plot structure than B. One might expect that the terms of any successful theory would have an initial plausibility of this kind, but recent work in linguistics ought to have convinced us that it may be necessary to postulate rather recondite categories in order to explain empirical phenomena and that general notions of plausibility cannot be allowed to determine the shape and details of a theory. Notions of acceptability or plausibility do play an important role, but not in this way: they determine what the theory must explain but not the categories or rules to be used in explanation.

Indeed, we are constrained to say, it seems to me, that the only way to demonstrate the superiority of a theory of plot structure is to show that the descriptions of particular stories which it permits correspond with our intuitive sense of its plot and that it is sufficiently precise to prohibit descriptions which are manifestly wrong. 'Plot' is defined only by our interpersonal use of the concept, and any theory which isolates a set of propositions that could not be generally accepted as the plot of a particular story would thereby show its inadequacy. In short, competing theories of plot structure can only be evaluated by their success in serving as models of a particular aspect of literary competence: readers' abilities to recognize and summarize plots, to group together similar plots, etc. This intuitive knowledge constitutes the facts to be explained, and without this knowledge, which we display every time we recount or discuss a plot, there is simply no such subject as the analysis of plot structure because there is nothing for the analyst to be right or wrong about.

In order to illustrate this point and to offer some specific criteria by which theories might be judged, I should like first to discuss the plot of a short story and indicate some of the facts about it which a theory of plot structure ought to explicate. Then it will be possible to make some general observations on the advantages and disadvantages of the approaches proposed by French structuralists. The story is Joyce's 'Eveline' from *Dubliners*, which Seymour Chatman has analysed in terms of Barthes' model and which has the advantage of posing in its brief compass some of the basic problems that arise when one tries to analyse plots.[5]

One elementary fact about our literary competence is that when called upon to summarize a plot we can do so in a single sentence or in a long and detailed paragraph. There is, in other words, a hierarchy of appropriate plot summaries, running from the most succinct to the most detailed, and there would be substantial agreement among readers about what ought to be included at a particular level of generality. In the case of 'Eveline' one might offer three summaries:

(1) Eveline is supposed to elope and begin a new life but at the last minute refuses.

(2) Having decided to elope and begin a new life, Eveline muses on her past and present, wondering whether she should go through with it. She decides to go but at the last minute changes her mind and refuses.

(3) Eveline has agreed to elope to Argentina with Frank and start a new life, but on the afternoon of her departure she sits by the window looking out on the street where she has always lived, weighing her happy memories of childhood, her sense of attachment, and her duty to her family against her father's present brutality and her attraction to Frank and to the new life he will give her. She decides that she must escape and will elope, but when she is about to board the ship with him she has a violent, almost physical reaction and refuses to go.

One could obviously quarrel with particular details in these summaries, but they would be generally accepted as adequate accounts of the plot. What is striking is how much agreement there would be about what should *not* be included in these summaries: no one would claim, for example, that any of them should mention the fact that while she is sitting at the window

---

[5] Seymour Chatman, 'New Ways of Analyzing Narrative Structure', *Language and Style*, 2 (1969), 1–36.

'the man out of the last house passed on his way home' or that 'the station was full of soldiers with brown baggages'. We know that these are subsidiary elements and a proper theory of narrative should provide a model which explains how we know it.

Secondly, there are a number of important facts about the way in which we organize elements of the story into plot as we read. The story begins as follows:

She sat at the window watching the evening invade the avenue. Her head was leaned against the window curtains and in her nostrils was the odour of dusty cretonne. She was tired.

We do not as yet know how to relate this to the plot. Is she watching for something in particular and will these sentences come to be subsumed under that heading, or is this simply a setting with no importance for the plot? Only towards the end of the next paragraph, after various memories have been narrated and we are told 'Still, they seemed to have been rather happy then,' can we identify the first paragraph as 'musing' or 'reminiscing'.

At the beginning of the second paragraph we encounter the narration of an action: 'The man out of the last house passed on his way home; she heard his footsteps clacking along the concrete pavement and afterwards crunching on the cinder path before the new red houses.' We do not yet know whether this is an incident in the plot. If this man figured in Eveline's life and she were awaiting his return in order to go see him, or if she knew that he and his wife were about to quarrel and were awaiting the outcome, then his passing would be a minor event in the plot: the beginning of a sequence of actions. But as there is no further reference to him in the next three or four sentences we soon decide that the earlier sentence was not a component of the plot but a detail to be picked up and read as an illustration of her desultory observation.

On the other hand, the sequence 'She had consented to go away, to leave her home. Was that wise?' is immediately recognized as an important structuring element which enables us first of all to read the preceding reflections as musings inspired by this prospective change of state and thereby fit them into the plot, and secondly to structure the material which has already been assimilated as reminiscence into positive and negative categories: is going away wise or foolish, what are the advantages and disadvantages, are the memories good or bad? And this tells us that any actions reported in surrounding paragraphs (in the context of reflection and reminiscence) need not be interpreted as part of the plot but may be used solely for their thematic value, as evidence of her attitude.

These examples illustrate the kind of facts that a theory of plot structure ought to explicate. A theory is 'descriptively adequate', to use Chomsky's phrase, 'to the extent that it correctly describes the intrinsic competence of the idealized native speaker.'[6] The structural descriptions which it assigns to a text must correspond to the intuitions of the reader, or, to put it the other way around, the theory must account for the intuitions of the reader by providing a model of the competence which enables him to perceive structure. However, these examples also illustrate something of the complexity of 'literary competence', of the implicit knowledge which enables the reader to process the text. As he goes through it for the first time he can, retrospectively, resolve his initial uncertainties about the function of certain elements and recognize which are properly constitutive of the plot. But as yet we have very little idea of how he is able to do this, of what rules and procedures he is unconsciously following when he picks out the crucial items in the plot.

If we look to extant theories of plot structure for an account of this process, it becomes immediately apparent that they have not approached the problem in exactly this way. Nonetheless one can attempt to determine their descriptive value by treating their categories as hypotheses about readers' expectations. That is to say, a theory about the basic elements or forms of plot constitutes a hypothesis about what readers look for in identifying and constructing the plot of a story. None of the theories

6 *Aspects of the Theory of Syntax* (Cambridge, Mass.: MIT Press, 1965), p. 24.

proposed seems satisfactory—indeed, most of them are so very general that it is difficult to draw from them hypotheses precise enough to be verified or disproved—but most offer some suggestions which will doubtless aid in the development of better theories.

The basic problem which each theory must confront is how one moves from the sentences of a text to a representation of its plot, and three types of theory can be distinguished by the way in which they approach this problem. The first starts not with the text itself but with the most general and abstract level of plot structure, hypotheses about the essential structure of the *récit*, and then works up, as it were, to more specific units and elements. The second postulates a set of categories which can be applied both to individual sentences and to plot summaries, hoping in this way to bridge the gap between the two. And the third tries to define some formal categories which suggest how the reader might move from the text itself to more abstract summarizing descriptions of plot.

The most distinguished representatives of the first approach are Claude Lévi-Strauss and A. J. Greimas. They argue that the basic structure of a story is that of a four-term homology in which A is to B as C is to D. In the clearest statement of this position, Greimas argues that to grasp a story as a whole is to organize it according to a structure of this kind so that the initial situation is to the final situation as a problem is to its resolution.[7] By this theory, to identify the plot of a story is not simply to pick out a series of actions noted in the text but to isolate the central action or change which is correlated with the thematic development. In the case of 'Eveline', then, the plot at its most general and fundamental level consists of her failure to make the planned escape.

Elements of the story, Greimas argues, fit into this schema

[7] A. J. Greimas, *Du Sens* (Paris: Seuil, 1970), pp. 187–8. Cf. Greimas, *Sémantique structurale* (Paris: Larousse, 1966), Claude Lévi-Strauss, 'L'analyse morphologique des contes russes', *International Journal of Slavic Linguistics and Poetics*, 3 (1960), 122–49, and *Anthropologie structurale* (Paris: Plon, 1958), pp. 227–56.

in one of three ways: the most important are 'contractual' sequences which constitute an undertaking or a refusal to do something; the actual performance of the actions in question occurs in 'performative' sequences; and finally there are 'disjunctional' sequences which involve movement or displacement of various kinds.[8] Although Greimas does transcribe a story in these terms, neither the status of the categories nor their relationship to the homological structure is clear. The notion of disjunctional sequences seems otiose: movements fit into the plot according to their purposes and consequences and not simply as movement. 'Performative' sequences are of course important, but the category itself does not help to indicate how we select those that are central to the plot. However, the notion of contractual sequences may well prove useful: it suggests that states of affairs may not in themselves be central to the plot; what we look for are situations which contain an implicit contract or violation of a contract. Most stories, in Greimas's view, move either from a negative to a positive contract (alienation from society to reintegration with society) or from a positive contract to a breaking of that contract. In 'Eveline', as perhaps in most stories of any complexity, the two patterns interpenetrate: her contract with her mother and her past is first broken by the decision to escape and then re-established by the failure to leave; her contract with Frank is established and then broken. By Greimas's model the structure of 'Eveline' is a four-term homology in which 'desire to escape' is to 'reluctance to escape' as 'decision to go' is to 'decision to stay'.

In short, this theory offers a hypothesis about the conditions which actions and situations must fulfil to count as central to the plot and about the constraints on the most succinct and abstract plot summaries, but it does not go much beyond that and has nothing to say about the reader's processing of narrated actions.

The second approach, whose major proponent is Tzvetan Todorov but which is also used by Julia Kristeva and by

[8] *Du Sens*, pp. 191 ff.

Greimas in some of his work, postulates a set of basic categories which can apply both to the various plot summaries and to the actual sentences of the text.[9] Todorov calls them verb and adjective, Greimas 'function' and 'qualification', and Kristeva 'predicative adjunct' and 'qualifying adjunct'. The categories are, of course, derived from linguistics as the two types of predicate in the canonical sentence. Todorov in particular seems to assume that their source necessarily makes them valid components of a 'grammar of narrative'. 'Cette idée repose sur l'unité profonde du langage et du récit, unité qui nous oblige à réviser nos idées sur l'un et l'autre. On comprendra mieux le récit si l'on sait que le personnage est un nom, l'action, un verbe.'[10] But of course such labels do not in themselves bring illumination.

The reason for choosing verb and adjective or function and qualification as the basic categories is that both the sentences of the text itself and those of the plot summary can be rewritten in these terms. Todorov observes that 'les structures restent toujours les mêmes, indépendamment du niveau d'abstraction', but this is true only because at every level of abstraction one is dealing with sentences and hence with predicates.[11] He offers no indications about the process of abstraction and combination which enables us to move from sentences in the text containing descriptions of states (adjectival predicates) or specification of actions (verbal predicates) to a summary of plot, and the fact that the same categories are used at both levels does not help us. Todorov divides verbs into three classes: to modify the situation, to commit a misdeed of some kind, and to punish. This suggests that there are two types of plot: those which involve the modifi-

[9] Tzvetan Todorov, *Grammaire du Décaméron* (The Hague: Mouton, 1969), Julia Kristeva, *Le Texte du roman* (The Hague: Mouton, 1970), Greimas, *Sémantique structurale.*

[10] 'This notion is based on the profound unity of language and story: a unity which compels us to revise our ideas about each. We shall understand plot better if we know that character is a proper name and action a verb.' *Grammaire du Décaméron*, p. 84.

[11] 'the structures remain the same, whatever the level of abstraction.' *Ibid.*, p. 19.

cation of a situation and those which involve transgression and punishment. It is not clear why the latter should be singled out for special attention; why not allow as separate types sequences involving a quest or a decision? In view of this obvious anomaly John Rutherford has suggested that transgression and punishment be dropped as special classes of verbs and that guilt be treated as an adjectival predicate (to commit a crime is to modify a situation and to change the adjective which describes one's state).[12] Though this is an improvement it destroys one of the claims which Todorov's theory makes, leaving only two hypotheses: that the constitutive feature of a plot is the modification of a situation—a claim which has scarcely ever been doubted—and that in reading a story we seek to distinguish between actions which modify a situation and elements which serve as the attributes or qualities involved in the modification. This latter hypothesis may be a useful though fairly obvious specification of the process of reading: as we move through 'Eveline' we must decide which actions serve only to characterize her and the situation in which she has placed herself, which of these are the crucial attributes involved in the change compassed by the plot, and which actions are in fact crucial as actions. Until something takes place which signals the actual or prospective modification of attributes, we do not know which are pertinent to the plot. Todorov's theory, however, does not enable one to say more than this about the process of reading.

In his 'Introduction à l'analyse structurale des récits' Roland Barthes tries to pay closer attention to the process of reading, and indeed his major categories, kernels (*noyaux*) and catalysts (*catalyses*) are simply a rough formulation of a distinction which the reader must make. Kernels are the elements picked out as essential to the plot and defined by their temporal and logical relations with one another. One kernel calls for completion by another kernel and they thus form a sequence of action. Catalysts, on the other hand—the term is most inappropriate and would well be replaced, as Seymour Chatman has proposed,

[12] See below.

by 'satellite'[13]—are attached to kernels as expansions which
'ne font que "remplir" l'espace narratif qui sépare les fonctions-
charnières.'[14] Kernels and satellites are not, of course, definable
classes of actions; they are relational terms only: what is a
kernel in one plot or at one level of description will be a satellite
at another. For the hero to lie in wait for the villain is, at one
level, a kernel, since it logically requires a temporal consequence: the villain arrives and is shot down. But at another
level these functions are satellites which expand the kernel
'revenge', a consequence of an initial kernel such as 'suffering
harm'. In 'Eveline', for example, the actions of the past which
the heroine recalls could be organized into kernels and satellites,
but within the story they become satellites or expansions of a
kernel such as 'weighing the evidence'.

The question of how kernels are identified and defined is of
course the crucial one, and Barthes' formulation leaves much to
be desired. Speaking of kernels as pivots of the story (*charnières
du récit*) which open at least two possible courses of action, he
implies that we recognize a function when we are uncertain
about the consequences of an action. Chatman, adopting this
point of view, even argues that the opening sentence of 'Eveline'
—'She sat at the window watching the evening invade the
avenue'—must be interpreted as a kernel because it raises the
question 'Why?'[15] But all opening sentences will raise some
question, leave some uncertainty about what is to follow. And
indeed the same is true for most actions, whatever their function
in the story. If kernels are to be units of the plot we must accept
that we recognize kernels only when we identify the role of an
action in the plot or, to put it another way, promote an action
to a constituent of plot.

This point was made by Vladimir Propp, the pioneer in the
analysis of plot structure, who asserted that the basic units of

[13] 'The Structure of Fiction', *University Review* [Kansas City] (Spring,
1971), p. 210.
[14] 'which only fill in the narrative space that separates nodal functions.'
'Introduction à l'analyse structurale des récits', p. 9.
[15] 'New Ways of Analyzing Narrative Structure', p. 13.

the story were not actions themselves but 'functions' or roles played by actions in a plot. One cannot determine the role or function of an action without considering its consequences and its place in the story as a whole. A given action can be used to manifest different functions, and it is the function which must be specified in an account of the plot.[16] Thus, a hero could build a large castle either as the fulfilment of a difficult task, or as a celebration of the successful end to his trials, or as an offering to the princess whom he wishes to marry, and in each case it will be an instance of a different function. Units must, in short, be defined retrospectively.

Some structuralists, particularly Claude Bremond, have attacked this view, arguing that a teleological conception of structure is unacceptable because it conceals the real alternatives which are experienced at crucial moments in the plot.[17] When the hero struggles with the villain he may either win or lose, and Propp's schema obscures this fact by making the struggle an instance either of villainy or of the hero's triumph, according to its consequences. But this is precisely what the analyst must do, for the role of the struggle in the plot will depend on its outcome, and the reader's uncertainty when faced with a struggle is in part an uncertainty as to how the sequence is to be named and integrated in the plot. To reject a teleological conception of structure is to condemn oneself to dealing with actions alone rather than with actions as structured in a plot.

That Barthes does not reject this conception of structure is clear from his remarks about the ways in which kernels combine to form plot sequences. A sequence is a logical series of kernels united in a relationship of mutual implication (*une relation de solidarité*).[18] Although when taken on its own 'battle' opens the possibility of either 'defeat' or 'victory', within a sequence such

[16] *Morphology of the Folktale*, trans. Laurence Scott, 2nd edition (Austin, Texas: University of Texas Press, 1968).

[17] 'Le message narratifs', *Communications*, 4 (1964), 4–32, and 'La logique des possibles narratifs', *Communications*, 8 (1966), 60–76.

[18] 'Introduction à l'analyse structurale des récits', p. 13.

as 'triumph of the hero' a battle implies victory and vice-versa. And it is when the reader begins to place actions in sequences, when he perceives teleologically organized structures, that he begins to grasp the plot. In the case of 'Eveline' we can say that the plot comes to take shape only when one retrospectively identifies the action of sitting by the window, reported in the opening sentence, as part of the process of musing or reflection that is an essential component of the sequence 'making a decision'. This constitutes the move from action to plot.

The retrospective definition of units relies to a considerable extent on a series of cultural models which readers have assimilated. 'Quiconque lit le texte', Barthes writes,

rassemble certaines informations sous quelque nom générique d'actions (Promenade, Assassinat, Rendez-vous), et c'est ce nom qui fait la séquence; la séquence n'existe qu'au moment où et parce qu'on peut la nommer, elle se développe au rythme de la nomination qui se cherche ou se confirme.[19]

Indeed, these cultural models operate in two ways: first of all, they provide classes into which actions fit, a set of categories which enable us to bring together bits of information and to construct wholes out of parts. Though we need not explicitly name actions while we read ('aha! she is reminiscing') it is our knowledge of these basic categories of human experience which enable us to hold together various things which the text tells us and to infer significant actions from the details presented. Secondly, these models provide a representation of culturally significant actions. Sitting by a window does not itself have enough force to found a story; we make it part of the plot by placing it under another heading. Leaving home is culturally marked as a significant action, so that once it is bruited in the text it assumes a dominant role in plot structure. Propp seems

---

[19] 'Whoever reads the text collects bits of information under the generic names of actions (Walk, Assassination, Rendez-vous), and it is the name which creates the sequence; the sequence comes to exist only when and because one succeeds in naming it; it develops according to the rhythm of the process by which names are sought or confirmed.' *S/Z* (Paris: Seuil, 1970), p. 26.

to have taken account of this aspect of plots in using, as the
names of most of his functions, general cultural stereotypes such
as villainy, struggle with the villain, rescue of the hero, difficult
task, etc. Novelistic models of the significant events in people's
lives serve as what Barthes calls a 'méta-langage intérieur au
lecteur lui-même':

la langue du récit, qui est en nous, comporte d'emblée ces rubriques
essentielles: la logique close qui structure une séquence est indis-
solublement liée à son nom: toute fonction qui inaugure une *séduction*
impose dès son apparition, dans le nom qu'elle fait surgir, le procès
entier de la séduction, tel que nous l'avons appris de tous les récits
qui ont formé en nous la langue du récit.[20]

The analyst must try to reconstruct this 'language' so as to
explain the way in which we implicitly name and thus make
sense of the sequence.

Barthes' general approach seems the most helpful, if only
because it does focus on the basic problem: that of explaining
how it is that we can select certain elements from a story,
organize them, and call that its plot. But his model remains
strangely atomistic, through the lack of any specification of what
one is moving towards as one collects kernels and satellites and
groups them into sequences. Seymour Chatman, in applying
Barthes' model to 'Eveline' identifies eight kernels, but he does
so by picking out the actual phrases which seem to him significant. Thus the kernel which I have called 'musing' or 'reminiscing' is somewhat arbitrarily represented by the phrase, 'One
time there used to be a field there'.[21] Chatman is able to pick
out this sentence as a kernel only because he has some sense of
an abstract structure towards which he is moving: there is

[20] 'The language of plot which exists within us already contains these
basic rubrics. The complete logical form which structures a sequence is
inextricably linked with its name: any function which initiates a *seduction*
imposes, as soon as it appears and by virtue of the name which it provokes,
the whole seduction, such as we have been taught it by all the tales which
have contributed to the formation within us of a language of plot.' 'Introduction à l'analyse structurale des récits', p. 14.
[21] 'New Ways of Analyzing Narrative Structure', p. 6.

nothing in the sentence itself or its relations with other sentences which would make it especially significant. And the theory ought to specify what kind of hypotheses the reader deploys in postulating abstract or general structures and relating them to the sentences of the text.

One requires, in short, a theory of the basic structures of plot and of the constraints which these goals impose on the process of assimilation and naming. It is perhaps here that the other approaches have something to offer. If we postulate that the hierarchy of kernels and sequences is governed by readers' desire to reach an ultimate summary in which the plot as a whole is grasped in a satisfying form, and if we take that form to be what Lévi-Strauss and Greimas call the four-term homology, Kristeva a transformation, and Todorov the modification of a situation, then we have at least a principle whose effects on the organization of plot we might investigate. What the reader is looking for in a plot is a passage from one state to another—a passage to which he can assign thematic value. This requirement imposes certain constraints on the units of the next level. First of all, the incidents of the plot must be organized into two groups and these groups must be named in such a way that they represent either an opposition (problem and solution, refusal and acceptance or vice versa) or a logical development (cause and effect, situation and result). Secondly, each of these groups can in turn be organized either as a series of actions with a common unifying factor which serves as name for the series, or as a dialectical movement in which incidents are related as contraries and named either by a temporary synthesis or by a transcendent term which covers both members of a contrast.

A model of this sort would help to explain the fact that in 'Eveline' we organize the plot around the dominant contrast between an initial decision to leave and a final refusal to leave. This basic structure, in turn, governs our organization of the two parts of the story: the first half becomes a logical sequence of reflection and decision; the latter half becomes an analogous sequence of doubt and refusal. And the sequence of reflection plus decision allows us to organize the sentences of the first half of the story into an oppositional series, where the salient feature of each narrated action is the contribution it makes to the debate about the advisability of leaving home. It is because our models of narration enable us to proceed in this way that we can pick out sentences such as 'One time there used to be a field there' as the manifestation of kernels. Without such general models, which we apply unconsciously in the process of reading, we would simply note that once there used to be a field there without knowing how to deal with that fact.

A model of this sort, taken in conjunction with the cultural codes which guide us in naming sequences and selecting certain actions as significant, might prove more fruitful in accounting for plot structure than taxonomic approaches which postulate new basic units and proceed to describe plot in these terms. For at the very least such a model would lead us to think seriously about the expectations of readers and their role in the perception of plot structure.

Anyone undertaking investigation of this kind will find a distinguished predecessor in the Russian Formalist Victor Shklovsky, who is one of the few to have realized that investigation of the construction of the novel and the short story is an attempt to explicate the structural intuitions of readers by studying their formal expectations. What do we require, he asks, in order to feel that a story is completed? In certain cases we feel that a story has not really ended; what is responsible for this impression? What kind of structure satisfies our formal expectations?

Shklovsky investigates some of the types of parallelism which seem to produce satisfactory structures: the move from one relationship to its opposite, from a prediction or fear to its realization, from an enigma or distorted presentation of a situation to its resolution. But his most interesting point, which illustrates the strength of readers' expectations, bears on the picaresque novel and what he calls the 'illusory ending'. The episodic novel requires an epilogue of some kind which, by differentiating itself from the series of events, closes the series and shows what kind of series it is (a description of the hero ten years later will show us whether the series should be read as steps in his decline, in his loss of illusion, in his expenditure of energy, etc.). The illusory ending, on the other hand, is a conclusion which exploits the reader's desire to round off the story. 'Generally it is descriptions of nature or of the weather that furnish material for these illusory endings. This new motif is inscribed in parallel to the preceding story, thanks to which the tale seems terminated.'[22]

A description of the weather provides a satisfactory conclusion because the reader can give it a metaphoric or synecdochic interpretation and then read this thematic statement against the actions themselves. By way of example Shklovsky cites a brief passage from *Le Diable boiteux* in which a passer-by, stopping to help a mortally-wounded man, is himself arrested. If the reader invents a description of the night in Seville or of the indifferent sky and adds it to the passage, Shklovsky argues, he will find that the tale seems complete. And certainly he is right: such a description gives the story a satisfying structure because the indifferent sky presents an image which can be read as confirming the implicit names which one might give to the preceding event. By confirming the irony of the story it isolates as plot the ironic movement of the action.

I cite Shklovsky's work because he seems one of the few who have asked the right kind of question and have sensed where the answers lie. He knew, that is to say, that the study of plot structure was largely a matter of formulating the expectations which guide the reader in structuring elements of the story into a plot, and he knew also that one of the best ways of discovering what norms are at work is to try altering the text and to see how its effect is changed. The analyst's task is not simply to develop a metalanguage for the description of plots but to bring to the surface and make explicit the 'metalanguage within the reader himself'. In evaluating proposals and theories concerning plot structure we must ask not whether every story can

[22] 'La construction de la nouvelle et du roman', in *Théorie de la littérature*, ed. Todorov (Paris: Seuil, 1965), p. 176.

be described in the terms proposed, for that is the weakest of requirements, but what generalizations their categories imply and how they account for the identification of plot. A successful theory must offer an explanation of the hierarchical structuring process by which we move from the text itself to plot summaries. Such a theory would be an integral part of a poetics of the novel, whose task would be to explain how, in organizing the sentences which we encounter, we make sense of a text. Much work remains to be done, but one should at least be able to proceed with a sense of the goals which make the study of plot structure worthwhile.

CHAPTER FIVE

ANALYTIC AND SYNTHETIC APPROACHES TO NARRATIVE STRUCTURE
Sherlock Holmes and 'The Sussex Vampire'

L. M. O'Toole

Writings of the Russian 'Structural Poetics' movement began to appear in the Soviet Union in the early 1960s, during the relatively liberal Khruschev era. The movement gathered momentum throughout the decade in spite of increasing opposition from the academic 'lit. crit.' establishment who wield a disproportionate amount of power in the institutes of the Academy of Science and on editorial boards.

Almost hermetically sealed off intellectually from the world outside the Soviet Union for more than twenty years, literary scholars with a commitment to 'poetika', the close study of the literary text, were unable to keep in touch with—still less contribute to—the exciting developments of the 1930s and 40s represented by 'Prague School' Structuralism and American 'New Criticism'. The debt they readily acknowledge is to the Russian Formalists of the 1920s who laid the foundations for new systematic ways of analysing literary texts and accounting for literature as a psychological and social phenomenon. In the study of the structure of narrative fiction the key Formalist figures were Shklovsky, Eikhenbaum, Propp and Tynyanov, with Vinogradov and Bakhtin active outside the movement proper. By its opponents, Formalism was seen as at once too radical (wedded as it was to the Futurist movement in poetry) and too reactionary (with a subtlety and flexibility in its approach to aesthetic and linguistic problems which betrayed the culture of its proponents as that of the pre-Revolutionary bourgeois intelligentsia rather than of the emergent proletariat), and was virtually stamped out by 'proletkult' obscurantism by the end of the decade. In a similar way—but, perhaps, for less respectable ideological reasons—Russian Structuralism, too, has been seen as being radical and even insidious by the conservative academic and literary establishment of the 1960s. This situation might seem to be exactly parallel to that of the French structuralists during the same period. In both countries a degree of academic notoriety has given the movement the moral advantage of being small, close-knit, relatively united ideologically and read avidly by younger students of literature. But there is a crucial difference in that individual structuralist critics in the Soviet Union have suffered the practical disadvantages of difficulties and delays in publishing their writings and in keeping in contact with fellow structuralists abroad, as well as having their books or symposia published in such absurdly small editions by state-owned publishing houses that they become bibliographical rarities as soon as they appear. If they operate from a rather restricted—and sometimes unexpected—range of university departments and research institutes, the best structuralists explore a vast range of related disciplines with impressive authority: general semiotics, the semiotics of literary forms, statistical literary studies, structural analyses of actual texts (usually from Russian literature and especially poetry, but happily compassing Asian and African myths and even such exotica as the *Kama Sutra* and English limericks), the problems of versification, linguistic problems of style, the cinema and the visual arts, mythology and folk-lore.[1]

The Formalists have often been criticized for the excessive

[1] A useful and comprehensive survey of the first decade of work by the Russian structuralists is provided by two of the movement's key scholars, E. Meletinsky and D. Segal, in 'Structuralism and Semiotics in the U.S.S.R.', *Diogenes*, 73 (1971), 88–115.

preoccupation some of them (notably Shklovsky in his more provocative early articles) showed with purely formal aspects of literary structure which they deliberately opposed to content and meaning. This may have been a necessary exaggeration at the beginning of the 1920s as they strove to propound a new way of looking at the literary work, but it has given rise to an absurd amount of acrimonious and ill-founded disputation since that time and, more seriously, tends to mask the degree to which form and content are indissolubly linked. Just as linguistics can not limit itself for long to the study of syntax alone, but must constantly refer back to semantics, so poetics, studying the phenomenon of literary art where, by definition, meaning and form reach their highest degree of integration, must analyse not merely the formal patterns but what is being expressed by those patterns. Vice versa, the Formalists were right in insisting that for too long literary scholarship had concerned itself with nothing but content. As we shall see later, one definition of the literary work of art might be that it is the syntactic expression of a deep semantic opposition.

The way structuralist theory (from the Prague School onwards) improved on Formalism by adding a semantic component may be illustrated by the case of the folk-tale. Vladimir Propp, in his seminal work *The Morphology of the Folk Tale*,[2] deliberately strove to isolate the syntactic features of the folk-tale: only a characterization of the thirty-one basic 'functions'[3] and their interrelationship would produce a model

[2] V. Ya. Propp, *Morphologiya skazki* (Leningrad, 1928; republished in Moscow in 1969 with an excellent post-script by Meletinsky). English translation: *Morphology of the Folktale*, trans. Laurence Scott, second, revised edition (Austin: University of Texas Press, 1968). The second Russian edition is available in French translation: *Morphologie du conte*, trans. Marguerite Derrida *et al.* (Paris: Seuil, 1970).

[3] As so often in literary criticism, there is a dearth of words with a single and precise meaning to denote new concepts. Propp and Shklovsky adopted the much-abused term 'function' but attempted to be precise about its new meaning, defining it as 'the most abstract and constant element of plot structure, . . . the act of a character (in a fairy tale) distinguished by its significance for the action as a whole' (cf. English translation of Propp, p. 21).

abstract enough to be universally valid. To this extent Propp was right: the most complex attempts by his predecessors at cataloguing folk-tales in terms of the character of their participants had contributed little. But, as Claude Lévi-Strauss was quick to point out when the English translation of Propp's book appeared in 1958, 'while he is able to define primary functions by exclusively morphological criteria, for their sub-divisions Propp is obliged to introduce certain aspects of content so that the function 'treachery' has 22 sub-divisions which reintroduce actual situations and characters . . .; rather than surreptitiously reintegrate content into form, form has to be kept at such an abstract level that it almost loses significance. Formalism reduces its own object to nothing . . . Before Formalism we certainly did not know what these tales had in common. After it we are deprived of all means of knowing how they differ. We have passed from concrete to abstract and can not get back . . . Propp discovered (magnificently) that the content of tales is permutable. He came to the odd conclusion that the permutations were arbitrary and had no laws of their own.'[4]

Propp's model for the structure of the folk tale might be characterized as a 'constituent structure grammar'[5] of narrative, consisting, as it does, of a series of functions, some obligatory, some optional, which 'slot in' to the text in a prescribed sequence. Victor Shklovsky proposed a similar 'constituent structure grammar' of the Sherlock Holmes detective story a few years before Propp's book appeared. As our discussion of analytic and synthetic approaches to narrative structure will be illustrated with reference to a Sherlock Holmes story, it

[4] C. Lévi-Strauss, 'L'analyse morphologique des contes russes', *International Journal of Slavic Linguistics and Poetics*, 3 (1960), 124 ff.

[5] Constituent structure grammars of natural language have been singled out for criticism by Chomsky in his *Syntactic Structures* (The Hague: Mouton, 1957) and later writings because they can only account for superficial relations between elements in a sentence and because they ignore all the logically and psychologically necessary semantic-syntactic processes which he and other transformational-generative grammarians have begun to uncover.

would be appropriate to list Shklovsky's functions in detail:

I. Waiting, discussion of earlier cases, analysis.

II. Appearance of client. The story proper begins.

III. Narrated evidence. The crucial secondary facts given in such a way that the reader fails to notice them. Also material for false surmises.

IV. Watson interprets the evidence wrongly.

V. Journey to the site of the crime: as this has often not yet been committed, the narrative is enlivened and the lines of the criminal's story and the detective's story merge. Evidence on the spot.

VI. An official police detective, if there is one, guesses wrongly, otherwise a newspaper, the victim, or Holmes himself, makes the wrong guess.

VII. An interval: Watson, not understanding Holmes's line of reasoning, tries to work things out. Holmes smokes or plays music. Sometimes he assembles groups of facts together without reaching any firm conclusion.

VIII The denouement, usually sudden. Often an attempt to commit the crime is made at this point.

IX. Holmes' analysis of the facts.[6]

Two of the Soviet structuralists, Alexander Zholkovsky and Yuri Scheglov, have paid tribute to Shklovsky and their other Formalist precursors in a paper given at one of the early conferences on structural poetics in 1961, but in their own work have rapidly moved away from the 'constituent structure grammar' of narrative and are regarded as the main exponents of the 'generative' model. As linguists they were well aware of the significance of the 'transformational-generative' revolution in linguistics, and their rather extreme stand in a semi-popular literary journal in 1967, 'Structural poetics—generative poetics' (where the dash means 'is', but implies 'should be') not only upset many pillars of the establishment, but nettled some of their more moderate allies by its strident tone and a number of

---

[6] V. Shklovsky, 'Novella tain' ('The Mystery Story') in *O teorii prozy* (Moscow, 1925).

148 L. M. O'TOOLE

exaggerated claims.[7] In a number of articles since, they have
explored the implications of this new approach and experi-
mented with mapping the 'transformational history' of narrative texts and episodes much as the generative linguist maps the
transformational history of a sentence.[8] The starting point for
such a process must be some kind of 'kernel' in the deep structure and the kernel of the literary work is what Zholkovsky and
Scheglov call the 'theme'. This is not the theme in the popular
meaning of the word, some kind of 'digest' of the plot, but a
scientific abstraction, a formulation in a more or less abstract
'metalanguage' of the irreducible meaning of the text. In their
most recent article[9] they discuss this concept of 'theme' in some
detail, seeing it as 'a primary element' out of which the whole
literary text is expanded,[10] via a variety of devices or processes
('priyomy'—a favourite word of the Formalists) such as plot-
building and realization in terms of character, setting, properties, etc. 'The theme is linked to the text not by an "equals" sign,
but by an inference arrow or, seen the other way round, "the
theme is the text minus the devices", or, more precisely—if
ponderously, "the theme is that invariant of which everything

[7] A. K. Zholkovsky and Yu. K. Scheglov, 'Strukturnaya poetika—
porozhdayuschaga poetika', *Voprosy literatury*, 1 (1967), 73–89.

[8] Yu. K. Scheglov, 'Opisanie struktury detektivnoi novelly', ('A descrip-
tion of detective story structure'), *Preprints for the International Symposium on
Semiotics* (Warsaw, 1968), reprinted in *Recherche sur les systèmes signifiantes*,
ed. J. Rey-Debove (The Hague: Mouton, 1973), pp. 343–72; 'Matrona iz
Efesa', ('The Widow of Ephesus'), in *Sign-Language-Culture*, ed. A. J. Greimas
(The Hague: Mouton, 1970), pp. 591–600; A. K. Zholkovsky, 'Somaliiskii
rasskaz Ispytanie proritsatelya (opyt porozhdayuschego opisanija)' ('The
Somali Story "Testing the Oracle" (an Attempt at a Generative Descrip-
tion)', *Narody Azii i Afriki*, 1 (1970), 104–15; 'Porozhdayuschaya poetika v
rabotakh S. M. Eizenshteina' ('Generative Poetics in the Writings of
Eisenstein'), in *Sign-Language-Culture*, pp. 451–68.

[9] A. K. Zholkovsky and Yu. K. Scheglov, *K opisaniyu smysla svyaznogo
teksta (na primere khudozhestvennykh tekstov)* (Institut russkogo yazyka AN SSSR,
predvaritel'nye publikatsii. Vypusk 22, 1971, 54 pp.). A translation will
appear shortly under the title 'Towards a "Theme . . . (Expression Devices)
. . . Text" Model of Literary Structure' (The Hague: Mouton, forthcoming).

[10] Ibid., p. 8.

in a work is a variation but which can not itself be represented as a variant of any more abstract invariant." '[11]

How near to the work itself will our exploration of the generation of a given sequence of textual elements out of some highly abstract theme actually take us? Although Zholkovsky and Scheglov have so far confined themselves largely to illustrating how elements of plot, character and the object world are generated through various operations on the theme, there need be no reason in principle why this process should not be extended all the way to the generation of actual linguistic structures in the text. Some of these will relate directly to (be generated directly from) the deep 'theme' while others will relate directly to intermediate stages in the process 'theme → text'. As we hope to show, it will be possible in this way to account adequately for many features of the style of a work.

The theme itself is not discovered through the generative process. Zholkovsky and Scheglov are not very explicit about how one arrives at the statement of theme, but imply that a combination of analysis and intuition enables one to make a provisional statement, a hypothesis which can then be tested through the process of synthesizing the text. With certain types of narrative genre the analysis needed to arrive at a satisfactory theme may be extremely complex. In order to focus the discussion primarily on the synthesis we have chosen a short, highly integrated, almost schematically simple, example of a highly stylized genre. 'The Sussex Vampire', one of Conan Doyle's

[11] Ibid., p. 33. This was expressed more elegantly by Edgar Allen Poe 130 years ago (though Poe probably did not see the scientific implications of his formulation): 'A skillful literary artist has constructed a tale. If wise, he has not fashioned his thoughts to accommodate his incidents; but having conceived, with deliberate care, a certain unique or single *effect* to be wrought out, he then invents such incidents—he then combines such events as may best aid him in establishing this preconceived effect. If his very initial sentence tends not to the outbringing of this effect, then he has failed in his first step. In the whole composition there should be no word written of which the tendency, direct or indirect, is not to the one pre-established design' (from a review (1842) of Hawthorne's *Twice Told Tales*, E. A. Poe, *Complete Works*, Vol. XIII (New York, 1965), p. 153).

later stories, from *The Case-Book of Sherlock Holmes*,[12] is so neat
in its structure, and so mannered in its style that one is tempted
to suspect Conan Doyle of mocking his readers (and himself)
with a piece of self-parody. We have chosen it above all because it is a whole story: up to now Zholkovsky and Scheglov
have tended to experiment in their articles (see Note 8) with
synthesizing only fragments of whole works, short anecdotes or
individual episodes. Scheglov's 1968 description of detective
story structure deals in detail only with the 'outer story' or
prelude to the Sherlock Holmes stories, i.e. the coming together of Holmes, Watson and the client and the initial narration of the problem situation before the investigation proper
begins. Although this restriction is deliberate and, perhaps,
necessary in the first stages of testing a new model, the full
generative potential needs to be demonstrated at every stage
in the synthesis of a complete work.

An analytic approach will help us at this stage to explore
the structure of the story in sufficient detail to arrive at a
provisional statement of the theme. This framework which is
being developed using a number of categories proposed by the
Formalists has proved useful in the analysis of more complex
types of short story.[13] This analytic approach also starts from
a provisional and very flexible statement of theme, testing it
against various structures in the work represented by the labels:
Fable, *Plot*, *Narrative Structure*, *Point of View*, *Character*, and
Setting. This approach is analogous to the kind of functional
models in linguistics developed by the Prague School linguists
and by M. A. K. Halliday,[14] in that it starts with an examination of features and relationships in the surface structure of the
text and systematically penetrates to deeper and more subtle

[12] Sir Arthur Conan Doyle, *The Complete Sherlock Holmes Stories* (London:
John Murray, 1928, repr. 1971), pp. 1178–96.

[13] L. M. O'Toole, 'Structure and Style in the Short Story: Chekhov's
"Student" ', *Slavonic and East European Review*, 48, No. 114 (January, 1971),
45–67; 'Structure and Style in the Short Story: Dostoevskij's "A Gentle
Spirit" ', *Tijdschrift voor Slavische Taalen Letterkunde*, 1 (1972), 81–116.

[14] Cf. M. A. K. Halliday, 'The Functional Basis of Language', in his
Explorations in the Function of Language (London: Edward Arnold, 1973).

ones. While dealing with formal syntactic categories, it treats form and meaning as inseparable, every formal choice (by language-user or literary artist) inevitably involving a semantic decision.

Something we have to take into account in stating the theme of any single Sherlock Holmes story is that it is one of a vast series of stories of a very highly stylized and conventionally structured type. The five books of short stories contain no less than fifty-six stories and one has, therefore, to think simultaneously in terms of an underlying theme for the individual story that should be consistent for the whole series. A formula which seems to me to offer 'an axis that maintains the unity and consistency of meaning'[15] not only in 'The Sussex Vampire' but through all the Sherlock Holmes stories is *the triumph of reason over the irrational*. The stories were written, like most popular works of suspense, detection and fantastic adventure, to titillate the reader's imagination with irrational fears and superstitions which they then reassuringly allay with rational, down-to-earth explanations. Sherlock Holmes, Conan Doyle's epitome of the rational, is explicit about this when he reacts to the various terrifying legends about vampires by demanding: 'But are we to give serious attention to such things? This Agency stands flat-footed on the ground, and there it must remain. The world is big enough for us. No ghosts need apply.' If there is one phrase that sums up Holmes for every Englishman, even if he has never read any of the stories, it is 'Elementary, my dear Watson.' Here this is elaborated to:

(Ferguson) 'It must be an exceedingly delicate and complex affair from your point of view'.

'It is certainly delicate', said my friend, with an amused smile, 'but I have not been struck up to now with its complexity. It has been a case for intellectual deduction, but when this original intellectual deduction is confirmed point by point by quite a number of independent incidents, then the subjective becomes objective and we can say confidently that we have reached our goal.'

[15] Oulanoff's formulation: H. Oulanoff, *The Serapion Brothers: Theory and Practice* (The Hague: Mouton, 1966), p. 122.

The *Fable* ('fabula' in Formalist theory) is the raw material
of situations and events in their original chronological order.
It is not a synopsis of the story in the sequence in which events
occur from page to page. How does 'The Sussex Vampire' look
if we see all the events in their original chronological order?
Certainly very different, because many of the vital events are
only seen in 'flashbacks'. Quite often the reconstruction of the
Fable is not a particularly interesting part of the analysis of a
short story, except that it provides a point of reference for the
order of events as actually narrated. In the detective story it is
very important because every stage in the *present* of the story
is designed to throw further light on certain aspects of the past
(except where the author lays false clues which obscure or
confuse the significance of past events). The typical Sherlock
Holmes story, in fact, involves two time sequences: that lived
by the detective (in this case Holmes and Watson together),
and that lived by the client whose past has its own distinct
chronology. The two chronologies merge once the investigation
gets under way, except that it is important if tension is to be
sustained, for the detective to be felt to be one step ahead of his
client (with us, the readers, perhaps, half a step between them,
half-conscious of the way his deductions are leading, pleasantly
mystified, yet gratified by our superiority over the client and the
stooge, Dr. Watson). Each new stage of the investigation then
fills in some more important details about the past of the client
and his problem.

I have attempted in Fig. 1 to map out these two chronologies
in detail. The horizontal axis represents the time sequence of
the events which we experience with, and through, Watson and
Holmes. Here the major 'functions' are boxed and in heavy
type. Each of these leads on to some disclosure which fulfils
its detective story role by simultaneously revealing some extra
information and deepening the mystery (at least for Watson
and us, the readers). The first three 'functions' are used to
provide necessary background knowledge to the case. They
therefore have no content in themselves except as acts of reading
or conversing. Their factual content lies along the vertical

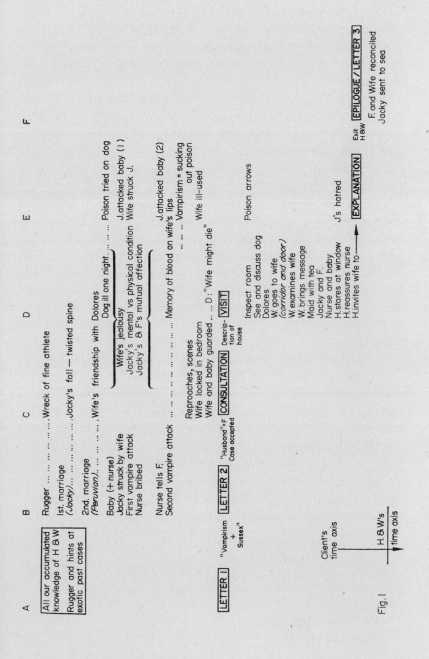

A B C D E F

All our accumulated
knowledge of H & W

Rugger and hints at
exotic past cases

Rugger ... ...Wreck of fine athlete

1st. marriage
(Jacky)... ... ...Jacky's fall — twisted spine

2nd. marriage
(Peruvian)... ... ...Wife's friendship with Dolores

Dog ill one night... ... . Poison tried on dog

Baby (+ nurse)
Jacky struck by wife
First vampire attack
Nurse bribed

Wife's jealousy
Jacky's mental vs physical condition   Wife struck J.
Jacky's & F's mutual affection

J. attacked baby (1)

Nurse tells F.
Second vampire attack

... ... Memory of blood on wife's lips

J. attacked baby (2)

... ... Vampirism = sucking
out poison

Reproaches, scenes
Wife locked in bedroom
Wife and baby guarded ... D: "Wife might die"

Wife ill-used

Descrip-
tion of
house

LETTER 2   CONSULTATION   VISIT

"Husband"= F
Case accepted

Inspect room
See and discuss dog
Dolores
W. goes to wife
(corridor and door)
W. examines wife
W. brings message
Maid with tea
Jacky and F.
Nurse and baby
H. stares at window
H. reassures nurse
H. invites wife to

Poison arrows

J's hatred

EXPLANATION   EPILOGUE / LETTER 3

Exit
H & W

F. and Wife reconciled
Jacky sent to sea

LETTER 1

"Vampirism
+
Sussex"

Client's
time axis

H. & W's
time axis

Fig. 1

axis, the time sequence of the client, Ferguson. As will be clear if we compare the colums A, B, and C, each successive stage of contact with the client gives us a more detailed knowledge of the period anterior to the opening of the story. Yet the details only mystify.

With the 'Visit' to the scene of the crime the two time-axes merge and the events are experienced simultaneously (though not, of course, with equal understanding) by Ferguson, Watson and Holmes. Retrospectively, i.e. above the horizontal, there is a further focus on those facts about the past which may provide the vital clue.

The 'Explanation' naturally only consists of past events illuminated in a crucially new way. With the 'Epilogue' the two time sequences continue along their separate dimensions.

The nine functions which Shklovsky distilled from the Sherlock Holmes corpus are not pure Fable, since they include flashbacks in the form of narrated evidence at several points. They are rather components of *Plot*, which may be defined as the *causal* unfolding of the narrative. The interplay between temporal and causal sequence, between *Fable* and *Plot* varies widely with different genres of prose narrative. If the Fable is temporality as perceived by the characters, Plot is causality only partly (and sometimes not at all) perceived by the characters, but gradually reconstructed by the reader. In our classic detective story we create chains of cause and effect out of interlocking patterns of motive and material, spatial and temporal evidence; the Plot is partly perceived through our reconstruction of the Fable. Holmes tantalizes his client and us with some partial reconstruction of this kind. Time becomes a crucial aspect of causality:

'What is it, Mr. Holmes?'
'The dog. What's the matter with it?'
'That's what puzzled the vet. A sort of paralysis. Spinal meningitis, he thought. But it's passing. He'll be all right soon—won't you Carlo?' . . .
'Did it come on suddenly?'
'In a single night.'

'How long ago?'
'It may have been four months ago.'
'Very remarkable. Very suggestive.'

Fable and Plot, then, are interacting chains but they do not make a story. This is the function of the Narrative Structure which builds events into an easily perceived and graspable pattern. The fundamental pattern for Narrative Structure in the short story and in chapters or episodes of the novel is that of Complication—Peripeteia—Denouement, where the Complication represents some kind of disturbance of a previously prevailing inertia, the Peripeteia a switch from this disturbed state to the state which prevails finally which may be the same as that before the story opened or some new state. We may define the short story as an idea given dynamic form; dynamic involves movement and this movement may be physical or psychological. We formulated the theme of 'The Sussex Vampire' provisionally as a semantic opposition: the Irrational/Reason. If we replace the oblique stroke by an arrow we have the bare bones of narrative structure, perhaps best summed up in a word by the *verbal noun* 'rationalization'.

The point at which the Peripeteia occurs is crucial to our understanding of the theme: indeed, in many subtly complex modern short stories initial statements of theme are frequently proved wrong or inadequate by the discovery of new peripeteia.[16] In our detective story this point of change occurs very near the end, although, if the author has played fair, it should have been anticipated by certain deductions that we and the detective can make on the strength of what we learn earlier. The complication, then, is the mystery, the irrational terror of apparent vampirism in the heart of the Sussex weald, which is resolved with a perfectly reasonable explanation in the denouement, as Holmes' hypothesis is borne out by the glimpse of the hatred on Jacky's face seen reflected in a shuttered window.

With most types of short story it is useful to follow Petrovsky[17]

---

[16] See the analyses cited in note 13.
[17] M. A. Petrovsky, 'Morfologiya novelly', *Ars Poetica* (Moscow, 1928).

in setting the basic narrative structure of Complication—
Peripeteia—Denouement within a framework of Prologue and
Epilogue, in each of which we can usually distinguish two
phases, the general and the specific. The General Prologue here
consists of all the relevant facts from beyond the past of the
story—all we already know of Holmes and Watson, their
earlier cases which are mentioned, their relations with the
machinery firm (the kind of exquisite irrelevance with which
Conan Doyle frequently embellishes his prologues) and what
we learn of Watson's youthful encounters with Ferguson on the
rugby field. Some detective stories use vital aspects of the
General Prologue as clues or motives in the main plot, but this
is not the case in 'The Sussex Vampire'. The Specific Prologue
is the way Holmes and Watson get involved in the case of the
Sussex Vampire: the two letters and Ferguson's visit to fill in
the details of the case. As Scheglov demonstrates,[18] such prologues in the Sherlock Holmes stories are all variations on a
pattern. Conan Doyle has to get his heroes acquainted with the
background of each new case and with the victim-hero. Usually
they are at home in Baker Street when they get a startling letter
followed by an interview (as here), or a coach pulls up, a ring
at the doorbell is followed by a clattering up the stairs and the
visitor is shown in to tell his story. There are all kinds of permutations of the details: Watson or Holmes may be preoccupied
with something when the interruption occurs; stormy weather
outside increases the air of tension and expectancy; the visitor
is variously greeted and welcomed to the fireside by Holmes;
the latter makes various deductions about the client's job, his
way of life, recent activities, or state of health from his minute
observation of his clothes, fingernails, hair, etc. But basically all
of the details are embellishments of the crucial mechanism of
getting Holmes and Watson in on a new case.

The Epilogues may be similarly divided into Specific (the
immediate future) and General (the longer-term future) and
may also be embellished to a greater or lesser degree. Here,
however, there is no longer the need to transmit a lot of basic

[18] Yu. K. Scheglov, 'Opisanie struktury detektivnoi novelly', pp. 355–62.

facts, to leave clues, or lay false trails, so the Epilogues are quite brief and factual—enough to dispose of the characters whose future is insufficiently resolved by the denouement: Ferguson and his wife are left embracing, Holmes and Watson tiptoe out of the bedroom with the ever-faithful maid, Dolores, and Jacky, we presume, will soon be packed off to the Merchant Navy for a spot of discipline. Finally (General Epilogue), back at the famous apartment, Holmes writes a letter in answer to the enquiry with which the story opened—a nice gratuitously circular touch, restoring the reassuring inertia of life with its 'feet firmly on the ground' as lived in the Edwardian image of London. Meanwhile, Watson, we presume, sits down to write up his latest case for the famous Case-Book.

The most intriguing level of analysis is *Point of View*. There are so many subtle variations in the type of narrator who may be chosen and in the way he stands in relation to the events and and the other characters that the possibilities are virtually infinite.[19] It is simply not enough to attach a label marked '1st person narrator' or 'third-person omniscient' as some of the text-books do. Many modern short stories since Chekhov have used the 'third person, limited omniscient' point of view, which has been defined as follows: 'The author narrates the story in the third person, but chooses one character as his "sentient center" whom he follows throughout the action, restricting the reader to the field of vision and range of knowledge of that character alone'.[20] But how much more is learned about such a story by applying the label? The necessary information is not who held the camera, but his angle and distance from the subject at any particular moment, his 'aperture' (or receptiveness), his 'focus' (or clarity of vision) and 'shutter speed' (or intelligence). The author may adjust these at different

---

[19] A stimulating attempt to explore the problem of point of view systematically is B. A. Uspensky's *Poetika kompozitsii* (Moscow, 1970); English translation, *The Poetics of Composition* (Berkeley: University of California Press, 1974).

[20] M. H. Abrams, *A Glossary of Literary Terms* (New York: 1957), p. 73.

points in the story and the pattern of his adjustments will probably bear some relation to elements in the Narrative Structure, as well as affecting the linguistic texture.

Now Conan Doyle uses Watson as a first person narrator of distinctly limited omniscience. Everything we learn is first distilled via his down-to-earth, literal-minded perception (in a sense he is the epitome—or reductio ad absurdum—of the 'Reason' pole of our thematic opposition; Holmes, although he reintroduces reason into wildly irrational situations, usually relies on a flash of the irrational inspiration of the creative genius for making all the facts and motives fall into place). Watson is the perfect stooge for the brilliant, mercurial Holmes, plodding along after a trail of clues, many of them false, missing the vital things that Holmes takes in at a glance and noticing irrelevant things which will lead us astray for a while:

'Of course I remember him,' said I, as I laid down the letter. 'Big Bob Ferguson, the finest three-quarter Richmond ever had. He was always a good-natured chap. It's like him to be so concerned over a friend's case.'

Holmes looked at me thoughtfully and shook his head. 'I never get your limits, Watson,' said he. 'There are unexplored possibilities about you. Take a wire down, like a good fellow. "Will examine your case with pleasure".'

'*Your* case!'

'We must not let him think that this Agency is a home for the weak-minded. Of course it is his case. Send him that wire and let the matter rest till morning.'

Holmes' explicit irony at Watson's expense—Watson, with his 'unexplored possibilities' is the only one who might be suspected of weak-mindedness—is carried implicitly by reference to their 'Agency', something much too official and institutionalized to represent adequately Holmes' approach to detection.

Watson's interpretations of what Holmes is up to also confuse the situation very conveniently and allow Conan Doyle to lay the beginnings of a trail without giving the secret away before Holmes can produce his final conjuring trick with the complete explanation:

'It was at this moment that I chanced to glance at Holmes, and saw a most singular intentness in his expression. His face was set as if it had been carved out of old ivory, and his eyes, which had glanced for a moment at father and child, were now fixed with eager curiosity upon something at the other side of the room. Following his gaze I could only guess that he was looking out of the window at the melancholy, dripping garden. It is true that a shutter had half closed outside and obstructed the view, but none the less it was certainly at the window that Holmes was fixing his concentrated attention.'

We do not, of course, discover until later that this is Holmes' crucial glimpse of Jacky's look of jealousy and hatred that solves the mystery, but we are alerted by the very explicit restrictions on Watson's point of view: 'fixed upon something . . .,' 'I could only guess . . .,' 'It is true that . . .,' 'none the less it was certainly . . .,' and even by Watson's rare, if rather mundane flight of fancy about the old ivory.

One of the other delights of the problem of Point of View is that modern authors can very rarely resist drawing our attention to what they are doing, to the relationship between the assumptions operating within the framework of the story and those of the real world outside. This is taken so far in some cases[21] that a whole story becomes a kind of dialogue between the narrator's view of the world and the view of the world the author assumes us to have. In a way, the author invents his reader as well as his narrator. Even in the relatively straightforward Sherlock Holmes stories we find a little of this interplay. The way Holmes teases Watson and casts doubts on his reliability as an observer, and even as a chronicler of events (where he is the only observer and chronicler we, as readers, have available), is an example of a temporary break in the Point of View framework: the created character, Holmes, is talking over the head of another created character, Watson, and addressing us, the readers, outside the story, directly. Watson's failure to recognize that the husband described in the letter is

[21] See my discussion of this aspect of Dostoevsky in the article cited in note 13 above.

Ferguson himself is a case in point. And as he reads through the accounts of past cases in the volume marked V, he reads:

Voyage of the *Gloria Scott* . . . That was a bad business. I have some recollection that you made a record of it, Watson, though I was unable to congratulate you on the result.

Although Watson is the one we are bound to trust for our information, he is not particularly trustworthy! Our minds and imaginations will be delightfully engaged in disentangling the truth and the distortion from the narrator's record as well as from the facts and evidence of other characters.[22]

It is clear from our discussion of Point of View how completely Holmes and Watson are designed as foils for each other. This is a universal throughout the series. If we analyse the problem of *Character* in 'The Sussex Vampire',[23] Ferguson and his wife are also foils for each other: Ferguson is so obvious, so English, so respectable, so recognizable, so easy to identify with, while his wife (who is the only character in the story who is given no name—'Mrs. Ferguson' would hardly do!) is dark, mysterious, passionate, foreign, alien to our (i.e. Holmes' and Watson's) way of life and full of potential threat, until we eventually learn how nobly she has been hiding the truth.

Most of the other characters, as usual in detective stories, simultaneously fulfil their functions as nurses, maids, offspring, pets, etc. and as potential villains. They are part of the pattern of true and false clues that we grope our way through, and Conan Doyle is very skilful in making Watson introduce them all equally carefully and dispassionately.

The *Setting*, too, is full of true and false clues: which are we to look at most closely in the large central room at Ferguson's

[22] A number of commentators have drawn attention to Agatha Christie's achievement in taking this aspect of point of view to its ultimate refinement in *The Murder of Roger Ackroyd*.

[23] Of course Point of View and Character are not really separable in this kind of story, since with Ferguson too we have to rely on his narrative for certain evidence from the past. Like all the analytical levels discussed here, these levels interact and reinforce one another: we separate them only as a descriptive and heuristic device.

home—the panelling on the walls, the modern watercolours, or the South American utensils and weapons? It turns out to be the latter, and we would have realized this if we were alert when Holmes' particular interest in them is alluded to. But it could have been the others. And again, what is the relevance of the shuttered window through which Holmes gazes so intently,[24] or is it another false clue like the door leading to Ferguson's wife's room?

'I followed the girl who was quivering with strong emotion, up the staircase and down an ancient corridor. At the end was an iron-clamped and massive door. It struck me as I looked at it that if Ferguson tried to force his way to his wife he would find it no easy matter. The girl drew a key from her pocket, and the heavy oaken planks creaked upon their old hinges'.

Apart from clues for the detection plot, the setting is most relevant to the theme. The very title of the story presents the basic opposition: *The Sussex Vampire*—what an oxymoron! The mysterious, threatening, terrifying, bloodthirsty world of vampires, normally restricted to Gothic castles in Hungary, Transylvania and other outlandishly un-English places. But all this in Sussex? In one of the cosiest and most familiar of the 'Home' Counties? In a part of England that is 'full of old houses which are named after the men who built them centuries ago. You get Odley's and Harvey's and Carriton's—the folk are forgotten but their names live in their houses'? Admittedly, Ferguson's house, like the man himself, is 'large and straggling, very old at the centre, very new at the wings' and 'the floors sagged into sharp curves,' but it still has 'towering Tudor chimneys and a lichen-spotted, high pitched roof of Horsham slabs,' and the ancient tiles which lined the porch still bear the original builder's trademark. A house, in a word, in the best of English traditions, secure in the clay weald between the North and the South Downs, not an hour's journey from safe-old, cosy-old London! Whatever could vampires be doing here?

[24] Surely Conan Doyle was not perpetrating an unconscious pun (that Freud himself might have been proud of) on the word *jalousie*, thereby anticipating Robbe-Grillet by some thirty years?

The setting seen in this light appears to substantiate Scheglov's formulation of the underlying theme of the Sherlock Holmes stories as the opposition Security/Adventure (here he is referring particularly to the 'outer', or 'basic' story prior to the appearance of an individual client):

The theme as a whole could be labelled 'security complex', and its sub-themes respectively—'possession of security' and 'provision of security' . . .

The basic requirement for building the world of Holmes and Watson (in its personal aspect) is that these characters, their activity, way of life, pastimes, interests, the accessories which surround them, etc., should combine the two opposing principles:

(a) adventure, dangers, changes of fortune, movement, drama;

(b) comfort, safety, domestic convenience, tranquillity, satisfaction;

It is the writer's task to look for conditions which will permit the foreground heroes (i.e. Holmes and Watson) simultaneously to receive a physical and spiritual 'shock' by getting involved in all kinds of dramas and adventures and yet not to quit their normal element, not to yield in any way their accustomed comforts, to enjoy full immunity. What is more, taking part in the drama which for the other directly interested characters may mean risking their lives, or at any rate security, family happiness or honour, must be for our heroes just a game, an amusement, a hedonistic pastime. This world, uniting the terrifying and the safe, movement with tranquillity, discomfort with comfort, offers a combination of conditions in which the most sober of citizens would agree, would even volunteer, to have adventures and to come face-to-face with danger and horrors and so on. The ethos of Holmes' and Watson's world is an ethos of 'excitement on the cheap'.

This theme is a sort of utopia created on behalf of the comfortably-off Victorian man-in-the-street: the educated middle-classes, small shopkeepers, men of property, etc. The theme is a product of the world-view peculiar to this social stratum: on the one hand, an attachment to his calm, enlightened, law-protected life and to the civilisation and progress which guarantee this comfort; on the other hand, a bit of 'romance,' excitement, contact with other, more cruel and sadistic, fiercer modes of conduct, in particular, the crime report provided John Citizen with his most vivid excitement.[25]

[25] Scheglov op. cit. (note 8 above), pp. 353–54.

Scheglov argues cogently for his 'Adventure/Security' formulation of the theme in terms of character, setting, etc. within the 'outer' story, but does not, perhaps, take fully into account the basic and universal mechanism of the detective genre—the intellectual pleasure the reader has in weighing the evidence in terms of facts and motives as the story proper progresses and in enjoying finally the elegant rationalization of apparently irrational behaviour. In some sense this opposition of the Irrational versus Reason is at a deeper thematic level than Scheglov's and is just as easy to relate to the unconscious needs of a positivist-minded educated middle-class reading public in Victorian and Edwardian England. If one confines one's analysis and synthesis to the prologue of the stories as Scheglov does, i.e. to the interplay between Holmes and Watson and the stages in the appearance of the client preceding the exposition and investigation of the case proper, the focus is too strongly on Holmes and Watson and on the emotional content of the notions Security, Comfort, etc. The fascination of the stories considered as whole units (and is it, in fact, valid to generate only a part, however consistently and predictably it recurs, from a 'theme' which is, by definition, relevant to the whole?) is surely in the mechanism of the deductive process whereby a rational solution is reached from an apparently irreconcilable mass of conflicting evidence.

We will attempt, therefore, to generate elements in the structure and text of 'The Sussex Vampire' out of our theme (the Irrational/Reason), seeing Scheglov's 'Security/Adventure' opposition rather as a first-stage realization of our more abstract formulation. We will follow as far as possible the principles which Zholkovsky and Scheglov have outlined in their papers, while representing the various stages in the generative process more schematically than they have done. This should clarify both the essential nature of the operations involved and the way they function in a particular case. The main operations that the two Russians have distinguished so far are shown in Fig. 2 in the order: Symbol (our convention)— Name of operation (the translation we have adopted)—

Transcription of the original Russian term—Alternative translations (in some cases).

Fig. 2

+	Combination	Sovmeschenie	—
→	Realization	Razvyertyvanie	unfolding, elaboration
<	Reinforcement	Usilenie	intensification, strengthening
‖	Repetition	Povtorenie	—
/	Juxtaposition	Protivopostavlenie	—
{ }	Multiple Realization	Vypolnenie odnoi i toi zhe funktsii tselym ryadom sredstv	Fulfilment of one and the same function by a number of means

⇒   Becomes, is transformed to

Generation of 'The Sussex Vampire' from Theme: Irrational/ Rational

1. (realization): Irrational/Rational → Adventure/Security

2. (multiple realization): Adventure → exotic (A)
sick (C)
Security → maternal love (B)
filial love (D)

(We may point out here, in order not to have to make the qualification at every stage in the generation, that the elements resulting from a realization of a realization still contain elements crucial to the original theme. This must be true by definition of the relationship between generated element and theme. So 'exotic' in the world of Holmes and Watson subsumes semantic components like 'foreign, alien, un-English, incomprehensible, threatening' and therefore viewed *irrationally*; similarly 'sick' subsumes 'abnormal, alien, contagious, impenetrable, threatening'; whereas 'maternal love' and 'filial love' in their normal, non-pathological manifestations are essentially '*reasonable*' emotions. The letters A, B, C, and D which we use to label the elements are merely a convenient shorthand to save lengthy repetition at later stages.)[26]

3. (combination and realization): A + B → Señora Ferguson

C + D → Jacky Ferguson

(This stage in the generation provides a starting-point for both characterization and plot. We may assume that a complex generative process takes place simultaneously on several levels, as in the author's mind, rather than linearly, as here. For convenience we will outline the generation of the plot first and then characterization, without, however, making any assumptions about the order of these two sets of operations.)

4. (combination) Add the plotting elements of detective fiction as a genre:

Mystery → Apparent (X)/Real (Y)

(The diagram from Zholkovsky and Scheglov (1971, op. cit.) shown in Fig. 3, p. 166, indicates how they conceive the relationship between universal genre elements and elements peculiar to a particular writer's canon).

This combination gives the following range of possibilities:

(a) AY + BX   / AX + BY
    (Señora Ferguson = villain)   (Senora Ferguson =
                                            innocent)

(b) CY + DX   / CX + DY
    (Jacky = villain)   (Jacky = innocent)

5. combination and juxtaposition):

(AY + BX) + (CX + DY) / (AX + BY) + (CY + DX)
(Ferguson's hypothesis)   (Holmes' explanation)

6. (realization) : replace / (above) by ⇒ and a semantic opposition becomes a syntactic process: the static becomes dynamic—

(AY + BX) + (CX + DY) ⇒ (AX + BY) + (CY + DX)[27]

---

[26] Note that these letters do not have the same significance as those used by John Rutherford in his paper below, pp. 196 ff.

[27] The story perhaps gains in power and universality by the fact that this formula could be restated, in the manner of Claude Lévi-Strauss, as an inversion of archetypes: problem stepmother ⇒ problem stepson.

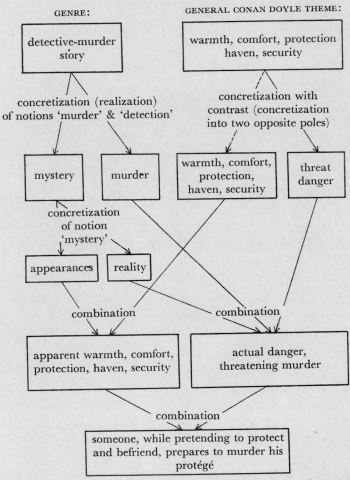

Note: a broken arrow indicates 'zero concretization', i.e. the transfer of some element directly to the next stage of the generative process without change.

7. (reinforcement) $AY + BX <$ vampirism

$\qquad AX + BY <$ warm latin love

$\qquad CY + DX <$ crippled soul

$\qquad CX + DY <$ dearest, most loving heart

(It might be argued here that this reinforcement need apply only to one of the elements, i.e. given AY (the reality of the exotic element), do we need BX (apparent maternal love)? We do, because, as the next stage (8) shows, each of these separate elements is elaborated at some point in the plot, the characterization or setting, or through combinations of these, and in the very language of the text.)

8. (realization of each element through plot, character, setting and language.)

$AY \rightarrow$ *Plot:* £5 for nurse's silence

                   Vampirism—some wild tale of foreign parts

                   'As if some frenzy had seized her'

                   'How do I know what strange impulse might come upon her?'

    Character: Peruvian: foreign birth and alien religion

                   Sides of her character which F. could never explore or understand

                   Traits alien to (BY) her ordinarily sweet and gentle disposition

                   Jealous with all the strength of her fiery tropical love

                   Frightened but (AX) beautiful eyes

                   flushed and (AX) handsome face

                   'She is ill but (AX) she is quite rational' (Watson)

                   Dolores as extension of Señora F.: a friend rather than servant;

                           ('wife's character would really be better known by D. than by you?') Tall, slim, brown-faced girl; indignant eyes; quivering with strong emotion; D's foreign accent.

                   Dog = 'Carlo'

	Setting:	Fine collection of S. American utensils and weapons
		Curare or some other devilish drug
		Vampirism—And yet here in the very heart of English Sussex
BX →	*Plot:*	Assaulting the poor lad in an unprovoked way

BX →   *Plot:* Assaulting the poor lad in an unprovoked way

Biting the baby's neck

Mother waiting to get at baby

'Day and night the silent, watchful mother seemed to be lying in wait . . .'

Blood all round her lips

Small angry red pucker → (BY) upon the cherub throat

Sucking blood   → (BY) sucking wound to draw poison

    Character: 'As a wolf waits for a lamb'

Jealousy of stepmothers

Again and again said she hated Jacky

    Setting: Nursery (scene of vampirism)

Señora F's room as prison/haven

AX → *Character:* Very beautiful

As loving a wife as a man could have

'She is a most loving woman'

Beautiful eyes . . . handsome face

BY →   *Plot:* 'Do I not love him—even to sacrifice myself rather than break his dear heart.'

'I want my child. I have a right to my child.'

'Cut to the heart.'

Assaults take different forms: a real clue (maternal ≠ stepmotherly)

upon the cherub throat—(BX) small angry pucker

Sucking wound to draw poison ⇒ (BX) sucking blood

Character: 'If ever a woman loved a man with all her heart and soul, she loves me.'
'A loving mother, (BX) save for assaults on stepson.'
'(Why wound—BX)—dear little baby?'
'Cut to the heart.'

Setting: Position at cot-side

CX → *Character:* Unhappily injured
Poor inoffensive cripple
Fall in childhood twisted spine
Shambling gait, etc.

DY → *Plot:* Flame of emotion and joy on seeing father
Boy cooed and nestled his head on father's breast

Character: Charming and affectionate
'Dearest, most loving heart'
Affection . . . great comrades
Devotion to memory of his mother

Setting: Comfortable drawing-room over tea

DX → *Plot:* Assaulted twice
Tried poison on dog
Pricked child with poison arrow

Character: Probably very developed in mind since his body circumscribed in action

CY → *Plot:* Penetrating and unfriendly gaze
Hatred and jealousy glimpsed on face in window reflection

Character: Maniacal, exaggerated love for Ferguson and his dead mother.

It will be clear from many of these elements that the combinations tend to generate pairs of opposing features: 'wild tale of foreign parts/and yet here in the very heart of English Sussex'; 'frightened/but beautiful'; 'flushed/and handsome face'; 'a loving mother/save for assaults on her stepson'; 'traits alien to/ordinarily sweet and gentle disposition'; 'Not very prepossessing externally/but a heart of gold, and devoted to the child', etc. Stylistically, then, many elements of plot, character and setting are presented in oxymoron-type structures reminiscent of the story's title. We will consider the implications of this after completing some further stages in the generative process:

9. (combination of clue elements)
   (a) Weapons, whereby AY $\Rightarrow$ AX + DX
   (b) Dog,   ,,   CX $\Rightarrow$ CY + DX
   (c) Window,   ,,   DY $\Rightarrow$ CY + DX
   (d) Baby's neck, ,,   AY $\Rightarrow$ BY + DX

All of these now point to the reality of Jacky's sickness (DX) and perversion of filial love (CY).

10. (reinforcement) enrich the mixture by strengthening:
    'Security' element in: Ferguson's character and back-
                          ground
                          London and Sussex setting
                          Holmes' and Watson's attitude
    'Adventure' element in: Ferguson's changed persona
                          Dog
                          'Walk-on parts' (nurse, Dolores)
                          Watson's and Ferguson's hypothe-
                          sis

11. (realization) all these elements in a style which is marked by alternations of the dramatic and reassuring, of doubt or fear (in the speech and thoughts of Ferguson (and Watson) and rationality or commonsense (with Holmes).

It would be absurd to claim that all the elements of structure, let alone all the elements of style are generated automatically and in a strictly predetermined way as if a computer were programmed to churn out Sherlock Holmes stories. Scheglov appears to be tempted by this mechanistic fallacy when he suggests that

a practical extension to descriptions of this kind would be the creation of 'new Sherlock Holmes stories' (attempts of this kind have,

of course, often been made, and with some success, although they have not been based on any such clearly formulated rules.) To achieve this, however, a great deal of work is needed to formalise the rules (if we have in mind the automatic rather than 'manual' generation of stories).[28]

—as if every theoretical discovery in science must instantly start spawning a new technology! No, the measure of the generative poetics hypothesis, as both Zholkovsky and Scheglov are normally at pains to make clear, is in its explanatory adequacy and descriptive power. Does it assist in explaining such relationships in a literary work as those between 'theme' and 'text', between 'form' and 'content', between the various devices a writer has at his disposal in delineating and mutually reinforcing plot, character, setting and so on? Does it enable us to account more adequately for the way certain underlying—and, at present, hypothetical—authorial skills, whether conscious or unconscious ('competence'), produce particular observable effects, and patterns in a literary text ('performance')? Does it provide systematic concepts and a terminology which help in the description of the work itself, of the process of communication in literature?

We have noted that a recurrent feature of the language in which characters are described is a pattern of antithesis. But this pattern is so marked at various linguistic levels throughout the greater part of this story that it becomes a kind of 'dominant'.[29] Some examples at the levels of nominal or adverbial phrase, clause and even paragraph will make clear how dominant is this juxtaposition of opposing notions of the rational and the irrational, of safety and adventure. We will use Scheglov's notation, S (security, safety) and A (adventure) to characterize the halves of the antithesis:

[28] Scheglov, 'Opisanie struktury detektivnoi novelly', pp. 353–4.

[29] A term used extensively in this sense by such Russian Formalists as Eikhenbaum and Tynyanov. The theoretical and descriptive implications of the term have been further explored by linguists and literary scholars of the Prague School.

PHRASE:

S   A
For a mixture of the *modern* / and the *mediaeval*
S   A
of the *practical* / and of the *wildly fanciful*
S   A
communication of even date / concerning *vampires*
A   S
Ferguson's *gaunt* features / *softened*
A   S
a pair of *frightened* / but *beautiful* eyes
A   S
her *flushed* / and *handsome* face
S   A
I could not see *honest Bob Ferguson* / in the character of
fiend or devil
S   A
a very *penetrating* / and, as it seemed to me, *unfriendly* gaze
A   S
small, *angry red pucker* / upon the *cherub* throat
S   A
on its *chubby* neck / there was this small *puckered mark*
S   A
Ferguson put *his big hand* / to his *furrowed forehead*
S   A
a cry in which *joy* / and *surprise* seemed to be blended

CLAUSE:

A   S
It was a ship which is associ- / a story for which the *world is*
ated with the *giant rat of*   *not yet prepared*
Sumatra

S	A
Anything is better than *stagnation*	/ but really we seem to have been switched on to a *Grimm's fairy tale*

S	A
The world is *big enough* for us	/ *No ghosts need apply*

S	A
a smile of *amusement* upon his face which gradually faded away	/ into an expression of intense *interest and concentration*

A	S
a *Peruvian* lady, the daughter of a Peruvian merchant	/ whom he had met in connection with the *importation of nitrates*

S	A
The lady was *very beautiful*	/ but for the fact of her *foreign birth* and of her *alien religion*

A	S
began to show some *curious* traits	/ quite alien to her ordinarily *sweet and gentle disposition*

S	A
a very *charming and affectionate* youth	/ though *unhappily injured* through an *accident* in childhood

S	A
Day and night the nurse *covered* the child	/ and day and night the silent, watchful mother seemed to be *lying in wait as a wolf waits for a lamb*

A	S
We had thought it was some *wild tale of foreign parts*	/ And yet here in the very heart of *English Sussex*

S	A
His *great frame*	/ had *fallen in*
His *flaxen hair*	/ was *scanty*
his *shoulders*	/ were *bowed*

A	S
A fall in childhood and a *twisted spine*	/ But the *dearest, most loving heart* within

S	A
It may be a *mere intellectual puzzle* to you	/ but it is *life and death* to me

A	S
'It is certainly *delicate*', / said my friend with an *amused* smile, 'but I have *not been struck up to now with its complexity*'	

A	S
The idea of a vampire was to	/ Such things do not

S	A
me absurd	happen in criminal practice in England

PARAGRAPH:

at this level we have: Holmes' eyes moving 'slowly and lovingly over the record of old cases' (S) juxtaposed with the adventure and terror of the irrational of their titles. (A)

A	S
horrified last paragraph of Ferguson's letter	/ the postscript about playing Rugby with Watson

A	S
'Is it madness, Mr. Holmes ... I am at my wits' end'	/ Very naturally, Mr. Ferguson. Now sit here and pull yourself together and give me a few clear answers. I can assure you that I am very far from being at my wits' end.

A	S
How can I ever forget how she rose from beside it with its blood upon her lips?	/ A smart maid ... brought in some tea

A	S
Do you like her, Jack? . . .	/ The boy cooed and nestled
His expressive mobile face	his head upon his father's
shadowed over, and he shook	breast
his head	

The Sherlock Holmes addict will recognize these and many similar antitheses as unmistakably typical of Conan Doyle's style, which, as we have seen, is largely the product of the mentality of Watson, his chosen mouthpiece. They occur so frequently in this story that the whole work becomes a sort of extension of the oxymoron of the title, almost a pastiche of his own canon. And yet we can now see this feature of the language not merely as decorative, a sort of embroidery of the surface texture, but as the expression of a crucial thematic opposition. Nor should we claim that the linguistic formulation all happens at our stage 11, as a culmination of the generative process. From experience and common sense we know that quite often linguistic form determines the precise notion being expressed ('How do I know what I mean until I hear what I say?'— W. H. Auden). As we have seen, certain phrases seem to emerge as a product of earlier stages of the synthesis. The sequence as we have expounded it is not conceived as the order of real processes, but as a model of the sequence of relationships from abstract theme to concrete text.

Our synthesis enables us to examine in detail the progression from the static to the dynamic: the way a fundamental semantic opposition is given syntactic form in art. From the title onwards elements at every level of the text, whether of plot, setting, characterization or language can, in principle, be accounted for as ultimate realizations of the theme.

A generative approach to poetics begins to make it possible to account for 'narrative universals', to study the interplay of a finite 'set of rules' operating on a finite 'lexicon' of people, actions and objects to produce an infinite variety of possible textual realizations. It provides instruments to help us explore some of the subtle and complex mechanisms of the human mind.

Of course, generative poetics is in its infancy, and (*pace* Zholkovsky and Scheglov) cannot claim to be the only structural poetics any more than generative grammar can claim exclusive validity in the study of language. It does not appear to be able to account adequately for purely linear or syntagmatic relations in the surface structure of a text (and may, indeed, obscure their significance at times). It is doubtful whether it can tell us anything about complex ironies or shifting and unreliable points of view. Side by side with a synthetic approach we need a 'functional poetics' which through analysis can begin, like functional linguistics, to describe not only the 'ideational', but the 'interpersonal' and 'textual' functions of elements in a text.[30]

Generative poetics, like other structural-semiotic approaches to the study of literature, offers a theory with considerable potential. Only detailed application of the theory to a large and varied range of texts will refine this, so far, tentative model and show its full potential. Exaggerated claims and bogus scientism must be avoided in the study of such complex organic structures as works of literature. Perhaps the best poetics will combine the virtues of the analytic, functional approach and the synthetic, generative approach. For the time being both can help thoughtful and sensitive critics to write good literary criticism.

[30] These terms are borrowed from M. A. K. Halliday, 'Linguistic Function and Literary Style: An Enquiry into the Language of William Golding's *The Inheritors*'', in *Literary Style: A Symposium*, ed. Seymour Chatman (New York and London: Oxford University Press, 1971), pp. 330–65. I have examined some manifestations of the interpersonal function in 'Speech Functions and the Study of Style', *Melbourne Slavonic Studies*, 5–6 (1971), 106–123.

CHAPTER SIX

STORY, CHARACTER, SETTING, AND NARRATIVE MODE IN GALDÓS'S
El amigo Manso

John Rutherford

Even though the aim of structural or semiological poetics is the comprehension of literature as a system rather than the interpretation or evaluation of individual texts, the poetician can hardly dispense with the analysis of texts as a basis for his investigations. One of the fundamental problems he has to face is that of segmentation. What are the component parts of literary works? At the purely verbal or stylistic level, the problem is not great: he can work in terms of immediately recognizable and universally accepted units such as the word, the sentence, the poetic line, the stanza, the simile, the metaphor, and so on. But narrative literature has another dimension, which is to some extent independent of language; for the 'world' that is created in, for example, a given novel can be described, using different words, accurately enough to be easily recognizable, as in translation or paraphrase. For the poetician who is concerned with narrative literature verbal analysis is, then, insufficient. He has also to attend to the analysis of the extra-linguistic 'world' of narrative texts, of their other dimension comprising—broadly speaking—all that which can be paraphrased. The problem of segmentation is more considerable for the non-verbal than for the verbal analysis of narrative literature. But this sort of analysis cannot proceed very far until there is some agreement about what the segments are to be and where the dividing lines between them are to be drawn.

It is the purpose of this paper to tackle the fundamental and elementary—yet still, I believe, unsolved—problem of the global segmentation of narrative texts' non-verbal, representational aspect; of the picture, that is, that they give of man situated in space and evolving in time.[1] Traditional novel criticism has often had recourse to three categories which can be adapted for the segmentation of the most representational aspects of narrative texts: character ('man'), setting ('space'), and story ('time'). But the approach of poetics to these three categories must be different from that of criticism, which tends to restrict itself to talking about the characters, locations and actions of novels in the same terms in which the characters, locations and actions of real life are commonly talked about. Poetics, concerned to formulate the norms governing literature as a system of communication, must direct its attention towards that which is specific to literature; and so the poetician's task is not to calculate the degree to which a novel apparently copies life, but rather to establish the principles according to which the novelist, consciously or unconsciously, makes a selection from life and orders that selection for the purpose, possibly, of giving the impression of a copy of life. The poetician will, then, look for non-psychological and non-sociological ways of discussing character, non-historical ways of discussing story, and non-geographical ways of discussing setting.

Character, story and setting do not, however, constitute the total representational structure of the novel. Just as in our everyday experience we find it necessary to draw distinctions between, on one hand, what we think of as 'external reality' and, on the other, the way in which we perceive this reality, so also, in the novel, it is useful to distinguish between an 'objective plane', of character, story and setting, and a 'subjective plane', of the means whereby this objective plane is presented to the reader. All that which concerns the presenta-

[1] Another application of the method outlined in this paper will be found in my forthcoming *Critical Guide to Leopoldo Alas (Clarín), 'La Regenta'* (London: Grant and Cutler, 1974).

tion of the world of the novel, rather than that world itself as
the reader is invited to imagine it, can be placed in a fourth
category, which I shall call 'narrative mode'. The analysis of
narrative mode can be seen as a bridge between the non-verbal
analysis of a novel's objective plane and the verbal analysis of
its style.

What I have suggested so far is straightforward enough, even
indeed banal. But it seems now even more necessary than ever
to go back to basic methodological questions like these. One of
the weaknesses of literary structuralism is its failure to resolve
such elementary problems and provide a framework for the
various analyses of literature that it has produced: its failure,
in a word, to structure itself. Some objections to specific structural analyses of literature can be simply answered on the basis of
even such rudimentary segmentation as I have so far outlined.
The criticism, for example, that recently developed methods for
story analysis[2] are inadequate because they fail to take account
of subtlety of presentation, manipulation of view-point, creation
of atmosphere (made insistently at the Norwich conference) can
be seen to be based on a misunderstanding, for such effects do
not belong to story at all, but to narrative mode.

I now want to look at each of the four categories and to
describe methods of analysis for each of them that seem to offer
interesting possibilities. I shall illustrate my arguments by
reference to the novel *El amigo Manso* (1882) by the Spanish
realist Benito Pérez Galdós. Although I believe that the methods
of analysis I am proposing are valid for all narrative fiction,
they are most obviously applicable to texts produced within
the nineteenth-century realistic tradition. For those who do not
know this novel, I offer a summary of it:

Máximo Manso is the narrator (the title means *Our Friend
Manso*). He is a young philosophy teacher, and he describes
himself as a rational and ordered man, abstemious and of simple
tastes. He recalls his childhood and youth in Asturias province;
his intellectual capabilities became evident at an early age,

[2] See below, pp. 186–200.

and he was hailed as a genius. His mother served his purposes and furthered his interests, dying only when his academic career was on a firm footing.

The novel's action starts. A neighbour, Doña Javiera, a butcher-woman who has some money and wants to improve her social status, asks Manso to take charge of the education of her son, Manolito Peña. Peña's education continues for two or three years. Then Manso's brother, José María, returns a rich man from Cuba. He needs a governess for his children, and Manso is able to help by introducing him to Irene, the nineteen-year-old poor, attractive and educated niece of Doña Cándida, a widow who had ruined her husband by her extravagance. All seem to be pleased with this arrangement. José María has political and social ambitions; Manso gets involved in his brother's affairs, and the orderly routine of his life begins to suffer. He is attracted towards Irene, whom he considers a perfect, rational being, whose tastes and beliefs coincide with his own. Doubts about her arise, however, when she suddenly reveals that she is unhappy, without giving any reasons. Manso's relationship with Peña continues meanwhile. Peña has not turned out as Manso intended: he is a man of action, an excellent orator, and of irregular habits. Under his influence the order of Manso's life suffers still more. Manso learns more disturbing news: José María is making advances to Irene, and his wife asks Manso to call him off. At a speech-giving occasion Manso's discourse is received coldly, while that of Peña arouses enthusiasm. The general opinion is that the latter has a splendid future in front of him.

The suspicion has been growing in Manso's mind that Irene is not as rational as he thought; but this suspicion increases rather than diminishes the strength of his feelings for her. Doña Cándida has mysteriously obtained some money, and Irene leaves José María's household in order to live with her. Manso perceives a certain furtiveness in the actions of both. His bewilderment is increased when José María's wife accuses Irene of encouraging her husband's attentions. Manso confronts José María, and the brothers argue angrily.

There is a diversion from the main action when the wet-nurse of José María's youngest child leaves suddenly; Manso steps in and puts an end to the state of emergency by finding a substitute. He is told, while on this mission, that José María is living with Doña Cándida and Irene. He goes to their house, and is there given conflicting explanations of the situation by Doña Cándida, Irene and José María. None of them is satisfactory, but one piece of new information which emerges is that Irene has a secret boyfriend. When, a little later, walking along the street attempting to analyse the situation, he meets Peña, the solution suddenly comes to him: his own protégé is the mysterious lover of Irene.

Manso's disintegration is almost complete, and it goes still further when Irene reveals herself to be a completely ordinary girl, totally uninterested in things of the mind, as full of social ambitions as most of the other personages in the novel, and concerned only to assure a secure and comfortable life for herself. Manso now finds to his horror that he is madly in love with Irene.

Doña Javiera is opposed to her son's relationship with Irene, for she sees a marriage with this humble girl as a blow to her chances of improving her social status. She asks Manso to intervene; and he does so, impulsed largely by his own need to obtain Irene for himself. When Peña rejects Manso's blatantly cynical reasoning, the latter states that it was merely a test of the firmness of the young man's love (the reader is left to decide the truth for himself). Manso now puts all his efforts into bringing about the marriage; he succeeds and the wedding takes place; Manso falls ill and dies, and is immediately forgotten by all.[3]

[3] The only important parts of the text I believe I have omitted in this summary are its anti-realistic opening and concluding chapters. Its first words are 'Yo no existo'—'I do not exist'—and the first chapter insists at length on the fact that Manso is a fictional, not a real being; and the last chapter elaborates and expands the point, with the revelation that the narrator is not only fictional but also dead. It is not, however, my purpose here to discuss this fascinating aspect of the narrative mode of *El amigo Manso*, its twofold denial of the conventions of realism.

Character can be described as being made up of the personages of a novel, interrelated in various ways, and each one built
up of various traits of personality also variously interconnected.
But to talk about character solely in terms of personality traits
and social relationships, as literary critics usually do—declaring
some personages to be more convincing or lifelike than others
on the grounds that they are more consistent or more powerful,
or on the other hand more subtle or more dynamic—is not very
relevant to an enquiry into the nature of literature, for it
represents little more than a projection of the critic's particular
view of life into the novel he is criticizing, and is in no way
either analytical or specifically literary. What is required is a
theory of character that is capable of indicating the ways in
which the picture of man given in narrative literature is significantly different from man as he is in reality; that, in other words,
analyses character in terms of its function within the structure
of the narrative text rather than in terms of the structure of
human personality or of society; and that is consequently
capable of defining the specifically literary patterning of literary
character. Such a theory has proved elusive. Tzvetan Todorov,
in *Littérature et signification* (Paris: Larousse, 1967), has made one
of the most serious attempts to formulate the principles which
govern the relationships between personages; but his method
seems not to be sufficient when applied to texts in which the
characterization is complex.[4]

The approach to this problem outlined by L. M. O'Toole in
his paper appears, in the light of this, attractive and promising.
The concept of literary characterization as a permutation of
themes points the way to a theory which can satisfy the requirements I have just set down. O'Toole has necessarily taken a
simple example to illustrate the theory he expounds; yet the
same theory is applicable to complete texts, in which there are

[4] See the discussion by Seymour Chatman in 'New Ways of Analyzing
Narrative Structure, With an Example from Joyce's *Dubliners*', *Language and
Style*, 2 (1969), 3–36. For another approach to character analysis see Sorìn
Alexandrescu, 'A Project in the Semantic Analysis of the Characters in
William Faulkner's Work', *Semiotica*, 4 (1971), 37–51.

more basic (or 'deep') themes and hence many more possible permutations. In *The Sussex Vampire* the characterization is rudimentary: there are two central characters, Mrs. Ferguson and Jacky, and two themes, which could be formulated as pairs of opposites, appearance versus reality and good versus evil. There is, incidentally, a significant difference between the two themes, in that the former does not apply directly to the personages concerned but rather to the other theme, and hence is adverbial rather than adjectival: Jacky, for example, is not an illusory personage, but an apparently good—and really evil—one. O'Toole has examined the two permutations of these themes and personages upon which the characterization of *The Sussex Vampire* is based. But there are other permutations, which are not actualized in this text: both personages could seem guilty and in reality be innocent; both could seem innocent and in reality be guilty; both could both seem and be guilty; both could both seem and be innocent; one could both seem and be innocent and the other both seem and be guilty; and so on. There are in fact sixteen possible permutations, of which fourteen are excluded from *The Sussex Vampire*. Its system of characterization obeys a simple rule of complementarity or opposition: one personage is always the opposite of the other, and the real situation is always the opposite of the apparent situation.

In *El amigo Manso*, themes and characterization could be similarly formulated, with the substitution of 'rational/irrational' for 'good/evil'. Manso is confident of his own rationality and of that of Irene, but in the course of the novel he becomes convinced that both are really quite irrational. Out of the sixteen possible permutations the choice here is a different one, and it obeys a rule of parallelism: each personage is at every point a reflection of the other. But to stop here would give a weak and insufficient analysis of the characterization of *El amigo Manso*. There are other important personages to be taken into account, most notably Peña; and there are other basic themes which can also be represented as pairs of opposites and in terms of which the analysis can be made more complete. The pairs 'order/disorder', 'culture/ignorance', and 'confidence/doubt', elaborated in various ways throughout the text, can be regarded as particular aspects (or sub-themes) of 'rationality/irrationality', and subsumed under that category; just as, in *The Sussex Vampire*, the pairs 'Englishness/exoticism', 'health/sickness', and 'love/hate' can be subsumed in 'good/evil'. But in *El amigo Manso* it is necessary to pay separate attention to other pairs: 'superiority/inferiority'—Manso seems to be the master of all, and comes to be little more than their errand-boy; 'nobility/baseness'—the behaviour of all personages is laid open to question in these terms; and 'worldliness/unworldliness'—social ambitions are the guiding force behind nearly all the personages, except Manso. Thus the analysis must increase a little in complexity to take account of the greater complexity of the novel's characterization.

The important point, however, is that the same method of analysis that was used for the simple characterization of *The Sussex Vampire* can, without strain, be applied to richer narrative texts. What it points towards is, in fact, a system which has certain affinities with the analysis of distinctive features in phonetics.[5] The basic characterization of *El amigo Manso*, of which the actual characterization in the text is an expansion and elaboration, could be represented in tabular form as follows:

	Rationality		Superiority		Nobility		Worldliness	
	R	A	R	A	R	A	R	A
Manso	−	+	−	+	+?	+	−	−
Irene	−	+	+	−	−?	−	+	−
Peña	−	−	+	−	+	−	+	+

(R indicates 'reality' and A 'appearance'.)

The two queries indicate that the question of the moral status

[5] The reader will notice that throughout this paper I make frequent reference to linguistics in explaining poetical methods and theories. In doing so I do not want to suggest that modern theoretical poetics is a simple matter of forcing literary structures into linguistic categories; I am merely drawing on a useful parallel for exegetic convenience. The poetician will not, of course, disdain whatever help older and more developed sciences may offer him; but poetics must be a science of literature built on the foundations of the intrinsic qualities of literature itself, and it must create its own methods, theories and terminology.

of Irene's and Manso's behaviour is left unanswered: although
much of Manso's behaviour is altruistic, it is not clear that some
of his actions are not less nobly motivated; and although Irene
reveals at the end that her conduct has throughout been underhand, it is implied that she could hardly have gone about things
in any other way. This type of ambiguity is, of course, characteristic of literature, and any method of analysis should take it
into account. Such a table as I have set out summarizes
both the individual personages, reading horizontally, and the
relations between personages, reading vertically. The next step
in this line of research is, perhaps, to produce, by applying this
method to a large number of texts, a universal vocabulary of
literary themes, in terms of which all narrative texts might be
analysed. I shall discuss this point later in this paper.

Setting involves the physical surroundings that are described
in the narrative text and within which the personages live their
imaginary lives. Its importance varies from novel to novel.
In many nineteenth century novels it is fundamental, while in
some modern ones it is almost suppressed. It has two main
functions. Firstly, it provides an explicit grounding in material
reality for the narrative, and hence enhances its sense of realism,
especially if the setting is, as in *El amigo Manso* (which takes
place in contemporary Madrid), identified as a real place.
And secondly it serves as a reinforcement for the text's themes:
themes that are combined in story and character are also
projected into the setting, which thus acquires symbolic values.
Analysis of setting can be performed in terms of these two functions, in order to discover the principles according to which
certain features of landscape or townscape are described in
preference to all the other features that might have been included but are not mentioned. An analysis of setting in *El amigo
Manso* might thus draw attention to the prominence of locations
which are presented as being characteristically Spanish in the
chaotic exuberance of their atmosphere, like the theatre, the
buñolería (working-class bun-shop), and José María's house,
and which contrast violently with Manso's aspirations to severe
Nordic orderliness. The theme rationality/irrationality is thus

projected, and the motif of the alienation of the intellectual is elaborated. Another point worth attention is the shift of location in both *El amigo Manso* and *The Sussex Vampire* to the centre of mystery—projection of the theme reality/appearance—for the solution of the enigmas around which both texts are built. The difference is that in the Spanish novel the solution does not smoothly emerge as a result of the investigations carried out at the 'scene of the crime', but rather—in a haphazard and irrational way—as the defeated investigator is walking back home. One is almost tempted to see *El amigo Manso* as an anticipatory parody of detective fiction.

Story can be seen as a complete series of interlinked actions and situations. Any kind of action or situation can enter into a story; but a story is not, clearly, any random series of situations and actions. Just as the linguistician who is concerned with syntax has the task of discovering the principles governing those strings of words that we recognize as sentences, so the poetician who is concerned with story analysis should try to discover the principles which govern those strings of actions and situations which we recognize as stories. It will be recalled that story belongs solely to the objective plane of the narrative text: it is composed of actions and situations as the reader, when he has finished reading the text, imagines them to have occurred; which is by no means how they are actually presented in many texts. We are concerned, to pursue the parallel with linguistics, with underlying structures rather than with those derived structures that are actualized in texts.

A theory of story can start from an obvious and unoriginal, yet important observation: the central feature of all stories—the 'verb', as it were, in story 'syntax'—is change, reversal of fortune, peripeteia. A working hypothesis about story structure can, then, be formulated: there is one basic kind of action in the absence of which no story can exist: the modification, or the attempted or prospective modification, of a situation which affects personages in some significant way; that is to say, which they regard as being either desirable or undesirable. It follows that the effect of a successful modifying action is not only to alter, but also to either improve or worsen, a situation. Stories, then, develop dialectically in three stages: (a) an initial situation; (b) an action which modifies, or which is intended or threatens to modify, the initial situation; and (c) the new situation which emerges as a result of the effects of (b) upon (a). In any given story the process of modification may be repeated a number of times, the resultant situation (c) of one sequence being in turn (for example) subject to change and hence becoming the initial situation (a) of a new sequence. Thus the simplified modern version of the story of *Cinderella* has a tripartite structure, for it contains three modifying actions and therefore three sequences, which can be represented as follows:

1 (a) Cinders is unhappy. (b) Godmother casts spell. (c) Cinders is happy.

2 (a) Cinders is happy. (b) Godmother retracts spell. (c) Cinders is unhappy.

3 (a) Cinders is unhappy. (b) Prince searches for her. (c) Cinders is happy.

Within the pair happiness/unhappiness are subsumed many other pairs of opposites, which are thus implicitly equated in this text: wealth/poverty, love/malevolence, leisure/work, light/darkness, cleanliness/dirt, social superiority/inferiority, integration/rejection. The story turns about this single basic theme, with its constituent sub-themes; it involves two movements, a temporary one followed by a permanent one, of the passive heroine from the negative, undesirable situation represented by the conjunction of the second terms of all the oppositions to the positive, desirable situation represented by the conjunction of the first terms.

Tzvetan Todorov, in *Grammaire du Décaméron* (The Hague: Mouton, 1969) has elaborated a system of story analysis which is based on the hypothesis that change is the defining feature of story.[6] The units of a story are propositions: each proposition

[6] The following account is a simplification of Todorov's method; I indicate in footnotes the principal modifications that I propose.

corresponds to a certain action or situation. Thus (a), (b), and (c) in each of the *Cinderella* sequences are propositions. A proposition is a combination of one or more personages and a predicate, which gives information either about what personages are or about what they do; the former are adjectives, the latter verbs. Propositions which correspond to situations, like (a) and (c) in each sequence of the *Cinderella* story, consist of a personage or personages and an adjective; and propositions which correspond to actions, like the central propositions (b) in each of the sequences of *Cinderella*, consist of a personage or personages and a verb. Each process which takes the personages

Among other investigations into story structure, the following are worth attention: C. Bremond, 'Combinaisons syntaxiques entre fonctions et séquences narratives', in *Sign, Language, Culture*, ed. A. J. Greimas *et al.* (The Hague: Mouton, 1970), pp. 585–90; Bremond, 'Morphology of the French Folktale, *Semiotica*, 2 (1970), 247–76; Bremond, Observations sur la *Grammaire du Décaméron', Poétique*, 6 (1971), 200–22; Seymour Chatman, 'New Ways of Analyzing Narrative Structure'; *Communications*, 8 (1966): 'L'analyse structurale du récit'; Eugene Dorfman, *The Narreme in the Medieval Romance Epic: An Introduction to Narrative Structures* (Manchester: Manchester University Press, 1969); Alan Dundes, *The Morphology of North American Indian Folktales* (Helsinki, 1964); Gérard Genette, 'Vraisemblance et motivation', *Figures II* (Paris: Seuil, 1969), pp. 71–99; A. J. Greimas, *Sémantique structurale* (Paris: Larousse, 1966); Greimas, *Du sens* (Paris: Seuil, 1970); Frank Kermode, *The Sense of an Ending* (New York and London: Oxford University Press, 1967); Edmund Leach, ed., *The Structural Study of Myth and Totemism*, A.S.A. Monographs, No. 5 (London: Tavistock, 1967); Claude Lévi-Strauss, 'The Structural Study of Myth', *Structural Anthropology*, trans. Claire Jacobson and Brooke Grundfest Schoepf (London: Allen Lane, 1968), pp. 206–31; Bertel Nathhorst, *Formal or Structural Studies of Traditional Tales*, Stockholm University Studies in Comparative Religion, No. 9 (Stockholm, 1969); Vladimir Propp, *Morphology of the Folktale*, trans. Laurence Scott, second ed., rev. and ed. by Louis A. Wagner (Austin: University of Texas Press, 1968); Propp, 'Les transformations des contes fantastiques', in *Théorie de la littérature: Textes des formalistes russes*, trans. and ed. Tzvetan Todorov (Paris: Seuil, 1965), pp. 234–62; Tzvetan Todorov, 'Poétique', in O. Ducrot *et al.*, *Qu'est-ce que le structuralisme?* (Paris: Seuil, 1968), pp. 97–166; Todorov, 'La grammaire du récit' and 'Les transformations narratives', in *Poétique de la prose* (Paris: Seuil, 1971), pp. 118–28 and 225–40; B. Tomachevski, 'Thématique', in *Théorie de la littérature*, ed. Todorov, pp. 263–307.

from an initial situation, which will be represented by one or more adjectival propositions, through a modification or threatened or attempted modification, represented by one or more verbal propositions, to a resultant situation, represented by one or more adjectival propositions, is a complete sequence. A story is composed either of one such sequence, or of several interrelated sequences.[7]

Within each sequence propositions can be related in two ways: logically, where one proposition represents the direct result of the preceding one, and temporally, where one proposition simply follows another in time, or is concurrent with it. In the *Cinderella* story, propositions (a) and (b) are in each sequence related temporally, and (b) and (c) logically: a verbal proposition is always related logically with an immediately succeeding proposition, which by definition must represent the direct result of the action concerned.

Todorov proposes some simple formulae to represent all this. Personages are indicated by the use of capitals X, Y, etc.; adjectives by A, B, etc.; and verbs by a, b, etc.[8] The logical

[7] Parts of Todorov's terminology can be improved. He uses the term 'agent' for all personages involved in a story. In fact personages can properly be called agents only when they are related to predicates representing actions, while the term 'patient' would be more accurate for personages when they are related to predicates representing situations. In addition, recent developments in linguistics cast doubt on the traditional distinction between verbs and adjectives. What Todorov calls 'verbs' would, for example, be called 'action verbs' by Chafe; he would re-christen 'adjectives' as 'state verbs' (Wallace L. Chafe, *Meaning and the Structure of Language*, Chicago: University of Chicago Press, 1970; see also Charles J. Fillmore, 'The Case for Case', in Emmon Bach and Robert T. Harms, eds., *Universals in Linguistic Theory*, New York: Holt, Rinehart and Winston, 1968, pp. 1–88). I retain the traditional terms for the sake of convenience.

Todorov's definition of the sequence is uncertain. Some of the sequences he formulates involve a chain of separate processes of modification. He would probably represent *Cinderella* as one sequence: Cinders is unhappy/Godmother casts spell/Cinders is happy/Godmother retracts spell/Cinders is unhappy/Prince searches/Cinders is happy. It seems sounder to use a constant definition of the sequence as a unitary process.

[8] Todorov's postulation of two other types of verb, 'to sin' and 'to punish', is an unnecessary and arbitrary complication of his system. However often

relationship between propositions is indicated by an arrow, $\Rightarrow$; the temporal relationship by a plus sign, $+$. If adjectives are seen in terms of pairs of opposites, then positive adjectives, standing for what are presented in the text as desirable situations, can be left unmarked, and their opposites (or negations) can be represented by the sign $-$. Verbs, also, can be opposed or negated: an actual or threatened modification can be met by an attempt to forestall or counter it. But it is not in practice convenient to represent such counter-modifying actions as $-a$, $-b$, etc., since it often happens in complex sequences, where the initial situation affects various personages in different ways and therefore has to be represented by several different propositions standing for conflicting desires and interests, that the same action is a modifier of some preceding propositions and a counter-modifier of others. It is better, then, to use the letters a, b, etc., both for modifiers and for counter-modifiers.[9]

The analysis of the story of *Cinderella* could, then, be re-written thus:

X Cinderella   Y Godmother   Z Prince
a to transform   b to search   A happy

(1) X–A + Ya $\Rightarrow$ XA

(2) XA + Ya $\Rightarrow$ X–A

(3) X–A + Zb $\Rightarrow$ XA

Such use of formulae provokes immediate hostility in many quarters; but I do not believe that there is really anything so inherently objectionable about it, and it does seem to offer certain important advantages. It would not be very sensible to reject a tool of analysis on the grounds of mere instinctive prejudice without seeing if it has anything positive to offer. Formulae are, at the very least, a convenient shorthand, which

situations of sinfulness and retribution may occur in the *Decameron*, they should be considered as adjectives, together with all the other types of situation in which personages can find themselves in stories; and verbs should be regarded as exclusively representing acts of modification.

[9] Todorov does not discuss the concept of the counter-modifier.

enables much more information to be set down in a given space than would otherwise be possible. The analysis of complex stories consisting of many long sequences intricately interrelated in various ways would simply not fit on to a page if presented in words. But there is another even more important point. The formulaic diagram, unlike any description in words, represents an abstract model of a story: the formulae give, in a precise and unambiguous way, its 'syntactic' structure (or, at least, they give a precise and unambiguous representation of my reading and analysis of its 'syntactic' structure), for which the key provides 'semantic' clothing. The use of neutral letters like X, Y, A, B, a, b, makes for a useful gain in generality; the *Cinderella* key can be replaced by others, to generate other stories that might appear to be quite disparate, but which can thus be shown to be isomorphic. If, for example, we rewrite the key as: X, a political leader; Y, the electorate; Z, the military; a, to vote; b, to rebel; A, powerful: then we have the basic story of many political novels. Or: X, an English Army officer; Y, a German guard; Z, a brave English private; a, to act treacherously; b, to sacrifice oneself; A, free: and we have the broad outlines of a characteristic story of a wartime escape from a concentration camp. Or yet again: X, Segismundo; Y, Basilio; Z, a soldier; a, to impose authority; b, to rebel; A, free: and there is the main plot of Calderón's *La vida es sueño*.

It is thus possible to distinguish between a story's 'syntactic' and its 'semantic' structures. The analysis of the former concerns the patterns of relationship between propositions within sequences, and between sequences within the story as a whole; the analysis of the latter concerns the verbs and adjectives that occur in the story, and brings us back to the study of themes, conceived as a series of oppositions combined in dialectical interplay. To return yet again to the parallel with linguistics, one could say that just as the linguisticians' concern is not so much the individual sentences that he studies but rather, through them, the sentence as an abstract concept, so story analysis should not stop with the particular features of individual stories but should direct itself at the abstract concept of the story. Formulae make it possible to achieve the necessary generalization and abstraction. To put it at its most extreme, they give the poetician, in principle, the chance of constructing a finite number of models which, together with the application of a set of transformational rules, will generate all the stories possible in narrative literature.[10]

This is indeed an extreme claim; for one thing, because what Todorov's method analyses is not in fact the story itself but a paraphrase of the story; and there is, as yet, no method for achieving a consistent degree of paraphrase for all stories. In my simple *Cinderella* illustration, for example, I have omitted such details as the mother's death and the father's remarriage, the conversion of the pumpkin into a stagecoach and of the mice into footmen, Cinderella's relationship with her stepsisters, her loss of a slipper, and so on—or rather I have abstracted them and included them in such generalized propositions as 'the God-mother transforms', 'the Prince searches', 'Cinderella is un-happy'. What I have attempted to do is to reduce the story to its necessary bare outlines; and, indeed, for any overall analysis of the story of a novel to be practicable it is necessary to proceed in this way. Having performed an analysis at this basic level, the incidental details can be seen as expansions or elaborations of the underlying structure it reveals. But according to what criteria are the 'necessary bare outlines' of a story to be traced, and distinguished from its 'incidental details'? For of any story there are many possible paraphrases, ranging from the single sentence to the summary which includes so much detail as to be scarcely shorter than the original. How, other than by instinct, can we decide how much in a story is vital and how much accessory, and establish an appropriate and consistent

[10] Todorov's system is unnecessarily complicated in several other ways. His five moods are, at the moment, a superfluous sophistication, for his analytic method is equally powerful without them; and the notion of sequential ambiguity is dispensable, for two sequences thus interrelated can always in practice be written as one complex sequence. The distinction between opposition and negation, which Todorov makes in his theoretical exposition but not in its practical application, is useful; I have left it aside here only for the sake of simplicity.

level of paraphrase for all stories? These are crucial questions facing story analysis at its present stage of development.

So far little progress has been made in providing answers. Todorov proposes a finite set of fundamental adjectives and verbs; but his proposals are clearly inadequate outside the *Decameron*, and unconvincing even within it, because of wide divergences in degrees of abstraction.[11] But a rationalization and extension of his list could perhaps provide a practical guide for paraphrase. Thus if it were agreed that 'to transform' and 'to search' are among the recurrent basic predicates, then these would be regarded as the verbs of *Cinderella* rather than, for example, the more particularizing 'to cast a spell', 'to retract a spell', or the even more particularizing 'to change a pumpkin into a stagecoach', 'to change mice into footmen', 'to try a slipper on young ladies', and so on. One might, then, try to draw up a list of predicates stated in the most basic possible terms—predicates which, in other words, are incapable of being simplified any further. And certainly, in practical story analysis, the beginnings of such a list does seem to emerge, as predicates fulfilling this condition recur in different texts. But a list compiled on the basis of trial and error—useful as it might be as a rule of thumb—is unlikely to satisfy theoretical demands. For if it is true, as I have suggested, that story predicates can largely be identified with literary themes, and if it is also true—as it surely is, to the point of being a truism—that there are no limits to the scope of literature in its portrayal of the human condition, then a list of universal predicates could hardly be other than an abstracted inventory of human actions and situations, and would therefore be irrelevant to the enquiry of poetics into the distinctive nature of literature. It would follow that the job of poetics is to investigate not themes in themselves but rather the selection and permutation of themes that is at the core of literary texts. Maybe, after all, the only principles needed—or possible—for establishing the appropriate level of paraphrase

[11] Todorov's list of verbs, for example, is as follows: 'travestir ou détravestir; faire un jeu de mots; faire une action physique; appeler à l'aide quelqu'un de plus fort que soi; changer de place; instaurer un système d'échange'.

are those of economy and irreducibility: that the verbs and adjectives be expressed in the fewest and the most abstract terms compatible with that expression remaining meaningful, that is to say with the propositions thus formulated retaining their full functional value within the structure of the story, and with the network of relationships which constitutes the story being left intact. Similar principles apply to establishment of the themes in terms of which character and setting analysis are to be carried out, where the same problem of paraphrase and abstraction has to be confronted.[12]

The modifications I have proposed to Todorov's method of story analysis simplify it to such an extent that it might seem, as Jonathan Culler (to whom I am indebted for many helpful suggestions) has proposed, that what I am left with is no longer a theory of story at all, but merely a metalanguage for talking about story. I believe, however, that the development of this metalanguage supposes and implies a theory about the way stories work. The method of analysis I have described produces at this stage only the most elementary theory; but it is surely necessary to proceed systematically and begin with fundamental problems before moving on to more complex considerations.

[12] An approach to the paraphrase problem which appears more theoretical has been essayed in a recent article by L. Doležel, 'Toward a Structural Theory of Content in Prose Fiction', in *Literary Style: A Symposium*, ed. Seymour Chatman (New York and London: Oxford University Press, 1971), pp. 95–110. Doležel suggests the idea of a 'set of explicit and controlled rewrite instructions' for the production of paraphrases of narrative texts at a consistent level of condensation. Yet 'the critical point in the paraphrasing procedure' is the assignment of terms in the text to 'their abstract equivalence classes' (in my terms, predicates or themes), for which operation Doležel admits that 'no satisfactory criterion ... is known', concluding that 'we are entirely dependent on trial and error': back, then, to square one.

In terms of 'semanticist' linguistics (see above, note 7), one could formulate a paraphrase rule for this primary stage of story analysis as follows: reduce the story to the central action verbs and state verbs involved and the personages related to them as, respectively, agents and patients; and eliminate all other elements, such as nouns which are not personages, nouns related to verbs in other ways, noun and verb inflection, etc.

In examining narrative mode one is concerned with the ways in which the novel's objective world of character, story and setting may be actualized in the text itself. Hence a narrator may report the events of his story in detail, dramatizing them, giving full accounts of conversations in direct speech, and generally seeking to give the reader the impression of witnessing events as they happen, with little or no mediation; or he may prefer economy to vividness, summarizing events more or less briefly. Any single proposition might, then, be actualized in a few words or in many pages; and the same distinction between specific and general methods of narration applies to character and setting. Furthermore, the narrator may write about his created world in the guise of an omniscient observer, who is free to tell the reader at any time anything about this world he thinks the reader ought to know; or he may write from the point of view of one of his personages, pretending to suppress himself and report only that which the personage could be aware of; or he may describe events as an unknowing independent witness would see them. The narrator's attitude towards his reader can vary from the remote to the intimate. He is always in a position to control the flow of time at will, speeding or slowing it as he sees fit, or disordering it completely. Such narrative techniques, as they actualize character, story and setting, add to their complexity by creating new combinations and relationships. What Wayne C. Booth has called the 'implied author' and has studied in *The Rhetoric of Fiction* (Chicago: University of Chicago Press, 1961) is another aspect of narrative mode, as I define the term. An important function of the implied author is that of moral definition: the establishment, either by direct statement or indirectly, through irony, humour, or simple unspoken assumption, of the standards according to which the reader is required to interpret the text. The implied author, in other words, provides a moral framework for the text, which limits its plurality. A literary work has a multiplicity of meanings, but not an infinity of meanings: indeed an infinity of meanings—total freedom for the reader to interpret the work as he pleases—would be the same as no meaning. The implied author lays down these necessary limits, without necessarily restricting the work to just one fundamental meaning, as Booth would have it. The framework that the implied author establishes may leave room for multiple interpretations of the text, but it rules some interpretations quite firmly out.

The interest of many narrative texts, especially modern ones, is centred on narrative mode rather than story, character or setting: the application of Todorov's method of story analysis to a text like *Eveline* does not, by itself, produce very interesting results (one sequence involving the eventual non-modification of the heroine's initial situation, after the intervention of various modifying and counter-modifying actions) precisely because it is not the story of *Eveline* but its narrative mode which is interesting. Narrative mode is such an important, extensive and complex concept that there is room here for an investigation of only one aspect of its functioning in *El amigo Manso*: the use of a protagonist-narrator to facilitate the development of an extensive enigma surrounding the events of the story, which are thus confused and complicated in the course of their textual actualization.

In story analysis according to the principles I have outlined, one looks for the various central processes of change each of which can be written out as one complete sequence. The basic story of *El amigo Manso* seems, then, to be composed of four sequences. The one which starts first in the text is that which involves Manso's education of Peña; it could be represented thus:

$$(1)\ XA + Y\text{--}A + YZ\text{--}B \Rightarrow Za \Rightarrow Xb \Rightarrow Y\text{--}A + YZB + X\text{--}A$$

where X stands for Manso, Y Peña, Z Doña Javiera, A 'rational, ordered', B 'socially superior', a 'to appeal for help', and b 'to help'. The two modifying propositions—the second direct, the first indirect, for it cannot give rise immediately to a resultant proposition, but only to another modifying proposition—fail to convert Y–A into YA, but ironically achieve another unintended modification, of XA into X–A, as Manso, under the influence of his pupil, loses serenity and orderliness. The roles

of the initial adjectival propositions XA and Y–A are reversed: Y–A originally represented the situation to be changed,
and XA the motivation of the personages who sought the
change: since Manso is rational, it appears to him and to
Doña Javiera that he is the one to impart rationality to Peña.
But in fact XA turns out to be the situation that is changed,
and Y–A the motivation. At the same time as all this is going
on, the intervention of Manso, while not making Peña into a
rational being, does give him enough polish and general knowledge to perfect his natural flair and turn him into a brilliant
orator, and thus opens the way to the social improvement of
him and his mother: YZ–B . . . $\Rightarrow$ YZB.

The second sequence to be initiated concerns Manso's helping
of his brother José María out of his various difficulties upon his
arrival in Madrid. The sequence involves several separate
actions, all of which contribute to this end: Manso finds accom-
modation for José María and his family when they arrive; he
finds a governess, Irene, for his children; and, finally, he even
searches out a wet-nurse for his infant. The effect of all this
activity is to establish José María in Madrid society and so to
make his rapid social climb possible. The most important of
the various actions summarized and brought together in this
sequence is the establishing of Irene in José María's house,
which should be seen in terms of social ambitions; she desires to
improve her humble status, and to this end she has acquired an
education—but her employment as governess does not, after
all, take her very far towards this goal. As Manso unwillingly
becomes involved in his brother's affairs, he sacrifices more of
the orderliness of his life. Hence:

$$(2)\ XA + V\text{–}B + W\text{–}B \Rightarrow Va \Rightarrow Xb \Rightarrow VB + W\text{–}B + X\text{–}A$$

where, in addition to the symbols already used and explained,
V represents José María and W Irene.

The third series of events is the central and most complex
one. It concerns the amatory interest of the three men, Manso,
José María and Peña, in Irene, her attitudes towards them, and
the resolution of the conflicts involved. Also bound up in this

process is Manso's most castastrophic loss of rationality, culminating in his death, as a result of the revelation of the truth about Irene and her marriage to Peña. It has to be written out as two sequences, the initial proposition of the second taking up the resultant proposition of the first:

$$(3)\ XA + W\text{--}A + XW\text{--}C + VW\text{--}C + W\text{--}B + YB + WY\text{--}C$$

$$\Rightarrow XVYc \Rightarrow WYd \Rightarrow XW\text{--}C + VW\text{--}C + WYC$$

$$(4)\ WYC + WY\text{--}D + ZB \Rightarrow WYe \Rightarrow Za \Rightarrow Xb$$

$$\Rightarrow WYa \Rightarrow Xb \Rightarrow WYD \Rightarrow WB \Rightarrow X\text{--}A$$

where, in addition to symbols already used, C represents 'in amatory relationship', D 'in marital relationship', c 'to woo', d 'to dissemble', and e 'to reveal'. Sequence 3 involves the three men's interest in Irene, each one's pursual of her, and the concealment she and Peña resort to in order to achieve the desired relationship.[13] Its initial situation is complex, affecting all the personages except Doña Javiera, and it therefore has to be broken down into several different propositions representing each of its relevant aspects. Not all the propositions are subject to modification: W–A and YB, and, in sequence 4, ZB, simply represent the motives of, respectively, Irene, for not being attracted to Manso, Irene again, for preferring Peña, and Doña Javiera, for opposing the prospective marriage between Peña and Irene and appealing to Manso for help in preventing it. Sequence 4 represents how Peña and Irene, having achieved the desired modification WY–C . . . $\Rightarrow$ WYC, now set about making their relationship permanent, WY–D . . . $\Rightarrow$ WYD. In order to do so it is necessary for them to undo the effects of the direct modifier WYd of sequence 3: hence WYe. This sets off a chain of verbal propositions, of which Za $\Rightarrow$ Xb are counter-modifiers, and the following VYa $\Rightarrow$ Xb,

[13] It will be remembered that it is the events of the narrative as they 'actually' happened that are analysed, not those events as the reader and Manso see—or fail to see—them at the time; and that a proposition containing a ' – ' sign represents not only the nonexistence of the situation indicated by the adjective but also the fact that this non-existence is undesirable from the point of view of the patient.

like WYe, modifiers. Sequence 4 contains two other modification processes, in addition to WY–D . . . ⇒ WYD: XA and W–B, both 'carried over' from a sequence 3, are inverted.

The three separate series of events are interrelated in a different way from the sequences in the other tripartite story I have analysed, that of *Cinderella*. Here the sequences do not follow each other, one starting with the situation left as a result of the previous one, though this is the type of relationship between sequences 3 and 4, and W–B from 2 is taken up in 3. They rather represent three more or less concurrent series of events; and their interrelationship is based on the fact that they all start at the same point, represented by the proposition XA, and end similarly with X–A. They show the various ways in which the ordered life of Manso—a man who has always lived in artificial isolation from the world and its problems—is disrupted and destroyed, as a result of his exposure to and involvement in everyday affairs, and in particular in the striving of others for precisely the sort of worldly success that Manso himself considers petty and unworthy. There is a repeated pattern in the sequences; some other personage addresses an appeal for help to Manso, and he responds positively; he helps the other towards his goal, which in each case ultimately amounts to social climbing, but in so doing loses his own most prized and vital attribute, rationality. In the course of the novel Manso responds to such appeals from every one of the other main personages:

$$XA + YZVW–B \Rightarrow YZVWa \Rightarrow Xb \Rightarrow YZVWB + X–A$$

The story of *El amigo Manso* is, then, a moderately complex intertwining of actions, situations and themes, in which Manso is clearly the central figure. He appears in a light both heroic and comic: he achieves for all others what they desire, which happens to be precisely what he disparages, yet in doing so he sacrifices his own most essential quality, and hence ultimately himself. Rather than the wise guide and teacher of others, as he fondly imagines himself to be, he is shown in practice to be their errandboy, or indeed their wet-nurse: a domesticated friend of the family (*manso* means 'tame') who earns his keep by making himself busy about the house, performing various humble, even degrading tasks.

Such is the underlying story structure of *El amigo Manso*; I now propose to examine the novel's enigma and its effects on the story. The enigma plays an important role in all narrative literature: Galdós makes much use of it; Roland Barthes, in *S/Z* (Paris: Seuil, 1970), has examined the development of the enigma in a short story of Balzac, in his study of what he calls its 'hermeneutic code'; and Todorov has done similar work with the stories of Henry James.[14]

The creation of an enigma is facilitated in *El amigo Manso* by the use of a protagonist-narrator whose view of events is severely impaired. What is hidden from Manso is also hidden from the reader, though the latter sometimes suspects certain facts before Manso does, as the implied author makes indirect comments behind his back, as it were. As the novel advances, a succession of questions presents itself to the reader; and as the questions accumulate so the enigma, built around the figure of Irene, grows and dominates the novel. The individual questions of which the enigma is built are the following, listed in order of appearance:[15]

1. What is Irene really like? (p. 62)
2. What does Irene read late at night? (p. 68)
3. Why is Irene unhappy as a governess? (p. 79)
4. What are Irene's reactions to José María's advances? (p. 98)
5. How cultured really is Irene? (p. 103)
6. How rational really is Irene? (p. 103)
7. What role has Irene played in Doña Cándida's move of house? (p. 111)
8. What is happening under the surface of events? (p. 132)

[14] 'Le secret du récit' and 'Les fantômes de Henry James', in *Poétique de la prose*, pp. 151–85 and 186–96.

[15] Page references throughout are to the 1954 Austral (Buenos Aires) edition.

9. What role has Irene played in Doña Cándida's enrichment? (p. 133)
10. Why is Irene leaving to live with Doña Cándida? (p. 134)
11 = 4. What are Irene's reactions to José María's advances? (p. 137)
12. Is Irene a hypocrite? (p. 138)
13. Is Irene receiving love-letters from José María? (p. 138)
14 = 9. What role has Irene played in Doña Cándida's enrichment? (p. 139)
15. What danger is Irene now in? (p. 143)
16 = 11 = 4. What are Irene's reactions to José María's advances? (p. 148)
17. Is Irene ill? (p. 151)
18 = 15. What danger is Irene in? (p. 151)
19. What is the relationship between Irene and Doña Cándida? (p. 151)
20. Who was hiding in Doña Cándida's house, and why? (p. 152)
21 = 10. Why did Irene leave to live with Doña Cándida? (p. 153)
22 = 8. What is happening under the surface of events? (p. 154)
23. What is Irene guilty of? (p. 155)
24. Who is Irene's boyfriend? (p. 158)
25. Did José María seriously pursue Irene? (p. 163)
26 = 12. Is Irene a hypocrite? (p. 166)
27 = 25. Did José María seriously pursue Irene? (p. 169)

Most of the questions are directly posed by the protagonist-narrator, like question 2:

What might she be reading? This was the subject of my profound meditation during the time I took to arrive home, and that enigma pursued me until I fell asleep, after reading a short while myself. And what did I read? I opened some of the books of my most ardent devotion—I cannot remember which ones—and I sated myself with poetry and idealism.

When I awoke, I asked myself once more, 'What might she be reading?' And while I was giving my lessons, I kept seeing, between the clauses and the maxims, just as one sees the light through the mesh of a sieve, the same question about Irene's reading. (p. 68)

A few pages later the question is repeated and elaborated, as Manso characteristically provides an optimistic and totally wrong answer:

I went to Irene's room, and I forgot everything upon seeing her. I did not hear her reply to my greeting, and I asked her, 'What were you reading last night?'
   And, like someone who sees one of his most precious secrets uncovered, she became confused, she could not answer, she hesitated, she pronounced two or three evasive phrases, and then asked me some question. I interpreted her question in a way favourable to my person, saying to myself, 'Perhaps she was reading something of mine.' But then I thought that, since I had not written any work of entertainment, if she was in fact reading anything of mine, it must have been either *Memorandum on Psychogenesis and Neurosis*, or *Commentaries on Du Bois-Raymond*, or *Translations from Hundt*, or maybe my articles refuting *Transformism* and Haeckel's crazy theories. The very dryness of these subjects provided a subtle explanation for the flush and the displeasure I noted in my friend's face, because 'no doubt', as I calculated, 'she does not wish to tell me she was reading such things, in order not to appear a pedantic know-all'. (p. 75)

The narrator thus provides an answer to his question, an answer which the implied author immediately—in the very process of its formulation, and through the manner of that formulation, a speciously logical argument which is patently no more than rationalized wish-fulfilment—invites the reader to reject. The question thus remains open, in an intensified form, after this elaboration in the shape of a false closure.

   Some questions are indirectly suggested by the implied author in the course of the narration, without Manso's having formulated them. Question 1 is of this sort. Manso's praise of Irene is so fulsome, he sees her as such an impossibly perfect woman, that the suspicion must arise in the reader's mind that Manso is not describing Irene at all, but rather a projection of his own abstract principles and ideals:

Fault could certainly be found with her physical features, but what rigid professor of aesthetics would dare to criticise her expression, that quivering surface of the soul, which could be seen in all of her and in no part of her, always and never, in her eyes and in the echo of her voice, where she was and where she was not, that shimmer of air that surrounded her, that hiatus she left behind when she went away—or, to put it more plainly, all those things that revealed her contentment with her condition, her serenity, the placid disposition of her spirit? Forming the nucleus of all these modes of expression I could perceive her pure conscience and the rectitude of her moral principles ... Her aplomb revealed a superior nature in splendid equilibrium. She seemed a woman of the North, born and brought up far from our enervating Spanish climate and this harmful moral environment ... Here was the perfect woman, positive woman, rational woman, the opposite of frivolous woman, capricious woman. (pp. 60–2)

In one of these two ways, explicitly or implicitly, each of the individual questions is articulated. The total enigma is a structure composed of these questions interrelated in various ways. Three types of relationships can be discerned:

Logical relationship; the posing of one question has as its direct logical consequence the posing of another, which thus immediately follows it. Questions 5 and 6, for example, are thus related: Irene's revelation that her general culture is less sound than Manso had assumed lays her rationality open to doubt.

Temporal relationship; one question follows another in the course of events, possibly in the absence of any other relationship with it. Thus new areas of enigma can suddenly be opened up. Questions 14 and 15 exemplify this process: the news that Irene is in danger introduces a fresh mystery into the narration, and intensifies the enigma by violently widening its perspectives.

Sequential relationship; one question takes up the area of enigma already explored by previous questions, and re-explores it, essaying new approaches. Thus sequences of questions, each sequence concerned with one aspect of the central enigma, are formed. This is the most important type of relationship between questions. In *El amigo Manso* there are three such sequences: questions 2, 3, 5 and 6 refer to Irene's intellectual standing and her rationality; questions 4, 7, 9, 10, 11, 12, 13, 14, 16, 19, 21, 23, 24, 25, 26 and 27 are about her morality, and more specifically her relations with José María: questions 15, 17, 18 and 20 concern her health and physical safety. Within any sequence there may be questions which are reiterations of earlier ones: this occurs when new circumstances, or the revelation of facts not previously known, give a question already asked a new relevance and thus turn it, in fact, into a different question even though it has the same form. The reader is likely to expect an answer to any question to suggest answers to the other questions in the same sequence, but not to questions in other sequences.

There remain three questions—1, 8, and its reiteration 22— that do not belong in any sequence: they are direct statements of the central enigma in general terms. The central enigma is only likely to be solved as a result of the answering of all the individual questions in all the sequences.

The structure of the enigma as it is posed in *El amigo Manso* can be represented by the following diagram. Only questions 1 to 20 are shown, because with question 21 the solution of the enigma commences, and this needs separate consideration:

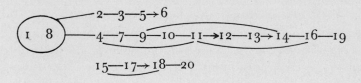

The numbers identify questions and indicate temporal relationships: the arrows indicate logical relationships; sequential relationships are indicated in the horizontal chains of questions; reiterations are indicated by curved lines.

The sequence concerning Irene's rationality dominates the narrative as far as page 111. Up to this point only question 4 suggests that the enigma is about anything other than Irene's intellectual status. The sequence concerning morality soon takes over, however, and once it is under way the interest in Irene's rationality fades; for Manso, though, moral uprightness is an integral part of true rationality.[16] After question 7, and as the morality sequence develops, the rate at which new questions are asked increases, and the enigma becomes more and more dominant in the novel. The second direct formulation of the enigma, question 8, occurs at this strategic point.

Throughout the morality sequence two associated suspicions develop, and create twin expectations: that Manso has a rival for Irene's affection, and that that rival is José María. At the moment of revelation the former, general suspicion will be confirmed, but the latter, specific one will be proved false. The revelation will come as at the same time a confirmation and a denial of expectations; it will be surprising yet not arbitrary, as a result of a controlled and modified use of the well-known technique of the red herring.

The sequence concerning Irene's physical well-being is the last of the three sequences to appear, shortly before the point where answers to the various questions begin to be suggested. It brings a new and unexpected perspective to the enigma; and in its way it is another red herring, for the suspicion it arouses that Irene is ill or in danger is unfounded: she is merely suffering from stress, which disappears as soon as things begin to go well for her. This sequence functions as a final pre-climactic diversion which further intensifies the enigma.

Just as the enigma grows gradually through a series of questions, so it is solved in a series of individual and partial answers. Each answer refers to a specific question, and in answering it provides consequential answers to other questions in the same sequence, as expected: but many answers fail to comply exactly with this pattern, either by not providing consequential answers to all the other questions in the sequence, or by unexpectedly suggesting answers to questions in other sequences, thus establishing new relationships between sequences, and disturbing the thematic grouping of the questions. Answers thus tend, either by doing less or by doing more than expected, to complicate matters still further, and so to add to rather than reduce the enigma, to open rather than close it. The effect of an

[16] See, for example, the passage quoted above, p. 203.

answer of this type is to generate a fresh question: questions 21 to 27 are all produced in this way. Things are further complicated by the fact that all answers in this novel are provided by personages who may well be mistaken or telling lies; no answer can be regarded as definitive, at least until some acceptable general solution is produced. The process of the solving of the enigma in *El amigo Manso* is as follows:

Answer 1; Irene states (p. 153) that Doña Cándida is attempting to procure her for José María. Question 19 is answered, and consequently (if the answer is accepted as correct) all the other questions in the morality sequence—except question 10. Questions 18 and 15, from the health sequence, are also answered: this answer both does more and does less than expected. The failure of answer 1 to provide any reply to question 10 is important, as Manso realizes. He therefore reiterates the latter (question 21). This in turn leads to the explicit reiteration of question 8 (as question 22), another direct articulation of the central enigma at a key point in the narrative. A partial, unsatisfactory answer only adds to the enigma.

Answer 2; Irene reveals (p. 155) that Manso's suspicions are well-founded, for she feels guilty about something. Answer 1 becomes even more suspect. The second partial answer further intensifies the enigma, giving rise to question 23: what is Irene guilty of? Suspense is now increased by the entry of Doña Cándida, which interrupts the dialogue between Manso and Irene and delays the answer to question 23.

Answer 3; according to Doña Cándida, Irene feels guilty because she has a secret boyfriend (p. 158). This answer, like the previous one, narrows the field of enquiry while generating another question: who is the boyfriend (question 24)? It also implies an answer to question 17, and hence establishes another relationship between the morality sequence and the health sequence: Irene is not so much ill as under strain because of the predicament in which she finds herself. An answer to question 12 is also implied: Irene is indeed a hypocrite, having been guilty of consistently underhand behaviour. In that case, answer 1 must be discounted, and all the questions that seemed to have been settled by it are reopened. Hence question 25: has José María's behaviour really been as wretched as Irene claimed? At this moment the entry of José María himself delays the answer to question 24, but facilitates an answer to question 25.

Answer 4; José María declares that he had merely made to Irene the kind of tentative overtures that any warm-blooded man would make to an attractive and possibly accessible woman (p. 163). After four contradictory and partial answers and three showdowns, the enigma is more dense and puzzling than ever. The accumulation of doubts leads to the explicit reiteration of questions 12 and 25, as 26 and 27.

Answer 5; Doña Cándida returns to state (p. 169) that the truth of the matter is that José María laid siege to the two women in order to gain access to Irene. Answers 1 and 4 are contradicted, and a third set of answers is suggested for the questions they refer to. The text itself gives no reason for preferring any one of the three conflicting answers.

Answer 6; Manso stumbles across the answer to what is now the key question, 24: Peña is Irene's boyfriend (p. 172). It is the first answer which seems truthful, for there is no element in it of self-justification; and now there are no new questions. Answer 6 also implies answers to questions 23, 22, 21, 12 and 10. It adds to the uncomfortable irony of Manso's position: his use of logical reasoning has led him to the conclusion that José María is his rival, and his interrogation of each of the individuals concerned has confirmed this belief; and now he discovers the truth in a quite irrational way, through a sudden hunch. So much for the values on which he has built his life.

Answer 7; Peña states (p. 173) that he was the man hiding in Doña Cándida's house, in order to attack his rival José María.

Answer 8; in the course of the conversation with Peña, Manso comes to the conclusion (p. 175) that Irene has, after all, been telling the truth about José María; and answer 1, which claims to settle many questions, is confirmed in his mind.

Answer 9; Irene reveals (p. 185) that she had stayed up late at night reading Peña's love-letters. Questions 2 and 13 are settled.

Answer 10; Manso finally comes to the conclusion (by p. 196) that Irene is not the rational being for which he had taken her. The remaining questions, 3, 5, and 6, are answered.

And so the enigma is solved—or is it? The contradiction between answers 1, 4 and 5 remains; for although answer 8 seems to confirm answer 1, the other possible solutions suggested by 4 and 5 are by no means overruled: Manso's willingness to believe Irene is not shared by the reader. Perhaps Doña Cándida was not so wicked and ruthless as Irene makes out, nor José María so insistent as the two women pretend: the truth about events is, maybe, not so clear-cut and melodramatic as answer 1 suggests. None of answers 1, 4 and 5 can be discounted, and the reader is not invited to make a final choice between them. Each contains a portion of the truth, and the three together build up a coherent picture of a complex situation. In the plurality of its solution the enigma in *El amigo Manso* differs from that in, for example, a detective tale like *The Sussex Vampire*, where answers are simple, definitive and absolute, and close all questions totally and unambiguously.

Three stages can be distinguished in the overall structure of the enigma in *El amigo Manso*: (i) the posing of the enigma, built up of a series of questions (1–20) which form sequences each one of which deals with a separate area of the enigma, whose rate of occurrence quickens throughout, and into which various types of diversion are introduced; leading into (ii) the development towards the climax, through a series of partial answers, delayed answers and suspect answers (1–5), all of which intensify the enigma, modifying and complicating its structure and generating new questions (21–7), at the same time as they narrow the field of enquiry, concentrating the area of the enigma; and so leading into (iii) the climax in the definitive answer (6), the anti-climax in the answering of remaining questions (7–10), and hence the solution of the enigma, the completion of its structure.

The effect of enigma on story is to place it in a new perspective, establishing a different but concurrent series of relationships between the propositions that constitute it. The morality sequence principally involves the attribute C, and the rationality sequence A; but all the story's propositions come into the enigma in one way or another. Because of the enigma, the full story structure only becomes apparent to narrator and reader towards the end of the text, when the enigma is solved. The enigma thus transforms the underlying story structure as it is actualized in the text: the order in which propositions are presented to the reader is not the same as the order in which I have represented them in the four sequences.

The study of narrative mode as it affects story, of which the study of enigma is one part, looks for the principles governing the relations between the underlying story strings (sequences) and their actualization in the text, presuming always that there are such principles, in other words that the processes of actualization are indeed rule-governed—that, for example, the propositions of a story cannot be actualized in absolutely any order, but that there are constraints to this reordering. The enigma causes the story of *El amigo Manso* to be revealed in two stages. Only the least important parts (sequences 1 and 2 except W–B . . . ⇒ W–B) are revealed as they 'actually' happen. Although the two sequences are intermingled in their exposition, the propositions of each sequence appear in the text in chronological order, and the relationships between them are immediately clear. Derived story structure is here, in other words, an elaboration and expansion but not a reshaping of underlying story structure. The truth about the events of the central sequences 3 and 4 is, however, revealed only after most of these events have taken place. The propositions are not actualized in the text in their chronological order, nor are any relations between them established, until the solution of the enigma reveals the structure of the underlying story strings. A few of the propositions (XA, XW–C, VW–C, W–B and YB) are actualized early in the text, but their relevance remains hidden; they are not interrelated in any way, their function in the story is not revealed. All the other propositions in the two sequences up to the key modifier WYe are also hidden, until that modifier sets in motion the process of the enigma's solution —that is to say, the full constitution in the reader's mind of the structure of the two sequences up to WYe. The remaining verbal and resultant propositions of sequence 4 are then actualized in chronological order.

El amigo Manso thus has, in a sense, two different but complementary narrative processes: one made up of the events themselves, and the other of Manso's and the reader's quest for the truth about those events. The story is an extended question directed at the future—what will happen? The enigma is an extended question directed at the present and the past—what is happening and what has happened?

The enigma in *El amigo Manso* does not only affect its story, however, but also its characterization, where its principal effect is to contribute to the establishment of relationships between Irene and Manso, and to strengthen the position of the former. Just as the story concentrates attention on Manso, so the enigma concentrates attention on Irene. Manso appears in the enigma as an impotent outsider, who is kept in the dark about events until it is too late to do anything about them: Irene the mystifier, Manso the mystified. Since intellectuals are supposed to find the answers to problems, the enigma accumulates irony at Manso's expense and thus contributes to the theme rationality/ irrationality.

Only some narrative texts are built, like *El amigo Manso*, round a major, extended enigma; but none is free from enigmas, even if they are of a more incidental, sporadic type. At the beginning of every novel there are many potential enigmas, regarding the antecedents of the personages that are introduced and often shown in action before anything is revealed about them. Some narrators go on to give a rapid solution to such enigmas in the summarized biography characteristic of much realistic fiction; others prolong the enigma by omitting any such survey and only allowing information about the personages to gradually emerge in the course of the narrative. The enigma is, at any rate, an important part of narrative mode, and any theory of narrative should include a theory of enigma.

Story, character, setting and narrative mode—the reader will now, I hope, be in a position to judge whether the division of texts into these four segments, and the methods of analysis I have suggested for each of them, show possibilities of contributing to a general theory of narrative. What I have proposed is a way of examining the various representational aspects of novels in terms not of their counterparts in real life but of the embodiment and combination in them of literary themes, which can be formulated as abstract oppositions. Themes thus appear as a text's nuclear structure of meaning that organizes the whole and is the purpose of its existence. Although, as I have argued, it seems likely that no general study of themes in themselves can be specifically literary and therefore of interest to the poetician, themes assume a central importance as basic elements of all texts whose structuring in them according to certain definable principles is the object of study. Character embodies various permutations of themes in personages; story works out a dialectical interplay between themes: setting projects the themes into the fictional external world containing story and character; narrative mode actualizes all this, producing as it does so its own combinations of themes on a different plane, that of the text itself, as opposed to that which is described in the text.

Jonathan Culler has set out in his paper some criteria by which I would be happy for the validity of the analytical methods I have sketched out to be assessed. My belief is that they do, on the whole, satisfy his demands. In one place, however, they seem to fail the test: they do not provide any direct explanations about how a reader assigns meanings to a text as he reads it—about, in other words, literary competence, which is the object of study of modern theoretical poetics. For what I have described is a retrospective analysis of a narrative text, an analysis from the point of view of the reader's total knowledge of it after he has read it. I am concerned with the general

principles of composition of a text, which can only be distinguished by, as it were, stepping back and observing it from a
certain distance as a whole structure: Culler is concerned with
methods of concomitant, or 'while-reading' analysis, analysis
from the point of view of the reader's successive states of partial
knowledge of a text at different stages of his progress through it.
I would argue that the two approaches complement each other,
and that both can reveal much about literary competence, the
latter directly and the former indirectly. Literary competence is
the product of the reader's exposure to a certain number of
literary texts; each new text is interpreted on the basis of the
set of expectations created by this exposure, and in turn modifies that set of expectations. The retrospective, overall analysis
of large numbers of texts should enable us to discover the principles according to which they are constructed, which can in
turn be identified with the set of expectations of a hypothetical
ideal or totally competent reader. One expects, for example,
the situation described in a novel one is beginning to be made
subject to forces tending to alter it, and one is guided by this
expectation in one's assignment of meanings and importances to
situations and actions described in the novel, simply because
the modification of an initial situation is one of the principles
governing the stories of all the novels one has previously read.
Barthes has developed in S/Z a method of concomitant analysis,
which sets out to show in concrete detail the way in which a
narrative text unfolds in a constant and intricate interweaving
of character, story, setting, enigma, etc. A retrospective, overall
analysis could provide the framework upon which a Barthes-
type approach, with its closer attention to the text's actual
words and the plurality of its realization, could hang. Both
approaches offer interesting possibilities, and there seems to be
no good reason for preferring one to the exclusion of the other.

CHAPTER SEVEN

THE STRUCTURE
OF NARRATIVE TRANSMISSION

Seymour Chatman

It is popular nowadays to assume that narrative is a semiological or quasi-semiological structure quite separate from the
language or other medium which communicates it. As such it
consists of an expression plane (called 'narrative discourse', or
simply 'discourse') and a content plane (called 'story').[1] The
expression plane contains the set of narrative *statements*, where
'statement' is independent of and more abstract than any
particular manifestation. A certain posture in the ballet, a series
of film shots, a whole paragraph in a novel, or only a single
word—any of these might be the actualizations of a single
narrative statement, since *narrative* as such is independent of
medium. The fundamental narrative verb is DO, or where the
subject is patient, rather than agent, HAPPEN. As Aristotle
maintains, *action* is the fundamental narrative element. Of
course, actions are only performed by (or happen to) actors,
upon or in reference to objects. So we must recognize not only
narrative statements of actions—I will call them PROCESS
statements—but also narrative statements of existence which
I will call EXISTENCE statements (these include descriptions).

Crosscutting this dichotomy is another which is based on
whether the statement is directly presented to the audience or

---

[1] This article is a development of work on the narrative, begun in 'New
Ways of Analyzing Narrative Structure', *Language and Style*, 2 (1969),
pp. 3–36, and continued in 'The Structure of Fiction', *University Review*, 37
(1971), pp. 190–214.

mediated by someone—the someone we call the narrator. Direct presentation presumes a kind of 'overhearing' or 'spying' on the audience's part; in mediated narration, on the other hand, the audience is directly addressed by a narrator. This is essentially the ancient distinction between *mimesis* and *diegesis*, or in modern terms between *showing* and *telling*. Insofar as there is telling, there must be a teller, a narrating voice. To specify the four consequent possibilities, I propose the terms ENACTS (the operation of an unmediated or 'shown' process statement), RECOUNTS (that of a 'told' process statement), PRESENTS (that of a 'shown' stasis statement) and DESCRIBES (that of a 'told' stasis statement). It is essential to understand that 'statement' is used here in an abstract sense, independent of any particular medium. We can still agree with Aristotle that mimesis is the mode of the drama and diegesis that of the dithyramb or pure lyric expression, and that epic or narrative is a mixed mode, combining elements both of direct and imitated speech. Cinema of course can also contain diegetic elements—for instance, captions and legends which help to set the scene or which recount intervening events. And Brecht has brought such devices into the theatre. But the medium of drama is more typically presentational; there do not need to be existence statements, since the existents are simply *there*, on the stage or screen—characters, props, stage-settings. Of course, mixed modes are possible: for instance, a character may narrate a story on stage, or the like. The cinema regularly uses a disembodied narrative voice (technically marked in scripts as 'Voice Over'). It sometimes happens that there is a virtual redundancy—the narrative voice telling exactly what the camera shows; good examples occur in Robert Bresson's film version of Bernanos' *Journal d'un Curé de Campagne*. For this, as for other reasons, the narrative film has affinities with literary narrative that it does not share with plays. Indeed, the term 'narrative film' is often used to distinguish this genre from the 'documentary'. Ballet, too, is radically mimetic; but comic-strips are generally mixed (although a fad for the pantomimic style has recently developed). Literary narrative can be more or less purely mimetic: stories can be written consisting solely of dialogue, for example.

So a central consideration for the theory of narrative is the transmitting source which is postulated. By 'transmission' I simply mean the class of kinds of narrative presentation which includes as its two subclasses showing and telling (always remembering that *narrative* showing is different from, say, theatrical showing). We can distinguish two broad categories, according to whether or not there is an explicit narrator, and if there is, whether his existence is obvious, that is overt, or covert. This distinction is often subsumed under the term 'point of view', but it is clear that that term can be seriously misleading and so will be avoided in the present work.[2]

The initial question, then, is whether a narrator is present, and if he is, how his presence is recognized and how strongly it is felt by the audience. The narrator comes into existence when the story itself is made to seem a demonstrable act of communication. If an audience feels that it is in some sense spoken *to* (regardless of the medium), then the existence of a teller must be presumed. In other cases, the audience feels that it is directly witnessing the action. Naturally, in all but the scenic arts—like drama and the ballet—pure mimesis, that is, direct witnessing, is an illusion. The question, then, is how this illusion is achieved, by what convention does a reader, for example, accept the idea that it is 'as if' he were personally on the scene, though the fact is that he comes to it by turning pages and reading words.

[2] The disabling ambiguity is discussed in an article by Sister Kristin Morrison called 'James's and Lubbock's Differing Points of View', *Nineteenth Century Fiction*, 16 (1961), 245–56. Sister Morrison shows that Lubbock and his followers used the term in the sense of the narrative perspective of the speaker (the narrator), that is, the inner workings of his mind; while James usually used it in the sense of the perspective of the knower or reader. Even more confusingly, the term often bears the non-literary sense of 'mental attitude or opinion' or 'interest' (as in 'From China's point of view, President Nixon's visit was very important'). To say that *The Ambassadors* everywhere presents Strether's 'point of view' is valid only if the latter sense is meant, for the speaker is clearly an outside narrator, and along with his *interpretation* of Strether's consciousness, he also gives us, sometimes ironically, his own view of Strether's situation.

It is clear that the author must make special efforts to preserve the illusion that the events are literally happening before the reader's eyes. And it is only very recently—within the last hundred years—that attempts at a purely 'dramatic' narrative have been made.

That it is essential not to confuse author and narrator is now a commonplace of modern criticism. As Monroe C. Beardsley argues, '. . . the speaker of a literary work cannot be identified with the author—and therefore the character and condition of the speaker can be known by internal evidence alone—unless the author has provided a pragmatic context, or a claim of one, that connects the speaker with himself.'[3] And even in such a context, it is preferable to speak not of the author, but of the 'author', or even better, ' "author"-narrator', for he is simply one of the possible kinds of narrators. The 'author'-narrator is never equivalent to the flesh-and-blood Dickens or Hemingway or Fielding. If he were, we could not account for the inevitable discrepancies between the values and ideas and experiences of authors as we know them from biographies, and the values, ideas and experiences implicit in their works. Or between two works by the same author, between the 'Fielding' of *Tom Jones* and the 'Fielding' of *Jonathan Wild*, or *Amelia*.[4] These considera-

[3] Monroe C. Beardsley, *Aesthetics* (New York: Harcourt, Brace and World, 1958), p. 240. Compare Kathleen Tillotson, *The Tale and the Teller* (London: Rupert Hart-Davis, 1959), p. 22: 'The "narrator" . . . is a method rather than a person; indeed the "narrator" never is the author as man; much confusion has arisen from the identification, and much conscious art has been overlooked. Writing on George Eliot in 1877, Dowden said that the form that most persists in the mind after reading her novels is not any of the characters, but "one who, if not the real George Eliot, is that second self who writes her books and lives and speaks through them." The "second self", he goes on, is "more substantial than any mere human personality", and has "fewer reserves"; while "behind it, lurks well pleased the veritable historical self secure from impertinent observation and criticism".'

[4] Wayne C. Booth, *The Rhetoric of Fiction* (Chicago: University of Chicago Press, 1961), p. 72 makes an excellent observation: 'the author of *Jonathan Wild* is by implication very much concerned with public affairs and with the effects of unchecked ambition on the "great men" who attain to power in the world,' while 'the author who greets us on page one of *Amelia* has none of that

tions have suggested the utility of a term like Wayne Booth's 'implied author':

> As he writes (the real author), creates not simply an ideal, impersonal 'man in general' but an implied version of 'himself' that is different from the implied authors we meet in other men's works. . . . Whether we call this implied author an 'official scribe', or adopt the term recently revived by Kathleen Tillotson—the author's 'second self'— it is clear that the picture the reader gets of this presence is one of the author's most important effects. However impersonal he may try to be, his reader will inevitably construct a picture of the official scribe who writes in this manner—and of course that official scribe will never be neutral toward all values.[5]

He is 'implied', i.e., he is a construction or reconstruction by the reader, and he is not the narrator, but rather the man who invented the narrator (if there is one), in short, the man who stacked the cards in this particular way, who had *these* things happen to *these* people. The distinction is particularly evident in the case of the 'unreliable narrator' (another of Booth's happy coinages). What makes a narrator unreliable is that his values diverge strikingly from that of the implied author's; that is, 'the norms of the work' conflict with the view of the events and existents that the narrator is presenting, and we become suspicious of his sincerity or competence to tell the 'truth'. The implied author can be at virtual odds with his 'author'-narrator. There is always an implied author, though there might not be a single real author in the ordinary sense (i.e., the narrative may have been composed by committee, by a disparate group of people over a long period of time, as were many folk ballads, by random-number generation by a computer, or whatever).[6] And what establishes the character of the implied author is the moral and other norms of the work taken as a whole.

---

air of facetiousness combined with general insouciance that we meet . . . in *Joseph Andrews*,' but rather imparts an 'air of sententious solemnity'.

[5] Booth, pp. 70–71. Booth discusses the problem of finding a good term for this entity on p. 73.

[6] These possibilities are suggested by Christian Metz, *Essais sur la signification au cinéma* (Paris: Klincksieck, 1968), p. 29.

Our sense of the implied author includes not only the extractable meanings but also the moral and emotional content of each bit of action and suffering of all of the characters. It includes, in short, the intuitive apprehension of a completed whole; the chief values to which this implied author is committed, regardless of what party his creator belongs to in real life, is that which is expressed by the total form.[7]

Preliminary to any discussion of the structure of discourse in literary narratives is an understanding of the linguistic and linguistic-philosophical basis for reports of speech, thought, physical action and so on, since it is at least partly on these grounds that the reader makes his decision about who is speaking, thinking or whatever, and in particular whether there is an express narrator or not.

The clearest evocations of a narrator are, of course, direct intrusions, the use of the personal pronoun 'I' or epithets like 'the author', or 'your narrator' and so on. Others (to be discussed below) are, rather, inferential: statements interpreting a

[7] Booth, pp. 73–4. At another point (p. 151) Booth states: 'Even the novel in which no narrator is dramatized creates an implicit picture of an author who stands behind the scenes, whether as stage manager, as puppeteer, or as an indifferent God, silently paring his fingernails . . . Insofar as a novel does not refer directly to this author, there will be no distinction between him and the implied, undramatized narrator; in Hemingway's "The Killers", for example, there is no narrator other than the implicit second self that Hemingway creates as he writes.' Here I must disagree: surely—if the terms are to mean anything at all—we must recognize the presence of the implied author, but not that of the narrator. Booth's term 'implied undramatized narrator' seems unnecessarily complex to describe what is nothing but the mere absence of a narrative voice. Why is it a 'mistake' typical of the 'unexperienced reader', as Booth claims, to assume that stories like 'The Killers' 'come to him unmediated' (p. 152)? Whatever mediation appears is surely that of the 'implied author', not that of a narrator: I assume that an example would be the fact that Nick and George and Henry are named from the outset (the reader 'knows' them even at the very first appearance) whereas the gangsters Al and Max are first 'the men', and the reader only learns their names as Nick, George, and Henry learn them, suggesting that the story occurs from the perspective of the latter. But the device of naming is surely that of the implied author, not that of the narrator. (I owe this example to Thomas O. Sloan.)

character's behaviour or action presuppose an interpreter, hence a narrator. (To say that it is the 'author'—i.e. the implied author—is simply to say that he elects to appear as a narrator). General commentaries on fate, the nature of the world or whatever presume a commentator, hence, again, a narrator. And so on. Somewhat less obvious are simple descriptions of a character's action or state of being. 'John sat in a chair' might in some sense be taken as the issue of a narrator's voice since John would not ordinarily be thought of as *saying* those words to himself. In this instance he would hardly verbalize to himself what he was doing. The ordinary convention is that a character is not verbally conscious of his location, or if he is, the consciousness would not take the bald form of mentally speaking the words 'I sat in the chair.'

There is then a set of sentences which by their form as well as content may be identified as utterances of a narrator. Clearly distinct from these are sentences attributable to the voices (external or internal) of characters, whose forms are more numerous and complex than is usually assumed. It is essential to be clear about them, since they are the elements of any discussion of the structure of literary narrative that pretends to exactness.

A convenient basis for such distinctions is provided by a recent movement in philosophy called 'speech act' theory. This is not linguistics in the strict sense: it is not concerned with the grammatical composition of sentences in a language, but rather with their role in the communication situation, particularly in their function as actual acts by speaker. We owe the theory to the English philosopher John Austin.[8] According to Austin, the intention of sentences—what he calls their 'illocutionary' aspect—is to be sharply distinguished from their grammatical, or 'locutionary' aspect, and from the effect which they achieve on the hearer, or 'perlocutionary' aspect. Thus, when a speaker utters a sentence in English (or any natural language), he is

[8] John Austin, *How to Do Things with Words* (New York: Oxford University Press, 1962). See also John Searle, *Speech Acts* (London: Cambridge University Press, 1969).

seen as doing at least two, and possibly three things: (1) he is
making that sentence, that is, forming it according to the rules
of English grammar, and (2) he is performing a quite separate
act *in* saying it, an act which might equally be performed by
non-linguistic means. For example, if he says 'Jump into the
water', he is performing (1) the locution 'Jump into the water'
according to the standard English rules for imperative constructions. At the same time, he is performing (2) the illocution
of *commanding*, an act corresponding in some way to non-linguistic acts like pushing his interlocutor toward the water. If he
accomplishes the intention of the illocution, in this case if he
succeeds in getting his interlocutor to jump into the pool, he has
performed (3) the perlocution of *persuading*. Note that perlocution, if it occurs, is the same whether the communicative act is
verbal, that is illocutionary, or not.

Perhaps the best way to distinguish between these categories
and to show that they are not cross-determined is to set up an
illustrative table. Take, for example the illocutionary act of
'predicting':[9]

Locution	*Illocution*	*Possible Perlocution*
'John will doubtless go mad'		persuade the inter-locutor
'It is probable that John will ultimately be crazy'		deceive
		irritate
'John's insanity probably will manifest itself' etc.	predicting	frighten amuse etc.

That is, any given illocution, say, prediction, can be couched

[9] William Alston, in *Philosophy of Language* (Englewood Cliffs, N.J.:
Prentice-Hall, 1964), p. 35, proposes this as one of a number of other illocutionary acts, including reporting, announcing, admitting, opining, asking,
reprimanding, requesting, suggesting, ordering, proposing, expressing, con-
gratulating, promising, thanking, and exhorting.

in any one of a number of locutions, using different syntactic and lexical elements. At the same time, the illocution might give rise to a bewildering variety of effects, that is, perlocutions in the interlocutor (including no effect at all), depending upon the context and the interlocutor's relationship to the particulars of the utterance.

It is now possible to go into greater detail concerning the illocutionary definition of literature and hence of the distinction between fictive and nonfictive narration, proposed by Richard Ohmann. Ohmann's thesis[10] is that 'a literary work (for our purposes 'a fictive narrative') is a discourse abstracted, or detached from the circumstances and conditions which make illocutionary acts possible; hence it is a discourse without illocutionary force. Or more exactly with *pretended* illocutionary force: 'Specifically, the reader constructs (imagines) a speaker and a set of circumstances to accompany the quasi speech-act, and make it felicitous.' The illocutionary force, then, is only 'mimetic', i.e., purportedly imitative:

. . . a literary work *purportedly imitates* (or reports) a series of speech acts, which in fact have no other existence. By doing so, it leads the reader to imagine a speaker, a situation, a set of ancillary events, and so on. Thus one might say that the literary work is mimetic in an extended sense also: it 'imitates', not only action (Aristotle's term), but an indefinitely detailed imaginary setting for its quasi-speech-acts.

Having asserted this, Ohmann goes on to distinguish between, among other things, fictive and non-fictive narratives:

Notice that the imaginary speaker and his circumstances may be very dimly implied, as in a novel with an omniscient, third-person narrator. Nonetheless, a novel is mimetic of a narrative account, rather than simply *being* a narrative account, like Capote's *In Cold Blood*. Of the latter it makes sense to ask all the questions implied by Austin's rules (e.g., Is the particular person speaking appropriate for the invocation of the particular procedure invoked? Does he really have the thoughts or feelings invoked? Will he or the reader

---

[10] Richard Ohmann, 'Speech Acts and the Definition of Literature', *Philosophy of Rhetoric*, 1 (1968).

actually intend to conduct himself according to the thoughts and feelings invoked? Etc.) . . .'

But this procedure obviously will not be appropriate to a novel or to a poem.

Thus throughout the following discussion, the expressions 'purported' or 'pretended' should be assumed to precede 'speech act' or 'illocution' insofar as the discussion turns on fictive rather than historical narratives.

The theory of speech acts provides a very useful tool for the analysis of the sentences of literary narrative. We may divide these sentences into two broad classes: those which are the speech acts of the narrator vis-à-vis his narrative audience; and those of characters vis-à-vis each other. To illustrate, consider the first several sentences of Dostoevsky's *Brothers Karamazov*:

Alexey Fyodorovitch Karamazov was the third son of Fyodor Pavlovitch Karamazov, a landowner well known in our district in his own day, and still remembered among us owing to his gloomy and tragic death, which happened thirteen years ago, and which I shall describe in its proper place. For the present I will only say that this 'landowner'—for so we used to call him, although he hardly spent a day of his life on his own estate—was a strange type, yet one pretty frequently to be met with, a type abject and vicious and at the same time senseless. But he was one of those senseless persons who are very well capable of looking after their worldly affairs, and apparently, after nothing else.

There is a considerable amount of story information ('story' in the technical sense, as defined above) communicated by these three opening sentences, and it is conveyed in different ways by the actual syntax, but in every case the speech acts are those of a narrator.[11] For instance, the following existence statements may be inferred from the first sentence. From the illocutionary point of view these are narrative 'assertions' or the like:

[11] For an interesting account of how literary information is communicated in sentences see Richard Ohmann: 'Literature as Sentences', *Essays on the Language of Literature*, eds. Seymour B. Chatman and Samuel R. Levin (Boston: Houghton-Mifflin, 1962), pp. 231–8. Ohmann analyses several sentences from literary texts in terms of their syntactic structures.

> There was a man named Alexey Fyodorovitch Karamazov.
> There was a man named Fyodor Pavlovitch Karamazov.
> Alexey was the third son of Fyodor.
> Fyodor was a landowner.

They are 'assertions' in a logical sense of the word, that is, 'a' is said to be 'b', where both 'a' and 'b' are entities (or, grammatically, nouns). Other existence statements are, illocutionarily, 'descriptions' (or 'attributions') that is, a quality (in the predicate) is attributed to an entity which is subject.

> He was a strange type.
> He was abject and vicious, yet senseless.
> He was capable of looking after his wordly affairs and after nothing else.

Certain other statements or parts thereof, though they might appear superficially to be process statements, seem to be better analysed at the narrative level as existence statements and illocutionarily as descriptions:

> Fyodor was well known in our district in his day.
> Fyodor is still remembered among us.

In the early versions of transformational grammar, passive constructions were derived from their active counterparts, the first from 'People in our district knew him well in his day', and 'We still remember him', or the like. But fundamental narrative units—the story statements—are not to be equated simply with the underlying deep structures of sentences. On the contrary, the transformations whose effects appear on the surface linguistic manifestation of literary narratives may be clearer indications of the narrative structure. Here, whatever their derivation, the items 'known' and 'remembered' are clearly meant to point to qualities or traits attributed to Fyodor, in the same way as 'notorious' might have been applied, or as 'strange, abject, vicious and senseless' actually are.

Similarly, the narrative function of 'We used to call him a "landowner" ' and 'He hardly spent a day of his life on his own estate' is less one of action than description. The point for the *story* resides less in the fact that we *called* him a 'landowner' (though the use of the first person plural does give rise to some interesting secondary questions at the level of discourse), than that he was usually so-called, that is, that that was one of his attributes. As in the first sentence, the point of the second is that he was not concerned with the welfare of his estate, he was not industrious, prudent, or whatever. That these are *narratively* existence statements of traits despite their appearance in action sentences is also communicated by the occurrence of habitual forms—'used to' and (the negative) 'hardly'. Such words also suggest the primacy of description, since the repetitions of the same actions in narrative clearly tend to characterize rather than to advance the plot.

'Owing to his gloomy and tragic death', on the other hand, however much it may relate syntactically to structures like 'His death was gloomy and tragic' does not have a primarily descriptive function. Rather, it states an event, the manner of which is, in the unfolding of the plot, secondary to the event itself; thus a narrative-statement paraphrase might be something like *He died gloomily and tragically.* (I am not, of course, presuming to rewrite Dostoevsky, but simply to highlight the purely narrative aspect of these sentences.)

There occurs in this passage still another category of speech acts that asserts neither actions nor description but does something that might be called 'generalizes' or 'opines'. This turns up in segments like 'yet one pretty frequently to be met with' and 'he was one of those senseless persons who . . .' The second may seem to take of the form of assertion, say 'There exists a class of senseless persons who . . .' But it differs in an important way from a clear-cut narrative assertion like 'There was a man named Fyodor Pavlovitch Karamazov'. A true narrative assertion is always integral to the story, and cannot be questioned by a reader, since to do so is to prevent the narrative from proceeding, to deny its very fabric. The author must be granted, by convention, the right to posit all those entities and actions necessary to his narrative. But assertions which are opinions do not have this warranty: they refer to the narrator's view of the world at large, not to the infraworld of the story, and the reader can immediately recognize this departure from the necessities of that infraworld. When the narrator says that there are persons who are senseless and yet capable of looking after their affairs, and that such fellows are frequently met with, he is presumably referring to the real world, the world outside the fiction; such fellows could be met on the streets of Moscow. Since it bears on the outside world, an 'opinion' in the strict speech-act sense makes an apparent truth-claim; one can reasonably ask whether the narrator is right or wrong on independent grounds. But it would not be meaningful to ask whether there was or was not such a person named Fyodor Pavlovitch Karamazov. The same point can be made about the difference between descriptive opinions, like 'Such a class is frequently met with . . .' and genuine descriptions like 'He was vicious', and so on. A statistical survey of personality types of the nineteenth century is a logical possibility; but since no claims that Fyodor ever existed can be made, it is impossible to judge whether or not he was vicious.[12] The speech-acts of *characters*, on the other hand, tend to be different. Although a character can, of course, tell a story within the main story, most of his speech acts will be appropriate to that actual framing scene and those will have all the variety in the (imagined) world: that is, his speech acts, like his other acts, will be addressed to the other characters and objects around him. So he enters into a wider set of relationships than do the narrator and the (implied)reader. To give just two brief examples: When Clarissa Harlowe in Richardson's novel writes 'I beg your excuse for not writing sooner,' the purported illocution is *apologizing*. When her mother writes 'I cannot but

[12] 'Opining' is like the narrative function called 'referential' (or 'cultural' or 'gnomic') which Roland Barthes (*S/Z*, Paris: Seuil, 1970, p. 25) applies to passages like the following (from Balzac's 'Sarrasine'): 'J'étais plongé dans une de ces rêveries profondes qui saisissent tout le monde, même un homme frivole, au sein des fêtes les plus tumultueuses'. ('Referential' in the sense that it permits the discourse to *refer outward* into the real world, to some kind of scientific or moral authority.) Note, again, the use of a certain kind of vocabulary that reveals the function, i.e. '*one of those* profound reveries that seizes *everybody* . . .'. And so on.

renew my cautions on your master's kindness,' there is a *warning*. And so on. Now of course a narrator can—and Fielding's narrators often do—apologize and warn. But they can only perform these acts in relation to the present situation, namely the narrative relationship which they have with their reader—they can only apologize or warn about the narrative itself, if they are to remain merely narrators. In Book II of *Tom Jones*, Fielding performs the speech act of *stating an intention*, but the intention is clearly in reference to the narrative:

Though we have properly enough entitled this our work, a history, and not a life; nor an apology for a life, as is more in fashion; yet we intend in it rather to pursue the method of those writers, who profess to disclose the revolutions of countries, than to imitate the painful and voluminous historian . . . Now it is our purpose, in the ensuing pages, to pursue a contrary method. When any extraordinary scene presents itself (as we trust will often be the case), we shall spare no pains nor paper to open it at large to our reader; but if whole years should pass without producing anything worthy his notice, we shall not be afraid of a chasm in our history; but shall hasten on to matters of consequence, and leave such periods of time totally unobserved.

And it is clear that such passages must always be ancillary to the central speech-act function of a narrator, namely to narrate. That cannot be a character's central function, for then he would become a narrator (a 'character-narrator' to be sure). Rather, characters use language to argue, to make love, carry on business, rhapsodize, cogitate, promise, make commitments, lie, and so on, always within the boundaries of the fictive world of the story.

Of course, it is possible to introduce illocutionary anomalies; consider the following passage from Samuel Beckett's *Watt*:

And then to pass on to the next generation there was Tom's boy young Simon aged twenty, whose it is painful to relate

?

and his young cousin wife his uncle Sam's girl Ann, aged nineteen, whose it will be learnt with regret beauty and utility were greatly diminished by two withered arms and a lame leg of unsuspected tubercular origin, and Sam's two surviving boys Bill and Mat aged eighteen and seventeen respectively, who having come into this world respectively blind and maim were known as Blind Bill and Maim Mat respectively, and Sam's other married daughter Kate aged twenty-one years, a fine girl but a bleeder (1), and her young cousin husband her uncle Jack's son Sean aged twenty-one years, a sterling fellow but a bleeder too . . .

To the word 'bleeder' Beckett has appended the following footnote: '(1) Haemophilia is, like enlargement of the prostate, an exclusively male disorder. But not in this work.' Richard Ohmann's interpretation of the anomaly is worth quoting *in extenso*:

Since our narrator has just told us that Kate is a bleeder, it is at best quixotic for him to inform us now that such a condition is medically impossible, and then to step out of his role *within* the novel altogether. What shall we say of the text? It is not exactly contradictory, since the statement about poor Kate is made within the fictive world of the novel, while that about haemophilia is outside it. (In this respect, the passage is akin to G. E. Moore's paradox—that one cannot say 'It's snowing, but I don't believe it's snowing.') Nor is it pertinent to say that the narrator has violated truth conditions: we don't *expect* a novel to tell truth in this sense. And certainly there is nothing syntactically wrong with the anomalous sequence. Yet I imagine many would share my feeling that what Beckett has written here is not simply unusual, or bizarre, or irregular, but un-English. That is to say, the passage violates some tacit rule for conducting discourse in English, some common understanding about how we will talk with one another. This understanding is perhaps roughly analogous to the rule violated by 'whose it will be learnt with regret beauty,' rather than to the expectations that make 'a sterling fellow but a bleeder' surprising.[13]

He analyses the anomaly by reference to the concept of that kind of speech act which Austin calls 'performative', a particularly pure speech act since it asserts nothing true or false, but simply performs the act in question. Where the performative is a 'statement', its requirements are something like the following:

[13] In *Literary Style: A Symposium*, ed. Seymour Chatman (New York: Oxford University Press, 1971), pp. 244–5.

To make a *statement* felicitously, I must, among other things, utter a declarative sentence (criterion 1). I must be the right person to make the *statement* (2). I will not get away with *stating* that a memory of your grandfather just crossed your mind. I must not mumble (3) or break off in the middle (4). I must believe what I say (5), and I must not ground my future conduct or speech in a contrary understanding of the state of the world [6].

Ohmann goes on to show that Beckett's footnote does not in fact satisfy these requirements:

It is here that the Beckett passage goes awry. Either it fails on rule 5, in that the narrator holds an improper set of beliefs for the act of stating that Kate was a bleeder, or it fails on rule 6, in that he comforts himself inappropriately afterward—namely, in writing the footnote. So one or the other of his statements is infelicitous—breaks the contract that exists between writer and reader. The second sentence of the footnote compounds the breach. For behind the act of stating is the all-encompassing illocutionary act of telling a story, and, by rule 5, the teller always endorses the fictive world of the story for its duration, and, again by convention, does not acknowledge that it *is* a fiction. When Beckett's narrator admits a discrepancy between his fictive world and the real world, he violates both rules. Hence he sets the reader at odds with the text, in a way that produces disorientation and amusement, but which, on a deeper plane, calls into question the very possibility, or at least the reasonableness, of building narratives or trying to make sense of human conduct, or indeed, maintaining a society.

This strikes me as an illuminating analysis, acceptable in every detail except the argument that the discrepancy is linguistic, that the anomaly is 'un-English'. I don't dispute it in the trivial sense that the anomaly could equally occur in German or Swahili, since I take Ohmann's 'un-English' to mean something like 'unlinguistic', but I would argue that it is not only unlinguistic, but 'unnarrative', since such an anomaly could be communicated even in another discursive medium. Consider, for example, trick photography in the cinema. Now it is perfectly conceivable that a trick-shot should occur—say a man flying unaided through the air—which is denied by the rest of the film (it never happens again, or no character sees it, or if one does, he simply shakes his head and dismisses it as 'seeing things'); yet the act may be perfectly 'true' in some deeper sense of the film's meaning. Wouldn't that be a parallel to Kate's being a bleeder in this fiction, even though that is not possible in the real world? Since there have been films made without words, without even captions, we must conclude that the anomaly is not in the language but in the discourse. To say that something is 'unnarrative' is simply to say that the discourse has introduced elements which are contradicted by reference to the ordinary laws of nature, and moreover that these have been called attention to within the work itself. As Ohmann points out, the narrator is here expressly withdrawing his 'endorsement' of the fictive world. However, it is not enough to say that he has violated rules and leave it at that. What has happened is that he has expanded into another kind of discourse, a kind of ironic narrative or narrative *manqué*, a narrative 'calling into question the building of narratives' which creates its own discursive form.

Fundamental to any analysis of the complex relations between speech acts of the narrator (if any) and of characters is a purely linguistic description of the basic ways of communicating speech (external voice) or thought (internal voice). A basic distinction is that between quotation and report, or in the more traditional terms, 'direct' and 'indirect' style. The distinction between *oratio recta* and *oratio obliqua* has been a grammatical commonplace for centuries. It is usually formulated in terms of speech— the difference between ' "I have to go," she said' and 'She said that she had to go'. But obviously the same applies to quotations and reports of thinking: ' "I have to go," she thought' and 'She thought that she had to go'. It seems worthwhile to maintain this dichotomy, since, in narrative, speech and thought are significantly different actions.

The grammatical differences between direct and indirect styles are quite clearcut. In both cases there are two clauses: for clarity's sake I shall call the introductory clause the 'tag',[14]

[14] Sometimes referred to as the 'verbum dicendi'; see, for example,

and the second clause the 'report'. The tag is the clause doing
the reporting or quoting (in the above case 'She said') and the
report clause contains that which is reported or quoted ('I have
to go' or 'She had to go'). The differences between the two
involve (1) the tense of the predicate of the report clause ('have'
becomes 'had'), and (2) the person of the subject of the report
clause ('I' becomes 'she').

But there has grown up within the last century another
distinction which crosscuts that between direct and indirect
style, namely that between normal, or, as I call them, 'tagged',
and 'free' style (*erlebte Rede, style indirect libre*).[15] Free sentences
are simply those with the tag clauses deleted: thus 'I have to go'
is the direct free counterpart of both the direct tagged speech
'She said, "I have to go" ' and of the direct tagged thought
'She thought, "I have to go" '; while 'She had to go' is the
indirect free counterpart of indirect tagged 'She said that she
had to go' and 'She thought that she had to go'. Or in tabular
form:

	Free	Tagged
Direct		
Speech	I have to go	'I have to go,' she said
Thought	I have to go	'I have to go,' she thought
Indirect		
Speech	She had to go	She said that she had to go
Thought	She had to go	She thought that she had to go

(Or better 'It occurred to her that she had to go,' since 'She
thought that she had to go' might be itself a free reduction of
'[She said] that she thought that she had to go'.) It is clear that
direct free speech and direct free thought are expressed iden-
tically and thus ambiguously, as are indirect free speech and

---

Dorrit Cohn, 'Narrated Monologue: Definition of a Fictional Style',
Comparative Literature, 18 (1966), 105.

[15] See the bibliography in footnotes to Dorrit Cohn's article and that in
Stephen Ullmann's 'Reported Speech and Internal Monologue in Flaubert',
Style in the French Novel (London: Cambridge University Press, 1957).

thought. Further, there is an additional ambiguity implicit in such indirect free constructions as 'She had to go', which might equally issue from the voice of the narrator.

Though narrative discourse is ultimately couched in words, it is not identical or coterminous with the linguistic manifestation. For example, we must recognize that the choice between indirect and direct discourse—between 'John said that he was fine' and 'John said "I am fine" '—is essentially discursive though its actualization happens to entail certain actual linguistic choices, for example 'that' vs. zero and 'he' vs. 'I'. But other, nonlinguistic features are also part of discourse. For example, the presence or absence of quotation marks (punctuation systems are not part of the 'natural language' but a separate superimposed system). 'Dots of ellipsis' ... showing change of time and place is another example of a non-linguistic signal in literary narrative. Such dots are not part of the language, not even of the written language, in the sense that a punctuation mark is, for example, the question mark, '?', which correlates with syntactic divisions and may also be a sign for a phonological feature like rising intonation. The fact that 'dots of ellipsis' may be used for other purposes—to show suspension of a structure, or to connect a title with a page number in the table of contents—is beside the point. In some narratives it is a signal of 'abrupt transition in time and place'; in others it may be used in quite another literary discursive function, for example, Virginia Woolf's short story 'The Mark on the Wall', where it signals the breaking in of reality on the free associative fantasy of the protagonist-narrator.[16] Another example of non-linguistic but discursive elements are the 'tears' to be found on several of the letters in *Les liaisons dangereuses*, or

---

[16] Its generalized, non-specific semantic import is, thus, like the various transitions between shots in the cinema: the simple cut, the dissolve, the fade-out and -in, the wipe, and so on. These clearly 'mean', but they do not have specific meanings, i.e. in some contexts the dissolve may mean 'at a place and time considerably different from that represented in the previous scene (as opposed to the cut which usually singals a briefer span)' or 'in the mind of the character', or 'a new motif in the action', and so on.

of *Pamela*. They are part of the larger semiotic context, the communication situation. The essential thing is not to confuse narrative discourse and linguistic manifestation, between which there is no necessary correlation.[17] Say that the author needs to express a certain action by John, for example, that John stole some money. Here the discourse is necessarily in the Process or Does mode. But the linguistic manifestation of such a narrative statement need not use a transitive verb at all. For example, the copula would work equally well: 'John's theft was in the headlines'. The discursive predication *Do* exists nonetheless; it is implicit in the noun phrase 'John's theft', and the mere surface manifestation, the actual choice of an English verb, is not significant at the narrative level.

So the expression 'process statements in the *Does* or *Happens* mode' must not be understood to mean any particular class of sentences in English or another language; it refers, rather, more abstractly, to a *narrative statement*, in the technical sense in which that term is being used. Narrative discourse may make use of the grammar of the language in ways that would be anomalous in other kinds of discourse. A short story by Truman Capote called 'A Christmas Memory'[18] is narrated by the protagonist, who was a child during the story time but who recounts the events retrospectively as an adult. Thus the first sentences are 'Imagine a morning in late November. A coming of winter morning more than twenty years ago': the illocution is *invitation* or the like. But in the third paragraph, after a description of an

[17] Though it contains many excellencies, David Lodge's *Language of Fiction* (London: Routledge and Kegan Paul, 1966) makes too much of the role of language in the narrative composite. There are other kinds of structures in narrative than linguistic, even though it is obvious, as Lodge urges, that 'the critic of the novel has no special dispensation from that close and sensitive engagement with language which we naturally expect from the critic of poetry' (p. 47). But language is no more basic than anything else that goes into the narrative. It is simply one of several systems, or codes, and there is no need to *rank* these, Aristotle to the contrary notwithstanding. Each code has its value, and different narrative styles highlight one system or the other. In James, language means a great deal, in Dreiser, relatively little.

[18] In *Breakfast at Tiffany's and Three Stories* (New York: Signet, 1959).

old woman, the boy's distant cousin, who is the other main character, we read: 'The person to whom she is speaking is myself. I am seven . . .' Other kinds of discourse could not allow the juxtaposition of 'I am seven' and 'This happened to me over twenty years ago'. But the logic here is perfectly clear: the simple present tense is used as a 'dramatic present', in other words we are to read it as if we had been transported backward in time and were witnessing the events with our very eyes. Or as if we were at a theatre (the next best thing), the narrator first appearing before the curtain and saying 'Imagine—so-and-so', and then stepping back as the curtain opened to reveal the very scene (though he will come back on-stage and continue to talk to the audience, standing immediately 'behind' the small boy).

A similar phenomenon is the use of the preterite with adverbs of present time: 'of course, she *was coming* to the party *tonight*'.

Much more could be said about the linguistic basis of literary narrative structure. But my ultimate goal is a description of the variety of narrative transmission. A logical way to proceed, I think, is from structures with the least presumption of a narrator's presence—that is, 'transcripts', through those where the narrator is indirectly present—to those in which he is not only present but highly vocal in his own person. I have space here for only the first end of the spectrum; I shall take up the question of more obvious intervention by narrators in a later paper.

First, an important theoretical presumption. Throughout, my discussion is based on the notion of the freedom of discourse *features* to combine in various ways, rather than that of homogeneous and fixed genres (although a rough generic classification will serve as a basis of organization). By discourse feature I mean a single property of the narrative discourse, for example, the use of the first person singular, or the use or non-use of time summary. Variety among narratives is thus accounted for in terms of various mixtures of independent features, not by an endless proliferation of categories or a Procrustean reduction of instances into normative types. Literary theory in general and narrative theories in particular have suffered from too powerful reduction into a small number of genres, with the consequence that the full discursive complexities of individual cases are missed because they don't 'fit' or get interpreted somehow as exceptional, or even worse, aberrant. The problem can be illustrated by reference to a recent book of F. Stanzel.[19] Stanzel reduces narrative discursive structure—what he calls the 'narrative situation' (*Erzählsituationen*)—to three types, 'authorial', 'first person' and 'figural':

If the author emerges by addressing the reader, by commenting on the action, by reflections, etc., the reader will bridge the gap between his own world and fictional reality under the guidance, so to speak, of the author. This is *authorial* narration. If the reader has the illusion of being present on the scene in one of the figures (characters), then *figural* narration is taking place. If the point of observation does not lie in any of the novel's figures, although the perspective gives the reader the feeling of being present as an imaginary witness of the events then the presentation can be called *neutral*.[20]

Examples are *Tom Jones, Moby Dick*, and *The Ambassadors*. He tries to account for non-canonic cases (of which there are an 'endless number', a 'continuous, ever-changing series',[21]) by means of the following model:

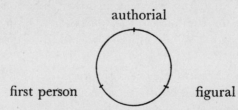

authorial

first person   figural

Mixed forms are explained as occupying midway positions on the circumference of the circle: '. . . the narrative situation of *Henry Esmond* (combining authorial and first-person forms) serves to prove that it is possible to realize intermediary forms which unite characteristic aspects of the surrounding novel

[19] Stanzel, *Narrative Situations in the Novel* (Bloomington: Indiana University Press, 1969).   [20] Stanzel, p. 23.   [21] Stanzel, p. 59.

types.[22] But when we consider these intermediary forms in detail, we begin to run into difficulty, a difficulty that derives from two related problems: (1) the categories are not genuinely parallel; and (2) the model seems to insist that a form must be transitional between two poles only. Obviously a narrative might contain features characteristic of all three classes (if there are only three).

Let us consider Stanzel's categories as if they were composites of distinctive features of the kind used in linguistic notation— use of the third (or first) person pronoun, existence of a narrator, and presence of the narrator in the fictional or experiencing world, the world of the characters.

	Third person	There is a Narrator[23]	Narrator is present in the fictional world
authorial	+	+	−
figural	+	−	−
first person	−	+	+

We are immediately struck by the fact that these features are not as clearly formulated nor as independent as this sort of display implies. The 'third-person' column and 'first-person' row betray a basic equivoque in the theory, an indication that the analysis hasn't gone far enough to uncover the really basic elements. In saying that the use of the first or third person is criterial, he is implying that the choice is made by each of the three narrative situations in the same way, for example, that the first person novel is narrated by a narrator who refers to himself in the first person, while 'The authorial novel is narrated in the third person'.[24] But 'narrated in the third person' cannot be parallel to 'narrated in the first person'. In a first-person

[22] Stanzel, p. 62.

[23] The distribution in this column is identical for certain other features mentioned by Stanzel, like temporal posteriority of the narrator to the events of the fictional world, and power to compress or summarize those events.

[24] Stanzel, p. 38. And later he speaks of 'the authorial narrator's characteristic reluctance to speak in the first person' (69).

narrative, it is the *narrator* who is referred to by the first person. In an 'authorial' narrative it is the *characters* (including the hero) who are referred to by the third person. The narrator of *Tom Jones*, refers to himself in the first person and to Tom in the third; on the first page,

The provision, then, which we have here made is no other than *Human Nature*. Nor do I fear that my sensible reader, though most luxurious in his taste, will start, cavil, or be offended, because I have named but one article.

Even where Fielding introduces a third-person expression like 'the author', it is clearly a euphemism of no structural importance, a mere stylistic variant of 'I'.

A similar point must be made about the figural form. Like other critics, Stanzel seems to be confused about who is actually speaking in a 'central consciousness' novel like *The Ambassadors*. He writes

The past perfect of the second verb can already be viewed from the experiential present of Strether: 'The Sunday of the next week was a wonderful day, and Chad Newsome had let his friend know in advance that he had provided for it. There had already been a question of his taking him to see the great Gloriani . . . (p. 133).' It subsequently becomes clear that this flashback represents a retrospection on the part of Strether. It takes place at the moment of his arrival at the home of the artist . . . [25]

But 'on the part of Strether' is surely incorrect if Stanzel means that Strether is *saying* this to himself; this is *not* a free reduction of the indirect thought form 'And Strether remembered that Chad had let him know . . .' or the like. On the contrary, a narrator and only a narrator could utter this particular sentence; it is precisely a narrator's epitome of what was understood between Chad and Strether.

The mere use of the first or third person is not a particularly powerful feature for distinguishing discursive types. Both Molly Bloom and Ishmael refer to themselves as 'I', but that hardly justifies placing *Ulysses* and *Moby Dick* in the same structural

[25] Stanzel, p. 107.

category—precisely because Molly is not a narrator. Indeed there *is* no narrator at this point in *Ulysses*, a situation which Stanzel's tripartite categorization does not easily allow for. For if we put interior monologue in the figural category, 'figural' cannot be equated with 'third-person narration'. In short, 'Third-' and 'First-person' are useless as features in themselves, without specification of the precise narrative element to which they refer.

The point of this critique of Stanzel is not to castigate the book, which I consider to be a useful contribution to our knowledge of narrative structure, but rather to demonstrate the difficulties of any system that reduces narratives to a limited number of set categories, in a taxonomic, rather than a feature kind of analysis. It is clearly preferable to consider the features separately, always allowing for a wide spectrum of possibilities of combination, and to think of the form of *any* narrative as built up out of its own congeries of features.

Since the narrator is a feature like any other and thus subject to dosage in any given narrative, a natural basis of discussion is the degree to which a narrative statement or a whole work presupposes his existence. The negative pole—the pole of pure mimesis—is that occupied by statements purporting to be direct transcripts of a character's behaviour. Properly speaking, in literature pure mimesis is only possible where that behaviour is only linguistic. The positive pole—the pole of pure diegesis—is where the narrator speaks in his proper voice, using the pronoun 'I' or the like and expresses views which are not so much the story as his *view* of the story (interpretations, general or moral observations and the like).

The negative pole, the absolutely unmediated story or pure transcript or record, consists of nothing beyond the speech or verbalized thoughts of characters, omitting even such minimal marks of narrative presence as 'he thought' or 'he said'. The use of such tags, however, is not a strong indicator of narrative mediation, for the convention of 'he said' is not much more conspicuous than that of the use of separate paragraphs to indicate a change of speaker in dialogue or of the character's name followed by a colon in printed forms of plays. (As such it is a feature of *discourse*, rather than of the medium.) Mediation does begin to appear when the tag employs certain 'interpretative' verbs—'he surmised' or 'he insinuated', or the like. The minimal phrases 'he said' or 'he felt' present a kind of norm; they add nothing—they represent a minimal representation in the process mode.

Theoretically, quoted dialogue is the minimal case; the only necessary assumption is that the author has copied the speech of the character. What we have is something like the transcript of a sound recording. We cannot avoid the implication that *somebody* has done the copying, but convention has it that we forget the act of transcription and assume that the expression is a pure act of mimesis. Even this form entails a transformation, from the modality of oral to that of written speech; the 'purest' instance of unmediated witnessing would have to be that in which the quoted text purported to be itself written—a letter, diary or whatever—in which a character's sentiments were depicted. The 'implied author' then is only a compiler.

Somewhat more distant from the pure mimetic pole is the depiction of actions other than overt speech, involving internal processes—thoughts, feelings, sense impressions, and so on—as well as external but non-verbal movement. In the first, the convention is that the author can read and copy out into words what is going on in the mind of a character. This obviously presupposes a machine somewhat more complex than a sound recorder—a machine for reading thoughts (including perceptions, sensations, unarticulated feelings), and putting them into linguistic form. It is not only the impregnability of the skull that makes this transcription difficult, but also the fact that a certain amount of mental activity is non-verbal and therefore verbal depiction entails the same minimal necessity for interpretation as does the depiction of more overtly visible non-verbal behaviour.[26]

[26] By the same token a purely physical act of this sort does not ordinarily presume consciousness on the part of the character, so that from the narrative-discursive point of view it is unlike a thought. Of course, 'John sat down'

Obviously, written narrative cannot directly imitate physical actions—like sitting down—the way drama does. When an actor sits down he imitates with the movements of his body the character's movements as he interprets them—it is he, not the playwright, who embodies the character. He performs the more immediate mimesis. And, as I have suggested, mediation always opens the possibility for interpretation: when we read in a narrative 'John fell into the chair' or 'John lounged about', there is obviously more than a mere imitation in words of John's action—there is a hint at least of a comment on that action. This is *logically* true to a certain degree even if the term is as neutral as can be—'sat' rather than 'lounged'. Even 'sat' implies something, if nothing more than the fact that more loaded terms have been avoided: perhaps something like 'John (*simply*) sat down'. The convention has it that there is a scale of interpretation: more neutral words suggest an avoidance of intervention. The bare description of physical action is felt to be essentially non-mediated. We make such assumptions as long as we feel that the implied author has done his best to avoid judging or commenting upon, interpreting (or whatever) the action. What these verbs precisely entail may not always be possible to specify, but, clearly, certain words and grammatical structures imply such judgement and others do not: for example, 'lounged' instead of 'sat'. Or syntactically, the whole class of sentence adverbs, which necessarily entail a speaker's judgement on the content of the sentence they modify: for example, 'Obviously, John was tired,' which is possibly a transformation of 'It is obvious *to me, the narrator,* that John was tired', that is, 'I have judged the matter and found it to be thus and so'.

I cannot attempt here a detailed account of the various forms

---

may mean that he not only sat down but that he was conscious of sitting down. But we assume that it doesn't, unless we have strong contextual evidence to the contrary, for example, where the mode is indirect free, so that every sentence bears a bit of the character's consciousness about it. However, many verbs imply in themselves an element of consciousness along with their physical aspects: verbs like 'wait', 'hand (something to)', and so on.

of mediated narrative transmission, and must content myself with a schema. The organization may be simple, proceeding from narratives involving *least* in the way of presuppositions about how the material reaches the audience to those pre-supposing the most. I am not presenting an air-tight taxonomy of narrative types but simply (hopefully) logical characteriza-tion of *one* feature of the narrative, namely the narrator.

WRITTEN RECORDS

Of all the forms of literary narrative, those imitating already written documents—like letters and journals—are most directly transcriptional. They reduce the implied author to a mere collector of documents; the only power he has is the narratively trivial one of collating the letters or editing the journal so that the typesetter could set the book. He is not even faced with the problem of transforming speech into writing, since he has before him the literal artifacts written by the characters; the only purported change is that of handwriting into print. He is not even a stenographer (with the stenographer's options about punctuation and so on), but merely a compiler. He may or may not make his presence known; if he does it is usually in the guise of 'editor' or the like.

The journal novel differs from the epistolary novel in respect to whom it implies to be the reader. The implied reader of a letter is the addressee and correspondent; the implied reader of a private journal is usually the writer himself. Its purpose is not informational but rather in the way of *aide-mémoire* or assessment and analysis of his developing situation. Like the letter-writer, and unlike the retrospective first-person narrator, the journal-writer does not know what will happen next, what will be the ultimate outcome of the plot.

Again, as in the epistolary narrative, the journal-writer may be a narrator, keeping track of events for his own edification and memory. But a simple transcription of things that have happened to him may not be his primary interest. Consider these passages from Sartre's *Nausea*; on the narrator's (Roquen-tin's) profession:

I don't think the historian's trade is much given to psychological analysis. In our work we have to do only with sentiments in the whole, to which we give generic titles such as Ambition and Interest.

On his own habits, seen at a neutral distance:

. . . there is something new about my hands, a certain way of picking up my pipe or fork. Or else it's the fork which now has a certain way of having itself picked up, I don't know. . . .

In such contexts, when narrative does appear, it often serves the function of example:

. . . a little while ago, just as I was coming into my room, I stopped short because I felt in my hand a cold object which held my attention through a sort of personality. I opened my hand, looked: I was simply holding the door-knob.

It is interesting to consider some of the possibilities of the journal convention in other narrative media, for instance, the film. Robert Bresson's *Diary of a Country Priest* (1950), after Bernanos' novel, illustrates some of the possibilities. Especially at the beginning, brief shots illustrating the quality of the curé's daily life in his tiny vicarage are interlaced with shots of his hand writing the journal (his physical and mental distress frequently being reflected in the blottings or erratic handwriting). At the same time his own voice—rather a voice-over, since his lips do not move—reads what he is writing in the journal. The peculiar narrative flexibility of the cinema is illustrated by the fact that the journal can continue to be *read aloud* by the 'voice-over' effect, even when the visual image is not of the journal but of the action depicted by the journal at that moment. Thus the action that we see, in the present tense, so to speak, is the visual counterpart of what we hear, in the past tense, from the curé's lips. This leads to certain interesting effects. At one point, for example, his voice breaks off and says that he must write down immediately what is happening; then there is a cut immediately to an action, as the voice-over ceases. This leaves the audience a bit disoriented. Are we to assume that the action has suddenly gone ahead of the journal, that what was only future and incipient in the journal has become present and actual in the image: that is, is it that the narrative convention is suddenly broken? Or is this simply a flashback without journal specification (as elsewhere: the voice-over says 'I arrived home', then stops speaking and the action continues purely visually)? Only the context helps us to figure out that the former is the case.

Another interesting effect is utilized several times to show that the mind of the curé is unable to grasp what is being said to him (not only illness but naiveté plagues him—he says plaintively at one point that he will never understand human beings). What happens is this: the action is completely in the dramatic rather than the narrative mode, that is, the narrative voice-over is still. He is conversing with another character, the countess, for example; the camera is focussed on him as he listens to her speak, though it is her voice we hear. Then her voice suddenly becomes weaker, though still audible, and the *journal*-voice-over starts speaking conjointly with her voice, though louder, as it explains why he cannot understand what she's saying. The multi-channel capacity of the cinema has only begun to make use of these interesting special effects.

SPEECH RECORDS

In the transcription of speech, the implied author is presumed to be nothing more than a stenographer. The unmediated record of speech can be that of a single character, the classic 'dramatic' monologue, or of two or more, that is, unmediated dialogue. In 'dramatic monologues' one character speaks to another, a silent listener (not to the 'reader', since there is no relationship established upon which this could be based).[27]

[27] There is no point, I think, in limiting 'dramatic monologue' to poetry and excluding it from prose, merely because its earliest and most famous exponent was Robert Browning (as Melvin Friedman does in *Stream of*

The essential characteristic of the dramatic monologue as of dialogue in general is that the speaker is *not* principally involved in recounting, since in that case, he would become a narrator, and the scene only the frame for a secondary narrative.

An example of rather pure dramatic monologue is Dorothy Parker's story 'Lady with a Lamp', the record of the speech of an unnamed character to her friend Mona, who is suffering a nervous breakdown and whom she is ostensibly trying to comfort but whom she only manages to make worse. The story begins and continues in the discursive technique of direct free speech:

Well, Mona! Well, you poor sick thing, you! Ah, you look so little and white and *little*, you do, lying there in that great big bed. That's what you do—go and look so childlike and pitiful nobody'd have the heart to scold you. And I ought to scold you, Mona. Oh, yes, I should so too. Never letting me know you were ill.

The expression 'I should so too' implies that at this point Mona has protested that she should not be scolded. Her verbal reaction never actually appears in print; but always is inferable from what her friend says.

I was mistaken, that's all. I simply thought that after—Oh, now, you don't have to do that. You never have to say you're sorry, to *me*. I understand.

(Mona's apology presumably interrupts the speaker at 'after'.)

You stay right the way you're lying, and I'll—Because you shouldn't move around, I'm sure. It must be terribly bad for you. All right, dear, you can move around all you want to. All right, I must be crazy. I'm crazy, then. We'll leave it like that.

(Mona presumably asks why she shouldn't move around, interrupting the speaker at 'I'll', to which the speaker responds

---

Consciousness (New Haven: Yale University Press, 1955), p. 26). A simple but useful definition appears in Joseph Shipley's *Dictionary of World Literature* (Paterson, N.J.: Littlefield, Adams and Co., 1960), p. 273: 'The dramatic monologue is a character sketch, or a drama condensed into a single episode, presented in a one-sided conversation by one person to another or to a group'.

'Because . . .' Then, presumably, Mona disagrees, so the speaker acquiesces, saying 'all right'.)

At the end the speaker has so upset Mona that she becomes alarmed herself at the reaction:

Mona, don't! Mona, stop it! Please, Mona! You mustn't talk like that, you mustn't say such things.

(Mona has perhaps threatened to do herself in.)

Finally, in desperation, the speaker calls to Mona's maid, Edie, the change of interlocutor being visually indicated by putting the paragraph in italics:

Edie, Oh, Edie! Edie, I think you'd better get Dr. Britton on the telephone, and tell him to come down and give Miss Morrison something to quiet her. I'm afraid she's got herself a bit upset.

Obviously, the dramatic monologue is so special an effect that there must be some overwhelming reason for its employment. It is clear that in 'Lady with a Lamp' the notion of a character's moral and psychological obtuseness and even unconscious malice is supported by the technique of keeping her interlocutor—her victim—unheard. Thus content finds a direct formal counterpart in technique.

Dialogue is so commonplace and well-understood that little comment need be made. Practically every novel or story contains narratives made up in smaller or greater part of quoted speeches of one character to another. What does need to be recognized is that narratives that rely totally or predominantly on records of characters' speeches—whether monologues or dialogues—entail more inference than other kinds of narrative, or if not more, at least a special kind of inference. To a greater degree than normal, the reader is required to interpret the illocutionary force of the sentences that are spoken by the characters; that is, he is supposed to infer what they 'mean' in the context of the action, even if there are no direct reports of that action, indeed even if the whole action can only be constructed through such inferences. It's as if he were supposed to supply, metatextually, the correct verb tag—'complained', 'argued', 'pleaded' or whatever—to characterize the speech act. Consider for example the following sentences from Hemingway's 'Hills Like White Elephants':

The girl was looking off at the line of hills. They were white in the sun and the country was brown and dry.

'They look like white elephants,' she said.

'I've never seen one.' The man drank his beer.

'No, you wouldn't have.'

'I might have,' the man said. 'Just because you say I wouldn't have doesn't prove anything.'

The girl first *poeticizes* or the like (italics for illocutions). The man may seem to be *admitting ignorance*, that is, at least, if the locution had occurred in another context; in this context, however, in response to the poeticism, the remark sounds more like a *rejection* of her flight of fancy, and is done with a hint of self-satisfaction. She then *criticizes* or *belittles* him. He in turn *defends* himself and *challenges her authority* to make judgements about him.

We make these inferences about speech-acts as we make all our inferences in reading—in terms of our ordinary knowledge of the world, our ordinary expectations of human behaviour in the society we know. That is perhaps why pure speech-report narratives are harder to understand across profound cultural borders.

Several narrative theorists[28] have used the word 'soliloquy' to describe another sort of unmediated narration of speech, citing as examples such works as Virginia Woolf's *The Waves*

---

[28] For example, Robert Humphrey, *Stream of Consciousness in the Modern Novel* (Berkeley and Los Angeles: University of California Press, 1959), pp. 35–8. For Humphrey, soliloquy is 'defined as the technique of representing the psychic content and processes of a character directly from character to reader without the presence of an author, but with an audience tacitly assumed' (whereas interior monologue does not acknowledge the presence of an audience). As I argue below, 'tacit assumption' should not be taken to mean that the character directly *names* the audience; rather, because he seems to be explaining or commenting upon what is happening or has happened and need not do so for his own sake, our presumption is that he is doing it for the reading audience.

and Faulkner's *As I Lay Dying*. Is the transfer of the term to narrative structure useful? Is this a separate narrative category? Let us recall its meaning in the drama. The standard examples —Hamlet's and Macbeth's soliloquies—contain at least the following features:

(*a*) the character does in fact speak (in the cinematic version, by a technical trick, his lips remain closed but we hear his voice);

(*b*) either he is alone, on stage, or if there are others they show by their demeanor and actions that they do not hear him;

(*c*) he traditionally faces the audience;

(*d*) but he does not necessarily name the audience; the second person pronoun or the imperative, if used, are addressed either to himself or, in formal apostrophe, to someone not present ('Oh ye Gods,' or the like);

(*e*) thus the audience is not being addressed, but rather overhears the character's address to himself or to someone not present;

(*f*) the style and diction of the soliloquy tend to be very much of a piece with the character's ordinary dialogue; thus if he speaks in a formal and poetic manner to the other characters, that is the style of the soliloquy, too; there is no attempt to modify his language to show that it is an *inner* phenomenon;

(*g*) the content often constitutes an explanation of or comment on the character's situation.

Features (*a*) and (*b*) are obligatory, the rest optional but usual.

Now in what sense can passages in narrative be called soliloquies? *The Waves* and *As I Lay Dying* do in fact exhibit some of these features.[29] In *The Waves* characters are said to *speak*: the tag 'he (she) said' is usually present, and passages attributed to each character are always in quotation marks:

'Susan has passed us,' said Bernard. 'She has passed the tool-house door with her handkerchief screwed into a ball. She was not crying, but her eyes, which are so beautiful, were narrow as cats' eyes before they spring. I shall follow her, Neville. I shall go gently behind her, to be at hand, with my curiosity, to comfort her when she bursts out in a rage and thinks, "I am alone".'

[29] Thus L. E. Bowling is incorrect in referring to *The Waves* as an 'interior monologue' novel: see 'What is the Stream of Consciousness Technique?', *PMLA*, 65 (1950), p. 339.

As I Lay Dying does not use tags, but name-captions are used to identify each speaker, as in a playscript.

DARL

Jewel and I come up from the field, following the path in single file. Although I am fifteen feet ahead of him, anyone watching us from the cotton-house can see Jewel's frayed and broken straw hat a full head above my own.

In neither novel do other characters respond directly to the statements of the speaker; thus we infer that the others have not 'heard' them. Thus the form cannot be 'dramatic monologue' or the like. Though Bernard seems to be addressing Neville directly, there is nothing in Neville's next speech (which occurs no less than four pages and ten speakers later) to suggest an acknowledgement of what Bernard has said; indeed, there is no way of knowing whether Bernard is even present at the moment he speaks (the scenic sense is very weak in *The Waves* in any case):

'Where is Bernard?' said Neville. 'He has my knife. We were in the tool-shed making boats, and Susan came past the door. . . .'

The same thing is true of *As I Lay Dying*; the only time there is an interchange between characters is when their conversation is reported by the soliloquizer, in which case the soliloquy itself has become a narrative within a narrative:

CORA

. . . 'She ought to taken those cakes anyway,' Kate says.
'Well,' I say, 'reckon she never had no use for them now'. 'She ought to taken them,' Kate says . . .

As for the optional features of soliloquy, discussed above, I cannot recall an instance where the reader is named or addressed in either *The Waves* or *As I Lay Dying*. In the rare cases that 'you' occurs in the former, it serves very much the apostrophe effect, as in Louis' speech upon finishing school:

'I am most grateful to you men in black gowns, and you, dead, for your leading, for your guardianship . . .'

It would seem then that soliloquies can only occur in a tagged, never a free format, for the simple reason that they must be recognized unambiguously as speech, not thought, or rather as a stylized, expressionistic form beyond mere thinking or speaking. As we have seen there is no way of telling, if the tags are removed, which is operative. In this sense, *As I Lay Dying* is more ambiguous than *The Waves*, since only the name-captions are given, but no specification as to whether the named character thinks or speaks the words that follow. My own feeling is that we are to assume that these words are neither spoken nor thought naturalistically by the characters, but rather are attributed to them in some extra-naturalistic way. And it may be that the form of *As I Lay Dying* warrants the establishment of a category separate from speech records.

RECORDS OF THOUGHT AND FEELING

The representation of a character's consciousness may also be unmediated (although the very fact that it is revealed may imply a shade more mediation than in the strict speech record). But 'consciousness' as a concept in narrative needs careful examination. I can only present a brief sketch, and attempt to account for a few cases which are often lumped together, under terms like 'stream of consciousness'.

Without plunging into psychology, one can distinguish on the basis of simple introspection, for the purposes of narrative analysis, two kinds of mental activity: that which entails language and that which does not.[30] I am sometimes conscious of *saying* to myself words like 'I must get milk and bread', but I am not ordinarily conscious of saying to myself as I pass a garden 'That rose is red' or 'See that red rose' of 'The redness of the rose'. It is the first kind of thinking, the kind that appar-

[30] The distinction is well emphasized in Bowling, p. 342; see below. Edouard Dujardin, *Le Monologue intérieur* (Paris: Messein, 1931) uses the term 'monologue traditionnel' to refer to this form, but this draws too close a parallel with theatrical monologue.

ently is already present in the mind in verbalized form, that appears in narrative as unmediated thought in the strict sense. A visual medium like the cinema can imitate a red rose directly, non-verbally, and it can show that it is the object of a character's perception by simple conventions, like first showing the character look offscreen, and then 'cutting' to the rose itself. The effect is equivalent to 'The character sees the red rose' or even, with contextual support, 'The character sees that the rose is red'. But literature is a verbal art, and even non-verbal sensations must be transformed into words; this inevitably raises the question of who is performing this transformation. But let us take these problems one at a time.

The most obvious and direct means of handling verbalized thoughts is to treat them as 'unspoken speech', placing them in quotation marks, accompanied by tags like 'he thought'. From *Pride and Prejudice*,

Elizabeth almost stared at her.—'Can this be Mr. Darcy!' thought she.

According to the schema presented above, this is direct tagged thought: the tense of the report clause is present, not past as it would be in the case of indirect style. The implied author has become mind-reader, in addition to stenographer. But he is no more than that; he does not interpret; he takes down only the words—and the exact words, diction and syntax—as they are 'spoken' in the character's mind. As such the tense remains present, and self-reference to the character is expressed in the first person.

But it is very easy—and has long been commonplace in European fiction—to drop quotation marks, and more recently to drop the tag. The result is direct free thought. This is a form of presentation or enactment which in extended form has often gone under the name of 'interior monologue' or 'stream of consciousness'. The features which characterize this kind of presentation are:

1. The character's self-reference, if any, is in the first person pronoun.

2. Verb predicates, if any, are in the present tense.

There are three additional logical implications:

3. The language—idiom, diction, word- and syntactic-choice—are appropriate to the character, whether or not a narrator is also present.
4. Allusions to anything in the character's experience are made with no more explanation than would be needed in his own thinking, that is,
5. There is no presumptive audience other than the thinker himself, no deference to the ignorance or expository needs of a reader or another character.

Conditions one, two, and four are not, of course, unique to direct free thought; they apply equally to any form of un-mediated speech—dramatic monologue, dialogue, and solilo-quy (but not to indirect free thought and speech, which are mediated, albeit minimally and sometimes ambiguously so).

For an example of free direct thought it is appropriate to turn to Joyce's *Ulysses*, say the first chapter of Section II, where we first meet Leopold Bloom:

(1) Mr. Leopold Bloom ate with relish the inner organs of beasts and fowls. (2) He liked thick giblet soup, nutty gizzards, a stuffed roast heart, liver slices fried with crustcrumbs, fried hencod's roes. (3) Most of all he liked grilled mutton kidneys which gave to his palate a fine tang of faintly scented urine.
(4) Kidneys were in his mind as he moved about the kitchen softly, righting her breakfast things on the humpy tray.
(5) Gelid light and air were in the kitchen but out of doors gently summer morning everywhere. (6) Made him feel a bit peckish.
(7) The coals were reddening.
(8) Another slice of bread and butter: three, four: right.
(9) She didn't like her plate full. (10) Right. (1) He turned from the tray, lifted the kettle off the hob and set it sideways on the fire. (12) It sat there, dull and squat, its spout stuck out. (13) Cup of tea soon. (14) Good. (15) Mouth dry. (16) The cat walked stiffly round a leg of the table with tail on high.
(17) —Mkgnao!
(18) —O, there you are, Mr. Bloom said, turning from the fire.

(19) The cat mewed in answer and stalked again stiffly round a leg of the table, mewing. (20) Just how she stalks over my writing-table. (21) Prr. (22) Scratch my head. (23) Prrr. (24) Mr. Bloom watched curiously, kindly, the lithe black form. (25) Clean to see: the gloss of her sleek hide, the white button under the butt of her tail, the green flashing eyes. (26) He bent down to her, his hands on his knees.

(27) —Milk for the pussens, he said.

(28) —Mrkgnao! the cat cried.

(29) The call them stupid. (30) They understand what we say better than we understand them. (31) She understands all she wants to. (32) Vindictive too. (33) Wonder what I look like to her. (34) Height of a tower? (35) No, she can jump me.

(36) —Afraid of the chickens she is, he said mockingly. (37) Afraid of the chookchooks. (38) I never saw such a stupid pussens as the pussens.

(39) Cruel. (40) Her nature. (41) Curious mice never squeal. (42) Seem to like it.

(43) Mrkrgnao! the cat said loudly.

(44) She blinked up out of her avid shameclosing eyes, mewing plaintively and long, showing him her milkwhite teeth. (45) He watched the dark eyeslits narrowing with greed till her eyes were green stones. (46) Then he went to the dresser, took the jug Hanlon's milkman had just filled for him, poured warm-bubbled milk on a saucer and set it slowly on the floor.

It is important to recognize that this passage, which is often cited as a standard example of 'stream of consciousness', only approaches free direct thought gradually. The first four sentences are straightforwardly narrated in conventional fashion, by an effaced narrator, whose existence is only known by the fact that the character is referred to in the third person and his actions represented in the past tense. Further, that such actions are summarized ('ate', 'liked') in the first paragraph posits a narrator who assumes somewhat more than the barest powers of observation—more than, say, the charge of the Hemingway-esque narrator. Joyce's narrator tells us what the character habitually did, and also verbalizes what we assume was only an unverbalized feeling in Bloom's own consciousness ('which gave to his palate a fine tang of faintly scented urine').

Joyce brings the narration into the present scene in the fourth sentence, preserving the narrator's right to pronounce upon the contents of the character's mind. The narrator continues to do so in the fifth, sixth and seventh sentences, although the truncated syntax (deletion of 'was' between 'morning' and 'everywhere' and of 'it' before 'made') hints at a move toward another kind of transmission.

That happens in sentence eight: 'Another slice of bread and butter: three, four: right'. Here the shift is to free thought; it is *not* the truncated syntax *per se* which makes it such, since we've already had that without a shift in transmissional mode, but rather the fact that, in context, any way we fill the syntax out will necessitate the recognition of ellipsis of the tag 'He thought'. In other words, it is not so much a question of whether this is short for 'I'd (or he'd) better prepare another slice of bread and butter' or 'It would be a good idea to have another slice of bread or butter' or whatever, but rather that regardless of the actual original content of that sentence, it is one that Bloom *thinks*. How do we know that? Simply because the word 'right' cannot be attributed to the narrator; it is Bloom's and not the narrator's word. In this context, the narrator could not possibly be imagined to be weighing the 'rightness' of Bloom's action; only Bloom can do so.

However, since so much is deleted, and in particular, the verb-tense, we cannot know if the mode is indirect or direct free thought. (The indirect form would be '(He thought) that was right', and the direct would be 'That's right (he thought)'.) The verb tense, however, is kept in sentence nine, which establishes it clearly as indirect free thought. Ten is ambiguous again, but on the principle of inertia, we assume that it is indirect. Eleven and twelve resume the direct narration.

'Soon', however, brings us back to Bloom's mind: it is a word actually reverberating in his mind or *could be* so reverberating (which is the most we can ever assume in the style of indirect free thought), but again for lack of verb tense we can't tell whether it is direct free or indirect free—'I'll have a cup of tea soon', or 'He'd have a cup of tea soon'. Similarly with fourteen and fifteen—'That's good' or 'That was good', 'My mouth's dry' or 'His mouth was dry'. Fifteen resumes the direct narration, and seventeen and eighteen, of course, are dialogue, that is direct tagged speech. Nineteen is narration.

But twenty resumes the quotation of Bloom's mind: it is the first unequivocal instance of his free *direct* thought, since the verb is in the present tense ('stalks'). Twenty-one through twenty-three, of course, are Bloom's 'quotations' of what the cat says: the full form would be ' " 'Purr. Scratch my head,' she's saying," he thought.' Twenty-four resumes the narration, while twenty-five goes back to the earlier ambiguous free style, without a verb. Twenty-six is narrative and twenty-seven and twenty-eight are direct tagged speech.

The next paragraph, sentences twenty-nine through thirty-five, is entirely in the direct free thought mode, with present tense verbs and first-person self-reference ('we', 'I'). Thirty-six is direct tagged speech, continued in thirty-seven and thirty-eight by direct free speech.

The next paragraph, thirty-nine through forty-two, is again indeterminately free thought. The rest of the passage is narrated.

So we can see that it takes relatively little in the way of direct free thought (in this case slightly less than half of the sentences) to suggest strongly the effect of 'stream of consciousness'. And further that though fragmentary syntax, free association and the like may accompany this style, the only *necessary* condition is the technique of free direct thought, meaning the use of self-reference by first person pronoun and present tense verbs; for even where these have been deleted, they must be presumed.

The use of direct free thought in mixed passages of 'stream of consciousness' permits the same sort of irony between character and narrator as does the sustained limited third person, 'central consciousness' manner of *The Ambassadors* or *Madame Bovary*. This is quite different from sustained indirect free style, where the effect is more often (though not necessarily) one of sympathy or identity of view between character and narrator. An example from the first page of Virginia Woolf's *Mrs. Dalloway*:

Mrs. Dalloway said she would buy the flowers herself. For Lucy had her work cut out for her. The doors would be taken off their hinges; Rumplemayer's men were coming.

The communal or sympathetic mode is established immediately in *Mrs. Dalloway* by means of indirect tagged leading to indirect free forms. The first sentence of the novel is indirect tagged speech: 'Mrs. Dalloway said she would buy the flowers herself'. (Speech is hardly ever communicated this way in the 'stream of consciousness' chapters in *Ulysses*. When it occurs, it is almost always in the direct form, set off by Joyce's own peculiar punctuation—an initial dash instead of quotation marks). The difference is fundamental; it is not that the words *are* the character's words: only that they *might* be. By establishing the indirect report, Virginia Woolf prepares the way for indirect free statements which are indifferently attributable to either narrator or character; and this is what I mean by calling it a 'sympathetic' mode—narrator and character are so close, in such sympathy, that it doesn't matter to whom the statement is attributed; either could have made it:

For Lucy had her work cut out for her.

Either 'For you see, dear reader, Lucy had her work cut out for her,' (i.e. 'I, the narrator observe that'), or 'Mrs. Dalloway remembered that Lucy had her work cut out for her.' Indeed the ambiguity goes even further, since in respect to Mrs. Dalloway the form is indifferently speech or thought; it could just as well mean 'Mrs. Dalloway *said* that Lucy had her work cut out for her.'[31] Since none of these is excluded, they all hover

[31] This 'triguity' among the possibilities—character's speaking voice or character's mental voice or narrator's voice—explains a line from Jane Austen's *Persuasion* that troubled David Lodge (*Language of Fiction*, p. 15): 'He had always been lucky; he knew that he should be still.' Lodge writes 'We seem to be hearing him speaking to Anne, or to himself . . . This is not obvious, but is, I think, indicated by the word *knew*. If the narrator's voice were speaking with full authority here, some more guarded word like *thought, supposed, believed* would have been used.' But the triguity would persist there too; the real source of it is the deletion (if there is such) of a possible *earlier* tag 'say': Is it 'He *said* that he knew that he should be still'

in suspension within the sentence, and there is established a sense that the narrator has not only access to but unusual affinity with the character's mind. She is part of an 'in'-group; we infer a communal form: 'It was understood by all parties (including the narrator) that Lucy had her work cut out for her.' And if we look back to the first sentence, we discover an interesting thing which prepares us for this consensus: Mrs. Dalloway is reported simply as saying she would buy the flowers, not as saying that to any particular person. It is a pronouncement, not a bit of dialogue. The implication again is communal, ridden with a sense of broader social context: Mrs. Dalloway is accustomed to having an audience, consisting of at least servants, attendants; the fact that it is not necessary, even in the first sentence, to specify her audience implies immediately that she regularly has one.

(The same kind of consensus operates at the beginning of Katherine Mansfield's 'The Garden Party': 'And after all the weather was ideal. They could not have had a more perfect day for a garden party if they had ordered it.' Indistinguishably the thought of one or all the family, or what one of them said to the others, or a report of the consensus of their attitudes, or the narrator's judgement—but which differs in no way from theirs.)

Thus the very narrative structure corroborates at the outset a fundamental distinction between *Mrs. Dalloway* and *Ulysses*: Mrs. Dalloway, the brilliant socialite, tied in so many ways to her society, always surrounded by people—husbands, friends, daughters, ex-lovers, servants, and even a sympathetic narrator —as opposed to those loners, Stephen Dedalus and Leopold Bloom, living on the margins of their society (for different reasons, of course), in conflict with it, unable to communicate with it—except obliquely, at odd moments. And their narrator distant, objective, even at times ironic:

---

or simply 'He knew that he should be still' (and if the latter, does it mean 'He knew: "I shall be still",' or 'I, the narrator, report that he knew he should be still (whether, perhaps, he was conscious of *saying* that to himself or not)")?

Mr. Leopold Bloom ate with relish the inner organs of beasts and fowls. He liked thick giblet soup, nutty gizzards, a stuffed roast heart, liver slices fried with crustcrumbs, fried hencod's roes. Most of all he liked grilled mutton kidneys which gave to his palate a fine tang of faintly scented urine.

The second sentence of *Mrs. Dalloway*:

The doors would be taken off their hinges; Rumplemayer's men were coming.

Again the effect is communal: it is the common understanding that Rumplemayer's men were coming. The future is conveyed by the past tense of 'will' and the past progressive 'were coming'. In *Ulysses*, on the other hand, the future only exists in the character's musings, and so is always in the present tense form (or in an elliptical non-finite verb form):

He heard then a warm heavy sigh, softer, as she turned over and the loose brass quoits of the bedstead jingled. Must get those settled really.
He pulled the halldoor to after him very quietly, more till the footleaf dropped gently over the threshold, a limp lid. Looked shut. All right till I come anyhow. He walked on, waiting to be spoken to, trailing his ashplant by his side. Its ferrule followed lightly on the path, squealing at his heels. My familiar, after me, calling Steeeeeee-eeephen. A wavering line along the path. They will walk on it tonight.

The detachment of interior monologue vs. the sympathy of the indirect free style: Professor Dorrit Cohn has well expressed the sense of intimacy between narrator and character in the latter:

By allowing the same tense to describe the individual's view of reality and that reality itself, inner and outer world become one, eliminating explicit distance between the narrator and his creature. Two linguistic levels, inner speech with its idiosyncrasy and author's report with its quasi-objectivity, become fused into one, so that the same current seems to pass through narrating and figural consciousness.[32]

[32] Cohn, p. 99. Others have also noted this effect: see, for example

At the same time, however, she shows that this is only one of the possibilities: the

narrator is, in a sense, the imitator of his character's silent utterances. This mimetic quality of the narrated monologue was repeatedly emphasized by its early theorists. Now imitation implies two basic possibilities: fusion with the subject, in which the actor identifies with, 'becomes' the person he imitates; or distance from the subject, a mock-identification that leads to caricature. Accordingly, there are two divergent directions open to the narrated monologue, depending on which imitative tendency prevails: the lyric and the ironic.[33]

So consensus or sympathy and intimacy between narrator and character is not the only aesthetic artifact of indirect free style. Consider the ironies in this passage from *Madame Bovary* which starts out as straight narrative and goes into indirect free style (ending up as direct tagged speech):

. . . Charles . . . attendit patiemment le retour de sa femme pour avoir des explications.
Si elle n'avait point instruit de ce billet, c'était afin de lui épargner des tracas domestiques; elle s'assit sur ses genoux, le caresse . . . (etc.)
—Enfin, tu conviendras que, vu la quantité, ce n'est pas trop cher.

Here the indirect free style supports rather the notion of the commonplaceness of Emma's action, how frequent an occurrence it was, how often she pulled the wool over Charles' eyes; and more generally the implication 'You know how it is done in petit-bourgeois circles'.

Indirect free style is one of the chief devices for indicating the speech and thinking of characters in partially unmediated narratives; it provides the structure for a middle ground of consciousness between total submersion in that consciousness, as in the 'stream of consciousness', and the Jamesian effect of relatively distanced observation by a narrator of a mediated 'central consciousness' or 'post of observation'—a topic for a later stage of this inquiry.

W. J. M. Bronzwaer, *Tense in the Novel* (Gronigen: Wolters-Noordhoff Publishing, 1970), ch. III, who uses the term 'emphatic'.
[33] Cohn, 110–11.

INDEX OF NAMES